EVERYONE'S GOT A STORY
AN ANTHROPOLOGIC MEMOIR

By

John Bishop

Ride Share Stories by an Uber/Lyft Driver

A Great Guide to
Green Chile, Gorgeous Skies and a Peaceful Mind

Santa Fe · Sedona · Washington, D.C.

First Published in 2019
By
Magic Publishing, LLC
P.O. Box 31279
Santa Fe, NM 87594

Email: john@everyonesgotastory.com

ISBN: 978-0-9819133-1-5

Library of Congress Control Number 2017918636

This book is dedicated to my three children
Tamara Ann Bishop-Amavilah
Kelly Sue Penuela
David Alexander Bishop
and a special thank you to
Glenys Carl

Table of Contents

PREFACE

I was attending a technology conference in San Francisco in February 2016. Prior to the conference one of my daughters suggested that I should really put the Uber app on my phone, so she downloaded it for me. I used it to ride around San Francisco, and was so impressed with the technology I wanted to get to know it better. Maybe I could start by being a driver around Santa Fe, where I live.

I'm a fairly unlikely person to be an Uber driver. For the past twenty years I have been President of a Portland, Oregon area company that works in the field of focused ion beam technology, a branch of nanoscience. We are essentially a nano machine shop making little parts for the semiconductor and related industries. I also started a high school in Santa Fe called The MASTERS Program, an early college charter high school where students can actually graduate with an Associate's Degree at the same time they graduate from high school.

After driving for a while I started to approach it as a sociologic and anthropologic study. I became fascinated by this intimate glimpse inside the lives of the riders and thought that others might be interested too. For a six-week period during the Spring, I interviewed many of my riders, recorded a lot of them with their permission, and kept extensive notes. Type in **bold** is me. Regular type is the rider. Type in italics is a second rider. Type in **CAPITALS** are my observations and thoughts after dropping the rider off.

While reading the book, when you see ∞ , it signifies the end of an interview. The quotation marks around the second paragraph on Page 388 regarding Light Language was the rider channeling a language I had never heard before, and then translating in spurts as she was talking. She identified this syllabic continuum of sound as Light Language. I have purposely left out references to the actual name of all the riders.

I hope you enjoy getting to know life and Santa Fe through the eyes of my riders as much as I have. Here is a special thanks to each rider interviewed.

Love to You,

John Bishop

v

WEEK ONE

— NORTH HOUSTON —

Hi. Airport, right?

Yes.

Say, I'm writing a book about my riders, just good stories and where they are from. Are you ok if I record our conversation and use it in my book?

Oh, great. Well, I'm originally from Houston, but I stay in Louisiana. I'm just coming on work, traveling, contracting. I get to see the world for free.

What kind of contracting do you do?

I'm contracted to Strategic Cart Service, the ones that deliver trash and recycling cans.

You've been doing that around town?

Yeah, for three weeks.

The blue ones?

Yes sir. And they had a special order for some pink ones, I guess, for breast cancer awareness.

Is that what those pink ones are for?

Yeah, you got the breast cancer awareness logo on the side of them.

Do they have new trucks that pick up these new recycle cans?

Yes.

So, they got a whole...

Yeah, they got like five new trucks coming, that's why they put them out now.

Five new trucks coming?

Yes sir, five new ones at $385,000 each. That's a couple of million dollars.

I see.

Yeah. But I enjoyed myself in Santa Fe. I enjoyed the climate. For me being down south from Louisiana, the weather was nice here because it was storming one day, the next day it was back sunny, yesterday it was raining, and now it's cool again. I love your mountains.

So, you work for a company that contracts with the city?

Yes. We contract all over the United States. Like last month we were in Rochester, New York, we have a few people in Detroit, Michigan, and next I'm going to Dallas.

Well, do you distribute things other than trash cans?

No, we just do cart delivery service. We just deal with new ones. We don't go and pick up trash carts or nothing like that. We just deliver new trash cans.

Do you do it all over the country?

Yes. All over the country, all over the United States.

Do they do it in any other countries?

No, I've never been out of the States. They are not international.

They are just nationwide. They are just United States. Yes, sir. So, how long have you been driving for Uber?

Little over one year.

Good pay?

Well, I don't do it for the pay; I do it for the fun and enjoyment of talking to people and interviewing them.

Socializing?

Yeah.

I'm a very social person too, coming from where I come from, the northside of Houston. It's kind of rough.

Did you grow up in a rough neighborhood?

Yes, sir. I grew up in the northside of Houston.

Tell me about it, what was it like growing up?

Well, you know, over there, there's a lot of poverty. It's low income. 75% of the homes are split up homes. No dad. Fortunately for me I had a step-father that raised me. Him and my mother have been together 28 years, but a lot of my friends and associates didn't have both parents. It's common, a lot of them go to jail, a lot of my childhood friends are dead.

From what?
From the violence. Usually over drugs.

I see.

Whenever there's drugs and money, there's violence. The generations are getting younger and younger. Today the grandmother might be 35, instead, like when I was growing up, my grandmother was 50. So yeah, it's a younger vibe. The grandmothers are younger. The mamas are younger, so the generations change. It's younger. There are no more values taught, no more respect for the elders. Like when I was coming up, you had to respect your elders. Even though we were raised poor, we still were taught morals, values of how to conduct yourself, good attitude and respect. These days it has all gone out of the window. Everything is shoot first, ask questions later. The teenagers are wild. There's more TV, more things on TV. The music plays a major part in the culture. They listen to a lot of rappers, and they don't realize that that's entertainment, because they were never taught no different.

When I was coming up, my mother sat me down and let me know the difference between real life and entertainment. These days they just let everything go. They go with the flow. Nobody is telling them the difference between right and wrong, or, what's reality and what's not reality. So, you know, a bunch of these teenagers, they are listening to music, and they are thinking that these guys that are rapping, that they look up to, that it is real for them. When you come from a broken family, sometimes you look up to other things. Sometimes you got to go outside the home to find a connection, and they are connecting with the hip hop and the videos and everything. They are just not knowing that it's really entertainment.

So, you might hear a dude saying, "I got 100 rounds in the clip." And they are thinking that that's cool, but not knowing that the man is in the studio booth with nobody, with no clips. He is just rapping for entertainment. He is saying what you want to hear, and he is not actually living that life. But the young generation think that he is actually living what he is saying, and they want to go out and copy. Because they look up to him. Because they are seeing the guy in the video with the nice girls, jewelry and foreign cars, not knowing that it's not really theirs. It's someone that's over them that has a big budget, that really doesn't care about the music that they put out, as long as it sells. They are not caring if the children hear this.

How old are you?

I'll be thirty-five in May.

Have you experienced much racism in America?

Yes, I'm not going to say much but I have experienced racism. It depends on where I travel to. Like I went to West Texas, and there weren't too many Afro Americans, so I saw it. I was thinking that maybe the times had changed. But when you go to different places you see that it still exists. It's not upfront racism, it's not upfront. It's more like hidden. But if you pay attention you can tell, because you look at the looks, and people when they go by you, they tense up. Yeah, it is racism. I'm from Louisiana. I stay in Louisiana. I've been in a couple of places where I felt the vibe that I wasn't invited. No one said anything, but I just felt, you know how you can feel? Body language is communication too. They never said it verbally, but physically and mentally, I could feel that there was tension because of my race. But me, I'm very religious, I believe in God. I've been through a lot of things where I know there had to be a higher power. I'm not saying that I know that there is God, but I know there has got to be a higher power, because I have been in situations, you know when you have been in situations in your life and things happen? Because I've been shot in Houston. That was one of the reasons why...

As a kid you were shot?

Yeah, I was shot as a teenager. And I shot someone too.

On purpose or...?

Yeah, on purpose. Because I went to prison for it. I've been in prison two times by being hard headed, and not doing what I was raised to do.

What kind of prison?

I went to prison in Louisiana. A lot of people would think, back in the old day, they would say, "Well, he's in jail. I don't have to worry about him. I know he'll be safe." No, that's not the case in prison these days. You might go in for a year and never come home again. It's a tough place particularly with all the sex stuff. But the penitentiary that I was in, they still get drugs in there. They say they are trying to rehabilitate you from drugs. That's not true, because the average correctional officer doesn't make enough. So, you know, money is the root of all evil. So, in jail you can say okay, let's say if I was a big-time drug dealer in the streets, and I go to jail. If I find the right correctional officer I could manipulate him like, "What do you make a week?" He might say, "I make $500 a week, $1,000 every two weeks." I could say like, "Well, if you bring this package in to me, I'll pay you $1,000 right now." Typically, most of them are going to do it. Yeah, that's why the penal system is growing rapidly. I even heard that Michael Jordan invested in prisons. He didn't become a billionaire by just selling sneakers. People stand outside for Michael Jordan tennis shoes, but he didn't become a billionaire until he invested in the prison system.

Really?

And by me being in prison and just going through life, I started to realize that prison was the biggest stock investment. I was just raised that it was the law, that people break the law, but as you look and start to research you will understand that it's really all about politics and money. Say, like I'm working right now. I'm free. I'm home and working. I might get paid $800 a week. But if I was in the penal system, I would do the same work, but the penal system would take 75% of my earnings. So, a job like right now where I make $800 in the penal system I'm working for them, I would probably take home $200, so they get the big end of it. And if you think about it, you are like, "Man, hold up. That's modern-day slavery. I'm doing all the labor, and you are getting most of the money."

That's interesting.

Yeah, so there's a lot of interesting things. I thank God for putting my head on straight and for what I've been able to realize. I got four children.

You have four?

Yeah, three girls, 15, 14 and 9 and a baby boy 2.

Hey man, it's been a pleasure.

It's been a pleasure too.

Thank you so much for sharing.

Not a problem. Anytime, sir. It was nice to meet you too. Good luck with your book.

I WISH I HAD MORE TIME WITH THIS RIDER. OUR LIFE STORIES ARE AMAZINGLY SIMILAR.

∞

— PARKING WHILE INTOXICATED —

Tell me about your story from last night.

So, I've been sober. I'm from Connecticut. I've been sober for four months. I came out here to help an ex-girlfriend with surgeries. I'd flown out here a few times, so I decided to drive back out here. I went out on St. Patrick's Day, met a couple, and just decided to have a couple cocktails with them. I ended up getting pretty drunk. I pulled over to an industrial park to like sleep it off a little bit. I was just about to leave, and I guess someone called, and the police showed up.

Well, you weren't driving.

I was, because I had admitted to having driven to that location.

You said it was like drunk while parking or something?

No, PWI. I call it PWI, "Parking While Intoxicated."

Yeah, right, which is far better than driving?

No, it's not. They arrest you. They gave me the same amount

of – it's really, really, really strict up here. I mean really bad. Basically, I spent two nights in jail. The first night I had to sleep on this really cold hard bench in the room. It was kind of a big room. There were a couple of other girls.

Did you have a blanket or anything?

They give you two blankets, and one to basically cover yourself. First, they put you in this take home dress browns they called them, like <u>Orange Is the New Black</u>.

The minute you arrived?

Yes. Brown is the new black, anyway. You normally sleep in your own clothes, but just whatever. Then the second night there's only – at that time there were only one or two other girls in that bedroom. I woke up, and there were like five other girls in that room. And two other girls that were in the room were frequent fliers; they have been in and out of there. And they're like, "this is bullshit, we should be able to get sent back." And I guess when you get sent back, you get sent back into this pod, which I never got to see, where they actually put beds and bunks and all that. So, by the second night there were seven girls in this one room. You have seven women, and you have to go to the bathroom a lot more than men do, and have to use toilet paper up more than men do. They give us a roll of toilet paper. One of the girls that was in there was detoxing extremely bad from heroin. She was having auditory and visual hallucinations, and running little gambits, and talking to people. Not making any sense. It was bad.

So, you had given up drinking four months ago?

Four years ago, I gave up drinking. Then in December, pretty much, things went kind of south with me and my ex. At that time, I guess I got a little depressed and I started drinking again.

What made you stop four years ago?

I almost died.

From drinking?

Yeah. I had cirrhosis and pancreatitis. I had neuropathy in both my legs and arms, I still have it in my legs. I was almost blind. I had gout. My liver was failing.

How much did you drink?

I was drinking at least two handles of vodka a day.

Two handles? What's a handle?

The big bottles that you...

Oh, my! You drank two of those a day?

Two of those a day, plus shots and going out. Then I became isolated.

For how many years did you do that?

Well, I've been drinking since I was 13. It became extremely elevated when my mother passed away in 2008.

So, at age 47 you were drinking ... I mean, 34 years you had been drinking?

Yeah, I think it's 35. Something like that. So, my mother passed away in 2008, and left me a ton of money, which I drank, mainly drank through. And I traveled a lot. I mean I woke up in Cabo San Lucas. Don't remember how I got there.

Oh, really.

I flew obviously. I mean, the only reason I knew where I was, is because I looked at the ticket stubs in my bag when I woke up in the morning. I'm like where the hell am I, because I'm seeing palm trees and water.

Did you have other blackout times?

Oh, god, yeah. Oh, yeah. Oh, yeah. Yeah, a lot. But I was a high functioning alcoholic. I was a creative director of a trade show firm. I flew around the country doing trade show jobs. And I would take the clients out. The clients loved me because I was fun. I did my job. I did my job well.

Vodka doesn't smell, does it?

It does. Absolutely.

Would you drink it with orange juice or straight?

Fresca.

Fresca?

Oh, man, plus I love Stoli Cosmos. I love those! But I traveled a lot. I went all over the place.

What I found with my addictions is that you can – I'm an addictive person. I was addicted to pot for a long time.

Pot?

Yeah.

Do you ever consider pot being medicine?

Well, it hurt my lungs.

Okay.

Okay, that's the issue primarily. But I found that once you just flip a channel in your brain ... Where is this place?

I don't know.

It says 2515, this way.

Okay. That's the police department.

Is it the police department?

Actually, if you don't mind going down the street, and let me see if there is a lot. I think I might just go to the police station like in ...

They say 2515 is down here, the courthouse, right here.

Well, I'm looking for the Impound Lot, but I think ...

So, it's got to be on this side, inside of this or the police station. Let me ask. You, ma'am, do you know where the Impound Lot is?

Yeah, it's going off Jaguar, but you need an appointment.

Actually no, I'm looking for... Yeah, I'm looking for Amanda Knox.

She's looking for Amanda Knox.

Oh, okay, so— you mean Amanda Kats?

Yeah, so I forget her last name.

Amanda Kats, thank you.

All right, thank you. She's cute. Yeah, I'm like really ... I'd like to be early. Keep all my ducks in a row.

Okay.

So, thinking about drinking. It's a cognitive behavioral therapy issue. It becomes a habit, and you become physically addicted. And my mother was an alcoholic. And they say that, I guess there's some connection between family members. It's a disease.

Well, I'm glad you got it handled.

Well, I'm now on a little breathalyzer thing that I have to blow every four hours, which is good.

You do that for the cops?

Yes. If you have the cops, it keeps you sober. I mean, I can't drive if I drink. If I blow anything over like point zero zero, I'm in trouble. And you can't, I mean, you can't drink.

Does it have some type of connection to the police department or by Wi-Fi or something?

Yeah, it does. It's all connected.

Okay. Well, thank you so much.

Thank you.

I NEVER KNEW SOMEONE COULD DRINK THAT MUCH ALCOHOL.

— ECUADOR ROSE FARM —

Hello, you're going to the convention center?

Yeah. Santa Fe Convention Center. We have a flower show there. I'm in the flower business in South America. We grow roses from Ecuador.

And then, do you fly them up here?

Yep. We fly them mostly to Miami, and then fly them all over throughout the States and Canada.

And do you have a season, or is it growing year around?

We grow year-round – year-round we have to sell, 52 weeks out of the year. We ship them also on big planes to Russia and Western Europe.

Do you rent airplanes?

No, there are cargo lines, and they make consolidations and fly them all over. So, quite a few Colombian and Ecuadorian farms are here.

That's interesting! "Roses from Ecuador," It's got a good ring to it. And what kind of trade show is this right here?

This is a particular group of wholesalers who consolidate their cargo from Colombia and Ecuador, and, I don't know, from other places as well, but mainly Colombia and Ecuador. And we all get together once a year.

Do any retailers come and buy?

Some retailers, local retailers, will come and see what their wholesalers have to offer and some of our products, but we do not sell straight to the retailers, rather to wholesalers throughout the states.

Throughout the states. Well, tell me, I love the smell of a really good rose. So many roses today they have no smell, what's the issue there?

Well, it has to do with the fact that the more smell the roses have, the less resistant they are to diseases and pests -- with the fragrance, insects are also more attracted to the roses.

That's interesting!

And therefore, the breeders who do bring out new varieties all the time are more looking into new colors, higher productivities, pest and disease resistance, and things like that. They do not breed for fragrance mainly. However, having said that, there are some varieties of garden roses, they are called, which have a lot of smell.

How many of you are doing this in Ecuador?

I don't know, maybe around 400 different growers.

Do you buy from some of these growers, and then resell it?

No, I don't. Some people do. I just grow my own, and I sell my own.

Do you grow them in green houses?

In green houses, yeah. I have close to 60 acres of green houses.

60 acres?

Yes, and close to 300 workers.

Oh, my lord!

Yeah, about 60,000 to 70,000 people work directly in the flower business in Ecuador. Same thing in Colombia, maybe a little bit more.

I saw something on TV around Valentine's Day about the growers of Colombia, how they are shipping them on airplanes.

Oh, yes. Valentine's, Mother's Day...

Are those the two busiest ...

Those are the two busiest ones, especially in the U.S.

Are there different days in other countries?

The most important date is International Women's Day, which is March the 8th. Russia and Europe are really big on this day.

And that's where they give out roses?

Yes.

Any other significant dates in other countries?

You have Mother's Day, like yesterday it was Mother's Day in England. Then you have a different Mother's Day in Sweden. You have Chinese New Year. We also ship into China, Japan and Australia.

Boy, oh boy! 60 acres, that's a lot of acreage.

Yes. And my farm is not the biggest. There are farms with over 250 acres of green houses. I'm a midsize farm, growing about 100 varieties of roses with many different colors.

Do you have a specialty?

Our specialty is actually to have a wide assortment. So, we don't have very large quantities of anything, but we have a little bit of everything. That's more or less the strategy here. So, a few farms come here, and we compete against each other, offering our products, some are the same varieties ...

How did they pick Santa Fe as a convention center?

Well there is a group of wholesalers, and they pick places for us all over the states and in Canada. We meet every time in different places.

And do you actually have a booth here?

Yes, we rented one of the larger salons there at the convention center. They are setting up the tables, and then we all have to make our own arrangements, so we hired a local flower arranger and - a florist actually.

How did you get into this kind of business?

I'm an agronomist by training, and got into that as Ecuador went into the flower business in general as a country. We are very agriculturally oriented in the country, looking for high cash crops to export.

You live outside of Quito?

I live outside of Quito, and the farm is about 50 miles outside of Quito. So, I don't know why they picked Santa Fe, but they look for places that are central for older wholesale members to come, because there are people coming from the state of Washington, from the east, all the way out from California, I don't know, Montana, Arizona - everywhere.

And they are primarily wholesalers?

Yes, almost exclusively wholesalers. They have invited some of the nearby retailers and florists just for them to see what all of them have to offer. We try to show new varieties, new products that come out into the market. So, we'll do that for – today we have to set up the booths, and the show will go on for tomorrow and Wednesday.

Had you rented a car?

I did, just as I arrived on Saturday, I rented one. Today we went to Taos Pueblo.

Pretty nice up there.

Very nice. And we are staying at the Eldorado Hotel, which is just around the corner from the convention center.

Is Ecuador a lot different than the United States?

Yes, quite different. Well, you find the same kind of malls and things like that, large cinema chains and things, but we have three different areas. We have the coastal area, which is warm, where I live, which is even higher than here, about 10,000 feet above sea level; and then we have the mountain area; and then on the back in the far east, we have the Amazon area. Both sides are warmer, and the mountains are rather cold, because of that.

Are your mountains part of the Andes chain?

Yes, yes. We even have a few very active volcanoes.

Ok, here we are. Nice chatting with you.

Thank you.

∞

— AUTISTIC —

Where are you headed today?

I'm headed back to Chicago.

I've been a Chicago Cubs fan for 71 years.

Well, congratulations. I used to say my condolences, but now I say congratulations. I couldn't be happier. My grandmother was -- is one of their biggest fans. What's that on our right, here?

That's the national cemetery.

Is it for soldiers?

Yeah.

Wow! That's impressive.

It really is. It goes on and on and on.

Oh, my god. You ever been to Normandy?

I've never been to Normandy.

They have a beautiful grave for the soldiers that died in D-Day. It's so impressive! I mean the white marble stones, they are all perfectly aligned in a row. Another one that's really impressive is the German one. They have a great site for the Germans. There was a famous Panzer Division general for the German army who is - it has been written up by all kinds of people, anyway, he had all of his soldiers buried around him. It's really cool. And it's all –

He had all of his soldiers buried around him?

All of his soldiers were buried around him. It's like –

Right there in Normandy?

It's in Normandy, yeah. Very few people go to the German one. I highly, highly recommend it. It's not anything like the allies. The allies are beautiful. It's pristine. It's maintained. It's right out on the ocean in the channel. I mean it's stunning, very moving. But the German one is, I would say, is equally impressive in a different way. It's not as organized. It's not as maintained. And all of the gravestones are black.

Really? What brought you to Santa Fe?

I had an interview for a job.

You were thinking about moving out here?

Yeah. I've been lifelong in Chicago. But this is an interesting opportunity, so I came out to look at it.

What do you do?

I'm a banker on the business side of things. I don't lend money or anything like that. I'm more on the executive management side. So, I am a lifelong White Sox fans. I have three kids, two boys and a girl. My daughter Darren and I used to have season tickets to the White Sox, 11th row right behind first base. I used to go a lot.

Oh, boy!

We used to give the tickets away to clients, but we used them a lot. The only one who would go with me was my daughter, and I think it was because she had ulterior motives. She really wanted the cotton candy and all of the goodies that came along with it, but she really got into baseball. And she still is. Her fiancé plays for the Oakland A's.

Really?

Yeah. And he is one of the nicest guys. I mean he is just an amazing, amazing guy.

Did you used to go to Comiskey Park?

Yeah. I used to go to Comiskey Park, and I like Cellular Field. It's absolutely come a long way. When they first opened it, it reminded you of like a mall or airport terminal. It didn't feel like a baseball stadium, but it's come a long way. It really is nice now. But I still call it Comiskey Park.

When I was eleven, my mother – I grew up in Sedona, Arizona, and we had a neighbor friend, Tim Fuller's mom Faith, who had a friend who pitched for the Chicago White Sox.

Oh, really?

A reliever, Jim Wilson, a long time ago, and so he got us first base side box seat tickets, right behind the dugout, I think it was in 1957. Well, it was a double header. The Sox won the first game, and in the second game the Sox were ahead. It was late in the game, the Yankees had the bases loaded, and they called in Jim Wilson to be the relief pitcher. Well, my lord! The first pitch he delivered, Moose Skowron hit a grand slam homerun and the Yankees won.

You know what? He can tell that to his grandchildren.

I know, but one of the thing that I remember most about this game, was that some of the fans, there were White Sox and Yankee fans, and first they started throwing popcorn at one another, then beer, then it got into a whole brawl right there in front of us. The cops came and everything.

Yeah. All of my brothers – I have nine brothers and sisters, all but one is a Cubs fan, and I mean they are fanatic Cubs fans. And my grandmother. My dad was a White Sox fan, and so he used to take us to White Sox Park. It was dangerous.

Yeah. I know.

It was dangerous. I mean there were times when we were a little concerned about this brawl kind of spilling over. The best thing they did was get really good security in there, and set up family sections and stuff like that. They weren't doing themselves any good.

I used to go to see the White Sox every once in a while, with my Irish Catholic girlfriend, Maureen, who was from the Bridgeport area. Her brother was a Chicago cop. I'd love to see a White Sox/Cubs World Series someday. Wouldn't that be classic?

That would be one of the best. But I can't go to the cross-town games, especially in Comiskey Park. I cannot stand to have Cubs fans in Comiskey Park, rooting against my White Sox. It just doesn't feel right.

I used to live at Belmont and Sheridan but before that Cleveland and Armitage area during the early seventies. I was an accountant for a bookbindery out in Cicero, just recently divorced, and living on my own. In the evening, I'd go up to Lincoln Avenue or Wells Street and check out the music. I'd sell this alternative magazine called The Seed, and I got exposed to alternative life styles. In August 1970, some friends invited me to go to Goose Lake International Music Festival which really opened my eyes to what was happening. I showed up in wing tipped shoes, white shirt and slacks. I mean there were 200,000 people rocking out all getting high and here I was in my wing tipped shoes and slacks. I think it was early 1971 when I went to the classic Auditorium Theater down on Congress and went to a Grateful Dead concert. My girlfriend gave me some mushrooms to take for the first time. I remember kissing her during the concert and these shooting golden pagoda images flying off in my mind. Later, when they were finished I had a telepathic communication with Jerry Garcia.

Wow. You did?

Yes indeed. What side of town do you live in?

I live in Oak Park.

My friend lives in Oak Park.

It's a nice little community. My ex-wife and I moved there, and raised our kids there. We moved about 1991. And I'm still in the same house. It's a Greek revival house.

Some of those houses in Oak Park are incredible classics.

Yeah. I actually sat in front of this house probably for about eight months before I bought it. I didn't have the money, and I couldn't afford it, but ...

You did it?

Yeah. I did it. I sure like the style over here in Santa Fe.

Yes, it's pretty interesting. Santa Fe is a great community.

Is it?

Yeah. And one of the great things about Santa Fe are the people who live here. You get to know these different communities and ...

Yeah. But my next destination is going to be in San Diego, because my oldest son, who has autism, wants to move there.

How old is he?

Thirty-two. He's living with me right now. He has lived out there for seven years with Kathy, his mom, who's a saint, and he moved back with me when I was taking time off from work right before here. It's been phenomenal. But he has a fiancée actually in there, so I've been, I've been teaching him ...

He has a fiancée?

Yeah, he does.

How is it with autism, with your son?

He is very high functioning. I often tell people he has an IQ that's in the 60 to 70 range, so academically he struggles, but he has a photographic memory. We've taught him how to learn in a way -- get the cards, and he will memorize all of the important stuff in a book, and it comes together like a mosaic. It's in his head. But he has an emotional IQ that is off the charts.

It would be equivalent to 150s, 160s. He just knows people. 90% of what comes out of his mouth is in the form of a question. If he was here and not me, by the time you got to the airport, he would know the lineage of your whole family, your grandparents and where they came from, and everything. And if you pick him up 20 years from now, he would remember. So, he has this way of moving with people, and he's also very sensitive. He always knows when someone is feeling bad or feeling, you know, however. He just says the right thing. It's really amazing. And his fiancée is disabled, and she has ...

What kind of disability does she have?

They don't really know exactly, but I do know that their strengths complement each other. We see for the first time that they can live compatibly, and that's been our dream.

Does he drive? No way?

He does. He has a license, but last October he had three seizures in one night for the first time. So, he's not going to drive now.

Do people with autism have a high rate of seizures?

Depends on the medication they are on, I think.

Oh, really? I have people around me that have Asperger's Syndrome and some of their relatives or siblings have autism.

Yeah. That's common. People are understanding it a lot better. He wasn't diagnosed until he was eleven, because people just didn't understand that it was a spectrum thing. They kind of had a certain notion that it was sort of these kids that are rocking back and forth, and can't talk. It's definitely on the spectrum, but that's not like ours.

San Diego is pretty nice.

Yeah, it is. Okay, from my knowledge – it's like $250 per square foot. It's a four-bedroom house. It's a Greek Revival. It's in Oak Park, and so it's roughly – let's just say it was appraised in the $800,000 range. That would be minimum, minimum, minimum here.

In San Diego? Yeah, I know.

Of course, depending on where you are at in San Diego. That's the one thing that I would not look forward to.

You are flying through Dallas or Denver?

Dallas. It's still -- the weather is going bad. I wonder if turbulence will be a factor.

It could be. Did you check your ...?

I did. I just assumed.

You never know about Santa Fe here with the airplanes.

Yes. I got to tell you, I've never been here before. When I got into the terminal I was like ...

This is our one gate wonder. Here we are. Have a good flight.

Thanks.

∞

— NEW ENGLAND —

You folks from Santa Fe?

No.

New Hampshire.

New Hampshire? Vermont. I get those two states mixed up sometimes.

Oh! They look pretty much the same, though just one is upside down.

Vermont doesn't have an ocean though. New Hampshire has a coastline?

Yeah, little bit of one.

Little bit.

Yeah, like a little bit and pretty directly into the Maine coastline.

What brings you to Santa Fe?

Just a little vacation, have a change of season, in different ways it is very different than New England.

I'll show you a really good gallery.

Oh, cool.

Yeah, we walked up—we walked a little way's up Canyon Road this morning and...

What do you all do in New Hampshire?

I work for a T-shirt company.

What do you do with T-Shirts?

I used to design them, but now I do all our social media marketing.

Oh! Is that how you primarily sell them?

Yeah, we have an online website, but we also sell wholesale. Actually, I wouldn't be surprised if there weren't one or two retailers around here that sold our shirts.

I used to sell 10,000 T-shirts a month.

Wow!

Really, for what? Just designs or--?

Designs that we came up with. They were sort of like not necessarily spiritual designs, but consciousness designs and they were all on natural cotton, organic cottons and natural packaging. It was many years ago.

That's cool.

We did a lot with Kanji, with the Kanji symbol for peace or for different things, and we put them right here in the center or on the pocket. One of the Kanji symbols for peace is a symbol for like the ocean being calm or flat. I heard of this rather buxom lady wearing this shirt, and this Asian lady came up to her and said, "Honey, you are wearing the wrong shirt."

Oh, how funny.

Yeah. I can't get over the architecture here. It's really neat and so different.

Is it like this in all of New Mexico.

No. Santa Fe is the city different. That's what they call it.

What do they call it?

The City Different. But northern New Mexico is a lot like this.

Oh, really?

Taos and some of the other areas are. Are you doing an Airbnb?

Yes.

How is it? How is it working out for you?

Yeah, it's nice.

Yeah, it's a little studio casita.

How much do you pay a night?

I don't know how much it was a night, but, so it's like six nights right, it was like $500 or something, so really not that bad.

Okay this gallery right in front of us with the flag is called Nedra Matteucci and you go, I mean the gallery itself is fantastic, but while there you go into their secret garden. There is a little door where you go into this garden. It's the most incredible sculpture garden.

What's it called again?

Nedra Matteucci.

Nedra Matteucci. It's right there on that corner.

We're going to try and bike down to the Plaza.

Because our little Airbnb comes with some bikes.

That's a good idea.

So many things. This is super cool! Did we get this far when we walking down it?

No, we didn't. Those are awesome! This is Canyon Road, right?

Yeah. And this one right here is a sister gallery to Nedra Matteucci.

Oh, Morning Star.

Yeah. And that's the back side of Nedra's house which is right down there. It's a phenomenal house that she has. The backside is the Morning Star Gallery and she owns that big gallery over there Nedra Matteucci.

Oh, it's named after her?

Yeah. We have a great granddaughter, who just loves, she is seven years old, and she just loves to go into Nedra's secret garden.

Yeah, sounds super fun.

Play with the sculptures. This gallery right up here is also exceptional.

Which one is it?

It's called Zaplin Lampert. They are rarely open, but if you ever catch them open go in. My lord, looks like they are open right now.

Oh good, we'd love to.

They have a bunch of the old Native American type stuff in there.

Native American. Oh, cool.

Yeah, wow! We didn't make it very far, we took like a walk this morning. Thank you!

Okay, Ladies. Thank you so much.

∞

— BANDELIER —

Welcome.

Thanks. We had an Uber ride yesterday, that took us all the up to Bandelier – about forty miles. Sorry this is such a short one.

My ex-wife and I were married up at Bandelier in the Ceremonial Cave.

Oh, really?

You have to climb these four ladders up the side of the cliff to the cave. There's a large kiva inside the cave.

Yeah, we went up to it yesterday.

We did it about 31 years ago.

That's heroic.

6:30 in the morning it was...

Oh, wow.

We got permission from the National Park Service and were married by a Sioux Medicine Man. We had 24 people standing in that kiva. Passed around the pipes and prayed. He hung these four different colored prayer flags representing the four directions on the rafters. As we were driving out of the park we were greeted with a huge double rainbow that enveloped the whole mesa up there.

That's so cool, 6:30 in the morning. So, you could see the sunrise kind of?

Yeah, and plus there were no other visitors. We took those banners and found a remote and isolated tree inside the park and tied the prayer flags to the tree. That tree was so special to us that we buried our son's placenta underneath that tree and sometimes we'd go and just sit underneath it. Some years later I was talking to a park ranger and telling her about this tree. She had seen the banners and knew the tree.

Well we really enjoyed Bandelier. Thanks for the ride and the story. Sorry the ride was so short.

Thank you.

— SOUTHWEST CLINIC —

People who travel here from other countries use Uber here all the time, right?

Yeah, right. You meet people from all over the place.

And it's very interesting because I meet all kinds of people from all kinds of backgrounds, like one young man was telling me he was musician, he was a serious musician. He recorded. He just didn't make enough as a musician, so he drove Uber.

Where do you primarily use Uber?

It depends on where I'm at.

Oh, you travel a lot?

So, my daughter who lives in Philadelphia, I've got them from Philadelphia. Most recently what? San Diego, San Francisco and wherever. Here too, coming from the airport in Albuquerque because that's where I live. It's always nice and I have always had a good experience.

That's good. I find my riders in general so fascinating as far as their professions, what they do, how they got to be what they are. It's very interesting.

I'm not very fascinating.

What do you do?

I'm a nurse in an HIV clinic.

Oh, my lord! My lady has a nonprofit here in town that provides free home care for people that fall through the gaps and cracks of our medical system.

That's a worthwhile endeavor.

And she started in the early 90's here in Santa Fe caring for all the AIDS patients.

What's the name of it?

Coming Home Connection. Now she's opening up a free hospice house in Santa Fe called Scott's House. I'll give you her card.

I'm in Albuquerque, so I work for Southwest CARE Center. They started here.

Well, she worked with Trevor for years.

Yeah, exactly. We came to work with Trevor and he retired shortly after he got us in Albuquerque. So, we opened the Albuquerque clinic there. Me, Dr. Michelle Iandiorio who was really great, who Trevor didn't want to see her leave the area because she's so talented. She's the associate medical director there.

Well, Glenys is her name and she's beginning to work in Albuquerque with the UNM Children's Hospital.

Oh, yeah, Carrie Tingley. It's good to know because I'm the nurse manager at the clinic. So, it's good for me to know, I mean, because – I have been working there for a year and a half now, so we get all kinds of people.

I thought so. You guys are new in joining it.

Yeah.

You took the whole thing over, Trevor moved, right?

Well, not the whole thing. Trevor is working now for Gilead, so before he retired he opened us up in Albuquerque.

I see.

So, we're the Albuquerque Southwest CARE Center office.

Yeah.

And we do primary care HIV services and PrEP, pre-exposure prophylaxis. We're getting a huge number of patients, which is really great, it's a wonderful thing to have in our toolbox against HIV, to be able to prevent it. It's a really amazing thing. So, Trevor went to work for Gilead and they're the manufactures of the drug that's used for PrEP.

I see. My brother died of AIDS in 1986 in Tucson. He was one of the early ones. I remember my dad and Reverend Sheldon holding watch all night long in his hospital room for days. Finally, he just withered away. He got so thin it was unbelievable. My mom just wanted to get in bed with him and hold him, but they wouldn't let her because he was quarantined,

And we're getting away from using that word AIDS – staging HIV. We're trying to...

Yeah, HIV, that's right. I think that's a good idea.

We're trying to have stage I, II and III catch on. We try to make sure that we always use those terms.

Yeah, okay, thank you.

It was a short ride for you. If you want to have your girlfriend step into the clinic one of these days, it would be so welcome.

Wonderful.

Yeah, because we might be able to do business.

Thank you.

Take care.

∞

— FASNACHT —

Tell me about Fasnacht.

It's called Fasnacht.

And it happens in Switzerland?

It happens in Switzerland. Now there's a small town in Switzerland called Basel. While in Basel, you literally can put your foot in Switzerland, France and Germany all at the same time because it's located there. A lot of fife and drum corps are there, they are called Cliques. And the Cliques get together, practice and play all kinds of fife and drum music. But they're not allowed to play out loud in the street or anything because there are strict ordnances against that. So, they have to go to the airport in France to practice. And then they also have some cellars that they can go into and practice. But Fasnacht is when they're allowed, all the cliques are all allowed to march through the town for four days and four nights, and you don't go to sleep.

You don't go to sleep?

You can if you want, but it's big and it's a parade, but there's no direction whatsoever. Like one Clique could walk down one street going one way, and another Clique could be walking through the town on the same street going the other way. Also at the same time they have these large, huge movement areas that they build. I'm talking like four or five feet tall, and they all have some sort of theme. One year when I went, one, Clique had a Marilyn Monroe theme. So they painted these big boxes and they light them up and then they carry them down and it looked...

Now what is Clique again?

Clique is a corps, fife and drum corps.

Okay. And how many people are in a Clique?

It doesn't matter. There could be twenty, there could be three. There could be forty it doesn't matter, whatever.

Okay.

So, but one of the times I went I saw them come down this hill, one of the Cliques came down the hill and looks like lava coming down a mountain, because the large movement areas. I'm talking these things are huge boxes that they build. And people throw oranges at you and that's to wish you good luck, and they throw -- what else they throw are these flowers, I forget the name of the flowers, orange flowers.

And is that held right after New Year?

No, it's in February I believe.

Oh, it's in February?

But it's called Fasnacht and then if you go to Wiesthal, Germany, oh my god, that's crazy -Wiesthal. They take carts like old wooden, like something you'd see out of Yentl, you know what I'm saying, that movie where they shovel wood and they light them on fire and they drag them down the street.

Oh, my lord.

And that is also part of -- it's like a combination of Fasnacht and then there is Wiesthal, Germany. And there are street lights in Wiesthal that the wires go across the road to the other side. There's like one light that hangs down in the middle of the road. That's how old the town is. And when the fire wagon is...

It's right in here, right?

Yes, it is. I think it's three or four nights of just mayhem and merriment and everyone is friendly, and I don't know, it's just a good time.

Great. Nice chatting with you.

You too, John.
You too, thank you very much.

— MEOW WOLF 1 —

Meow Wolf?

Yes.

Do you know anything about it?

We've heard about it. We've heard rumors about it.

It's like pretty nondescript. It's a bowling alley that's been gutted, and they put in a seventy room Victorian house.

Right.

That sounds really interesting.

Where you all from?

Los-Angeles.

The Hancock Park, Koreatown area.

That's sort of like a classic area near downtown, right? I used to live in L.A.

It's very central - west of downtown. It's very cool, yeah.

You would like it.

I had a business in L.A. that I helped start called Day Runner, making a thing called the Day Runner Organizer that you write your notes, addresses, meetings in. I sold that in 1986 and retired over here in Santa Fe.

Oh, cool.

But then I have done this and that here. I have no idea what will become of this book, but I interview all kinds of people.

What's your plan?

Well, I'm not sure yet. What I really want to do is a book and a movie, so I'm hoping to get a video thing and have little vignettes of people. Santa Fe is a very interesting place to pick up people. An eclectic group of people live here, and an eclectic group of people come here.

Yeah, the people from all over that you pick up?

Last opera season I picked up a lady just arriving from Dubai to visit the opening of the opera.

Oh, wow.

She lived in Dubai?

Yeah.

Wow.

Oh, that's cool. Haven't been there, but definitely on the list.

There seems to be a lot of good places to eat.

Unfortunately, the number one restaurant in town called Jambo Cafe, an 81 year lady drove through the plate glass window, when all the people were eating their lunch.

Oh, my gosh, was everyone okay?

No. No one died, but broken legs and –

Okay. No one died though.

So they were serving out of their truck in front of Jambo's in their parking lot.

Oh, my gosh, that's awful.

Sometimes they serve out there at Meow Wolf. Meow Wolf has some great food trucks.

Yeah, I saw that on their website. Very cool.

People go through Meow Wolf in different ways.
Yeah.

Yeah. Like kids go through just to experience each room, and the phenomena of each room. But a lot of people go there and start reading the material, and as you read the material you will read about this guy named Lex and his family, and how their sense of time and dimension sort of exploded. And they are trying to figure out reality, and teach Lex about what's real out there.

What's real?

Well, I mean, it's an interesting story. But everyone's got a different story going through, even though they read the same material. That's what's so artistic about the whole thing.

How many times have you gone?

Oh, did it once. I did it with my daughter and granddaughter. Both could have stayed there for days. I was on sensory overload after a couple of hours. But it is phenomenal! Our seven-year-old great granddaughter Aliyah would love it.

It's really cool, and it's good for so many different age groups.

Yeah. What do you do in L.A?

We are both psychologists. I'm a professor; she is a staff psychologist at USC.

Oh, my granddaughter is a senior at Xavier High School in Phoenix. USC just flew her out to L.A. for an interview.

Oh, cool, for a particular ...?

To see if she wants to go to school there. She's also going to visit Santa Cruz.

Yeah.

I mean Santa Clara. It has a program where they give a full scholarship, including room and board.

I went to Santa Cruz.

I don't think she checked out Santa Cruz. Did you go to Santa Cruz? Now tell me about it.

It's wonderful.

I'm a little biased, but it's the best.

It's the best?

It's the best, yeah, it just depends on what –

I'm going to play this for my granddaughter. What's so amazing about Santa Cruz?

Oh, my gosh, the people! Everyone is very genuine, and down to earth. It's slow and kind of laid back. I often would go to the ocean.

Gorgeous, yeah, beach town. It's very progressive.

It's a big surfing community, and it's definitely very different from USC. And I worked at USC before too, and I love USC.

They have a program up there in Santa Clara she is consid-

ering where you only get this particular kind of scholarship if you're chosen out of 10 kids They ask them to write some kind of an essay, or something like that. I don't know what it's about. But they judge these essays, and the winners, all of them get free tuition and room and board. She got accepted by Swarthmore, University of Chicago, Brown, pretty top-notch schools.

Yeah, sometimes it's a crap shoot.

It's just random.

If you were given a scholarship with full room and board between Stanford, Harvard, Brown and USC, how would you make your decision?

I think it would depend on her major. I don't know, like the culture of the place you want to be living in. They are all so different in terms of like –

Culture.

The environment.

I like Santa Cruz myself. At USC, the undergrads are pretty small.

Yeah, but it depends. I lived in Boston too, and Harvard, obviously, just has that really old history, and some people really like it. I also knew people who went there as undergraduates who didn't like it that much, because they just didn't feel connected to the other people who went there. So, thinking about what kind of people you want to be around and –

Yeah, I think that's the big thing.

Harvard attracts a certain kind of people. USC attracts a different kind of people. So, they are very different.

My other granddaughter was easy. She's going to go to the University of Arizona. She just finished high school in

three years, but, boy, I mean, these state schools are expensive too. She's thinking about joining a sorority. My mother was a Pi Beta Phi and it was a major part of her life, for her whole life, after college.

Yeah.

University of Arizona is $24,000 a year with in-state tuition and room and board in a dormitory. Ok, here we are. Enjoy Meow Wolf.

Ok, thanks. Bye.

∞

— SPEECH THERAPIST —

Good Morning. What brings you to town?

I'm visiting from Los Angeles. Yeah, we went to Ohio, picked up a car.

You're driving it all the way back?

Yeah, we flew to Ohio. My girlfriend got a car from her dad, and we are driving it back. She won't say, but I think she got it practically for free. And we're going to drive it to Los Angeles. We're stopping in different places.

What do you do in L.A.?

I'm a speech therapist. Yeah, I work with adults. I don't work with kids. I work with adults with strokes and things like that.

Oh, with strokes? That's wonderful. Is that the primary adult issue, strokes?

Yeah, usually that and heart attacks. But usually they have some type of neurological damage to your brain that affects your speech and swallowing. The two major things we work with are speech and swallowing. So, what is your book about? What is your angle?

My angle is to just create little vignettes of people. And just interesting stories. It's a lot of fun.

Yeah, interesting. You get politicians around here?

I do. State senators.

What about Richardson?

Never had Richardson. I've had dinner with Richardson and breakfast with him before. He's an interesting guy.

That's interesting. What do you think about this new one?

Susana Martinez?

Yeah, Trump supporter.

I don't think – she didn't support Trump.

No?

I think she may now, but she didn't during the election.

Because he was privy with her, I guess.

No, because he came into town, and said she wasn't doing a very good job. Did you purposely choose adults over children to work with, or did your profession just end up that way?

It just kind of ended up that way. I did choose. I didn't want to work with small kids. I wanted to work with adults from the beginning. I had a leaning that way. I wasn't sure at first, but I had a leaning that way, and it's way different work. When you work with kids you focus on articulation and delay in speech production, and things like that. With adults it's more neurological, and it's different.

My daughter works primarily with blind kids and then part time with blind adults.

How interesting.

Yeah. Canine and cane management, you know, dogs and canes – canine management and listening are two of the big deals.

Yeah, it is. There's a huge difference.

She was awarded blind teacher of the year several years ago for the states west of the Mississippi, or something like that.

Really? I will let the gate open. All right. Thank you, sir.

Ok. Thank you.

— HARRY'S MANAGER —

Hello.

Good morning. Let's see where are you headed? Ok, got it. What do you do here in town?

I am a restaurant manager.

Which restaurant?

Harry's Roadhouse.

Harry's? Oh, yeah. I love their veggie burger.

Oh, it's good. It's a great place.

It really is. And plus, you have gluten-free bread.

We do. We are super conscious of allergies and gluten-free and all that stuff, which I think is really cool, because, you know, we're so casual, but we take that stuff really seriously, which is awesome. Yeah, I love Harry's.

I had a party of eight out there three weeks ago. And a party of six two weeks ago because my lady's grandkids were here from Denmark. And their friends and nieces and great grandkids and so on.

Fun! Well, that's fun. I love when I meet people who love Harry's.

I've been eating at Harry's for 25 years so... for a long time! I don't know how long.

Yeah, they've been open 25, so probably that long.

Yeah.

You know, I was in fine dining for about a decade.

Here in town?

No, it was in Hawaii.

Oh, Hawaii! I love Hawaii, particularly Maui. The marine reserves they have there are unbelievable. We snorkeled at Ahihi Kinau and Kahekili reserves and saw all these brilliantly colored fish and marine life. But it was over on the Big Island that I went out into the ocean maybe 300 yards, dove down with my snorkeling equipment and about 10 spinner dolphins danced right in front of me for several minutes. Of course, the Road to Hana shouldn't be missed and seeing Ohe'o Gulch and the Seven Sacred Pools. It was on Big Island also where I couldn't proceed on the road because red hot lava was flowing across the road.

Yeah, Hawaii is great. I moved here, and I was at The Compound for a while and I just got so sick of fine dining.

Oh, my god. Do you know my son David Bishop?
Yeah.

Do you know David?

Yeah, yeah. I adore David. He's sweet as pie.

He just moved.

Did he? Where'd he go?

Initially Sonoma County up in northern California, but then Las Vegas.

Cool!

He moved to live with his girlfriend.

Oh, good! Cutie. He is such a sweetie pie. Yeah. Wow, small world.

It is. Listen, I pick up people all the time who know my son.

Yeah, I mean, in the restaurant industry, you know, you really get to know a lot of people. It is such a social job, you know?

You all know each other.

Yeah, we do. Especially in Santa Fe, you know? It is such a tight knit group. It's just a tight knit industry.

Do you know him from the Compound or from Coyote?

No, Arroyo Vino.

Oh, yeah?

Yeah. And then, I hired him at the Compound.

You hired my son?

Yeah, yeah. He's just so sweet.

He knows his wines.

He knows his wines so well. I was always so impressed. And

so, when he wanted to come over to The Compound, I was like, "Yes, we need people with your knowledge!" Yeah, he's great. I was so sick of fine dining and so, you know, Harry's put up an ad and I was like, you know, I am going to give it a shot. And it is the best job I've ever had.

It's consistent, isn't it? That's the major thing.

Yeah. Harry and Peyton take such good care of us. They are so sweet. They are just real genuine people. I just adore them.

That's wonderful.

Next time you are in, say hi. I'll buy you a margarita.

Well, thank you. Thank you so much.

Of course! Wow, small world. Well, tell David I said hi. Thanks for the ride. I appreciate it.

You're welcome.

Someone hit and run my Jeep the other day, so it has been in...

Oh, my Lord!

It's been in getting fixed. And I am just right here, yes. Thank you so much. It was nice to meet you. Yeah, tell David I said hi. Next time you are in Harry's, say hello.

I will. Thank you.

∞

— ALL ABOUT LUCRETIUS —

Are you both going to the dentist?

No. Mason wants to be let off at Smith's first.

I see.

Luckily its right across from the dentist I'm going to.

He sent me like six texts and my phone died.

Oh! Your phone died?

I didn't get any. I went up to the exhibit room and made some coffee. Then Alex showed up so we tried to talk...

Then I texted Devon to see if he wanted to join us for coffee. Eventually he showed up, and the three of us were talking. Somehow, we got on the subject of justice, and we got into an argument, because I was very passionately saying that I'm not okay with what's termed lawful killing, which is like...Let's say you get pulled over for a traffic violation, and you get out of your car. You happen to have like your phone in your hand. Cop thinks it's a gun, and just kills you.

And then the judge refuses the case, and says, "Oh, well, you know, the cop thought it was a gun, and that's why he killed him. That's lawful; that was okay." Then the case is closed. Meanwhile the person's brother or father or somebody died, and they just told him, "We are sorry for your loss. It was a lawful killing." And that's about all there is to it. I was upset! They were both trying to ... Rather than like sit with me, and be with my angst about that, they were trying to offer me explanations of why it's that way, and trying to explain that there is no better solution. And I was just getting more and more upset. It's not acceptable, even if there is no solution! At the very least, the very least, they should be outraged, and not accept it.

I was saying at the very least the state should give them a couple million dollars or something. At least then there would be some type of acknowledgement. The state would be saying to the cops, "We don't condone this either, even though we are not going to punish you."

That sounds like an interesting discussion. Did you try that coffee with them?

Yeah, I did.

Oh, cool! Do you like it?

Yeah, I did. It was quite delicious. I think I'm going to go buy myself a little water heater, like you have —

You can get one of those for $15 at like Wal-Mart or something.

Yeah. And I'm going to get one of those, and then I'm going to get those little filters. So I can just make one at home. You can't beat a good cup of coffee.

You can't - can you? He's made $70,000 so far out of a $100,000 goal on Kickstarter, and this is his first week.

Whoa! I really hope it gets out there. Where would he sell it? Online, or where do you think?

I don't know. Some company will probably buy him out, and sell it through all different types of channels. I don't know.

That's amazing! He managed to make that much in just one week?

I know.

That's incredible! I would buy it.

It sounds like a lot of people want this product. Sounds like he figured out a need, and figured out the technology required to fulfill the need.

Yeah. And he wrote his own patents.

Oh, really?

Yeah. He wrote four of them.

Wow! What's his profession?

He doesn't really have one. He never went to college, just one of those genius kids.

That's pretty cool. How old is he?

28 or 29. I think 29.

Pretty smart kid. Do you know how he figured out how to write those patents?

Studied.

Wow! Self-taught.

He studied online.

That's pretty awesome! Wow!

Where are you guys from?

I'm from Montana. I grew up on a ranch. It was really close to Canada.

What's it called?

It's called Thompson Falls. It's this really tiny town in the middle of nowhere. It has 1,400 people living in it. And Jackson where was it you lived?

I'm from California.

What part?

Santa Rosa. It's just 60 miles north of San Francisco. Pretty temperate weather. Hey what book is that you are reading.

Lucretius - The Swerve.

Tell me about Lucretius.

I suppose he was kind of like the Greek philosopher, Democritus. Democritus believed that if you kept chopping things up eventually you would get to a particle that's so small that you couldn't chop it up anymore. Basically, the idea of an atom, theoretically. But you know, they didn't have any ideas of protons and neutrons, or any of that, but just the philosophical concept.

Yeah.

And he took that philosophical concept, and expanded upon it a little bit more. He was a Roman guy as opposed to Greek. We read him at St. John's as opposed to Democritus. A lot of Democritus's work is lost, but a lot of Lucretius's work is still complete for the most part when it comes to like the idea of atoms. I forget what the idea of the Swerve was. He had some sort of idea about motion.

The idea was that in the very, very beginning, all of the infinite atoms were aligned and moving in perfect alignment, and then one, for some unknown, hypothesized reason, just swerved and created a collision. Then that collision began this kind of eternal...

Yeah.

Fusion?

Yeah, some sort of a creation process.

Is that what fusion is all about?

Well it's not necessarily intended ...It's really more ...

Philosophical?

I think he means it very literally. He really believed that there was this "Swerve,"-and he doesn't know what caused it.

A collision of atoms and matter, which certainly sounds a little bit similar to the Big Bang Theory of course. Obviously, he had no idea what our modern conception of an atom is. He just thought there is probably matter, which is the smallest matter ever, that you can't even see, and it doesn't stop.

That's what they are doing in the Swiss cyclotron. It's a big tunnel thing.

Oh, yeah, and they collide ...

Yeah, they collide atoms to try to experience the Big Bang.

Oh, that's so cool! I think they discovered sub atomic particles from doing a lot of collisions with like hydrogen atoms or something. Then they figured maybe if we collide sub atomic particles with sub atomic particles, we'll find more particles, like breaking them apart. At least, that's what I've have heard. I might be wrong. Lucretius was one of the first guys who like you weren't totally sure if he believed in God or not, like let's say that God is Venus, blah, blah, blah. It's almost like a poetic way, he starts his book. But then there are hints where it's like, does he actually believe in all these goddesses and gods, or is he just pretending so he doesn't get killed?

Which dialogue is it where Socrates is about to be killed, and he gives his full speech about there being an afterlife, so don't be sad for me ...

Oh, was that, "The Apology?"

"The Apology," maybe. I heard an interpretation that he didn't really believe in what he was saying, that he was trying to make his family feel better, like kind of manufacturing arguments, so that they were like, "Oh, okay, I don't feel bad about this anymore." He didn't really believe in what he was saying.

Yeah.

And, we kind of get that feeling from Lucretius too, because he ...

I mean you especially get it from Lucretius, because there are a lot of things he says that sort of subtly implied that he doesn't believe in God or anything like that. Some people argue that he might have even been an atheist, which is really weird at that particular time.

He was writing to his friend, and he was trying to give his friend a reason to enjoy life.

And he says, "There are little particles that you can't see."

Yeah.

What a very technical reason they give.

Now that it's coming back to me a little bit I think he actually disputed the very notion of life. You don't have to be unhappy about your life, because your unhappiness is based off of a paradigm that's obviously at fault. If you remove that paradigm you get reasons for your own happiness. I think the whole point is to remove the paradigm by stressing the argument of atoms, and basically saying everything is meaningless, and that's okay.

Some people take comfort in the idea of God, and that there is some sort of structure. Some people take more comfort in the idea that there isn't a God. It's really interesting! I suppose if you believe in God, then there is the problem of how do you justify it if bad things happen to you, or if you see some evil thing happen in the world. But I guess if you're an atheist and everything is random, that's just fortune, and you can't control it. I know, I guess that's comforting, but I guess it's sort of not very comforting at the same time. It's really weird!

I took a seminar training in the seventies called EST, later it was called The Landmark Forum, and one of their teachings was that life is empty and meaningless – it's whatever you create it to be. A lot of people had difficulty with the concept that "life is empty and meaningless." Belief in God, one way or the other, requires belief, so whether you believe or not believe, it's really two sides of the same coin, it's the psyche that requires a belief. I've tried to get rid of most of my beliefs, and am still working on it. Who you are, with no beliefs, gets close to your pure essence. Beliefs sometime clutter the way of most folks knowing more of who they are, and of knowing their pure essence. Can you image the world with no beliefs? Here we are. Thanks.

Yeah, thank you.

∞

— FRUIT LADY —

Do you get mostly tourists or townies when you drive around Santa Fe?

It's like 50/50. How long have you lived here in Santa Fe?

Six and a half years, coming up on seven.

Where are you from?

Mostly from Idaho. I wasn't born there, but I grew up there and consider it my home.

What do you do here in Santa Fe?

I came for an undergrad program. I graduated about three years ago.

Southwest or St. John's?

St. John's College. And now I do fulltime fundraising work for a non-profit, like grassroots, small dollar, you know.

Are you available to do grant writing?

Maybe. It's not something I have a ton of experience with, because I do grassroots fundraising, so like I can kind of help with our grant writing process.

What's grassroots funding?

Like small dollar, people who give $5.00 or $100, but not people who give $10,000.

I see.

I help with our grant work, but I don't write our grant proposals. Also, I'm on a board of a search and rescue team.

Oh, you are?

I'm angling toward learning how to do grant writing for them. **That's a good thing to know.**

Yeah. Good for the team, even if we get $1,000. We buy our own gear and the members pay to volunteer. We use that money to buy gear, certifications and all those kinds of things. So yeah, it would be good, a good thing to learn. What kind of a nonprofit are you involved in?

It's one called Coming Home Connection here in Santa Fe, and it provides free home care for people who fall through the gaps and cracks of our medical system.

Yeah, that's cool. It's a very necessary thing. I was talking with a friend of mine yesterday about nonprofits, right, because if we all did our jobs really well, we'd put ourselves out of work. Like in a perfect world, we wouldn't need anyone to provide the money to send healthcare home for folks.

Right.

In a perfect world, I wouldn't need to be working to fight climate change. But here we are. Nonprofits, that's pretty interesting.

I am also with the Rotary Foundation and we support a lot of nonprofits in Santa Fe.

What? Like the Rotary Club where I grew up is sort of this omnipresent name. But I don't think I actually know what they do.

Community service and global service. Our club has 65 local projects that we support.

Wow, that's ambitious. Is that...?

Different club members are interested in different things. We have a water project in Guatemala that our club supports. And some people down there do wells, and things

like that in rural areas where they've got no running water. We do medians here as part of our beatification project, we do the Santa Fe River cleanup. Our big project is Pancakes on the Plaza.

Oh, yeah.

We're always raising money in the community for Pancakes on the Plaza, then we give it away to nonprofits that support kids.

That's cool. It sort of serves as a hub for volunteering and support?

Yeah. We are all from the business community. We get together once a week and have since 1905. It was founded in Chicago by Paul Harris. We have over 1.2 million members worldwide in 33,000 clubs in 200 different countries.

So, like the members are all, like the volunteers are all members of the business community?

Yes. Rotarians come from the business community.

Interesting.

Members are like professional bankers, lawyers, members of nonprofits, entrepreneurs. People who just want to serve together.

Right, that's one of the tricky things. So many nonprofits are in their own bubble, they're not connected. It makes sense to have a kind of central network. I mean, of course some of the community foundations and stuff, they have networking events and bringing people together, but it's different. I have only been working fulltime in nonprofits for two years.

Well, it's a good way to serve. I mean some people, their entire career is served in nonprofits. They have to figure it out somehow.

I worked in restaurants for about 13 years or something, and I still cater on the side now and again, but I think that I'll be full time in nonprofits for quite a while.

Those clouds are amazing.

They're so pretty. It was beautiful after the storm last night. But it was pretty cold.

It was. I'm afraid we lost our apricot tree.

Yeah, I was thinking about that, all the fruit is going to be trashed.

I don't know if we got that cold even with the snow. I think maybe the apricot trees survived.

Definitely. Our cherry and crab apples near my office, most of the flowers were knocked off. They might still have their innards, you know, but the petals are knocked off.

Right.

They lost a lot of their beauty yesterday but hopefully they didn't freeze. Yeah, it's a real bummer. All of the trees are blooming for weeks. Then like three springs in a row, we had a late storm that froze everything. We had a peach tree and a couple of apple trees and stuff. Few years in a row we had no fruit because it all froze. So then one winter we decided we were going to watch the news every night, and we got out there. We had a system of a ladder and sheets, and covered everything, and we ended up with so many peaches on the tree that the big branches broke off under their own weight.

Aren't peaches just unbelievable sometimes?

They are. It's incredible.

To get a fresh sweet peach is like...

A fresh ripe peach, it's like Heaven.

A gift from the Gods.

Yeah, it really is. It's amazing. It's a shame you can hardly ever find them ripe.

There's a lady here in town named Margarite who has a fruit stand on the corner of Alameda and Saint Francis.

Oh, yeah.

On weekends, she's there sometimes. But I don't think she's started yet, but she has the best consistently good organic sweet peaches and tomatoes. They call her the Fruit Lady.

It's not far from my office.

Yeah, if you subscribe to her email list she keeps you posted of what she has. She brings them down from Southern Colorado. Of course, the best peaches I have ever had were as a kid growing up in Sedona.

Awesome! If it's easier for you, you can let me off on the corner, like right before Saint Francis.

Okay. Hey, thank you for letting me record this. Adios.

Thank you.

∞

— BEAD FEST —

So, tell me about Bead Fest.

Okay. Bead Fest is here every other year.

Every other year?

I'm not really sure how long it's been going on but this is my second time to come, so I was here two years ago. And Bead

Fest, they have them actually all across the country, but I come to this one because it's in Santa Fe, and because I live in Las Cruces.

Exactly. She lives in Las Cruces. I live in Virginia. So, I traveled to come here and that heavy case that you just lifted and put in the back is a bag of tools because I just took a workshop.

What is it that you do with beads, I mean buy beads, services or make jewelry?

Yes, they have workshops, and in the convention center, they have classes that are taught there. Also, they usually have a convention hotel where some of the classes are taught. This year it's at the Drury Plaza Hotel. And then they also have a sales floor at the convention center where there's all sorts of vendors with bead, tools and business systems. It brings people from all over.

So, are you bead professionals? Is that the way I would describe you?

Yes. Jewelry designers.

Jewelers.

Jewelry designers? I see, okay.

Yes. Bead professionals, I like that.

I am more a bead professional than you. You're more of a jeweler.

I do metal work.

You do metal work?

Yes.

Check out her website. She has beautiful jewelry.

I have a jewelry application. I'll send your information on my project.

Okay.

I write the Bible and other sacred texts on a nickel disc the size of a dime.

Now, I have heard of things like that, yeah.

And I'm looking for jewelry settings to place my nickel discs in.

How do you do this?

Well, I do it with a focused ion beam, but it can also be done with a laser.

Focused ion beam.

So, I've heard of it like writing data on a grain of rice.

Right. I can do that.

Oh, my goodness.

I work in focused ion beam technology. We do it for different things but my primary thing is machining diamond and different metals. We make little diamond tips and probes about 1/1000th the width of your hair that are primarily used in the semiconductor industry. We make little apertures down to like 100 nanometers.

So, do you work with Los Alamos or anyone?

My patents are originally from Los Alamos. I track what goes on up there, as do other patent attorneys. I have an exclusive license for three Los Alamos patents that happen to apply to the diamond industry. I was in the middle of negotiating a license with a large Tel Aviv diamond firm for them to utilize these patents, and right in the middle I get a call from this English sounding guy who said he was DeBeers. He said that DeBeers would like to talk to me immediately about licensing these patents. Seems like they had already produced 20000 millennium diamonds utilizing this technique. So, they flew me over to London immediately on Business Class, and I sat down with several DeBeers board members and attorneys in their board room, them on one side of the table and me on the other negotiating this deal. Finally, the DeBeers board member leading the negotiations put his half glasses down on the end of his nose and said, "We're just playing poker now, aren't we?" And finally, we shook hands, and finished the deal. So, for the past seventeen years I have worked at the highest echelons of the diamond industry licensing these patents to mark diamonds with logos, such as The Forever Mark by DeBeers. I also place spiritual marks and membership organization marks on the table of diamonds. You can see the marks with your iPhone.

That's cool.

Okay. Thank you, ladies.

∞

WEEK TWO

— MEOW WOLF 2 —

Have you got all your interesting's out?

Yeah, we just came down for the weekend to go to Meow Wolf.

Oh, what did you think of that?

It was awesome.

Yeah.

What an awesome night! There was a concert. A band called itchy-O played. We're all from Denver. They are a 32-piece percussionist group and really fun! They wear costumes. It's a perfect venue for them.

Did people hangout in the rooms or just in where they were playing?

You could do either.

Everything is open, so you could just wander around if you wanted to.

Can you still hear the music no matter what part of the building you were in?

I mean, I guess, but if you're pretty far away it's going to be hard. I didn't know what it would be like there. I was just walking around getting lost.

Actually, I was going to put a little saddle right on your back. Be like don't worry, to the left.

Did you all fly?

Yeah, we flew in a small airplane. I'm the pilot.

Is it a one engine?

Yeah, little four-seater. We came down through the San Luis Valley, cut out north about probably 30 miles north of Alamosa. There is a spot where you can cut over the San Juan's.

That valley is pretty nice.

Yeah, it was so beautiful during the flight. Our friend kept saying, "Keep your eyes peeled for UFOs." You just keep your eyes open for them, like every five minutes you keep looking.

Did you fly over Dulce?

No, that's where the UFOs are, right? We flew right past Crestone and up that valley.

Did you go over the Sand Dunes?

Yeah, we flew just west of the Sand Dunes. We didn't fly directly over them. It becomes the valley north, way north of where the Sand Dunes are. You can take a route that takes you right over the Sand Dunes, but then you are flying over mountainous terrain for a long time.

So, you guys flew down just to visit Meow Wolf?

Yeah, sure!

Did you do Airbnb?

Yeah.

You got a whole house that you rented?

Yeah.

The house is like a family therapy office, which was perfect for all of us because there is so much to play with. There's tons of books to read! I have learned so much.

It's a family therapy office?

Yeah, they use it as this like therapist office most of the time, but there are still bedrooms.

We are pretty sure there is some sort of sex therapy going on, because the bedrooms have cameras.

There is a big surveillance camera in each bedroom, so we covered them with a towel. It's kind of weird, but the owner was showing us that they don't work.

I would say the exact same thing, but she's probably just a fucking liar.

So, we were still going to cover it.

I'm also doing a movie with my riders, but I haven't set up a video. You guys would be perfect for my video!

I drove Lyft for a while in Denver. It was fun. I liked driving from when I got off work until 4 am. I would just have a lot of coffee before I drove, and then deal with the troublemakers.

I only work in the mornings and the afternoons. My lady likes me home at night. It's a completely different sensation driving at night for me.

Yeah, see I'm a bad driver. If I drove during the day people would give me bad reviews, but at night everybody's wasted.

So, you get good reviews?

Yeah. And you get tipped a lot at night. Lyft has given out something like $200 million in tips that Lyft drivers have received. Nice, yeah? I only use Lyft, and I always tip. Unless somebody is just...

Yeah, you can do it on the app.

A jerk. Do you have Lyft in Denver?

Yeah, but you get a lot of drivers who don't know where they are going, and get lost. And it's hard to tip after that. It's like, that's your job.

There was a big jet convention here in Santa Fe about six months ago where all the jet manufacturers of private jets flew their latest and greatest airplanes into Santa Fe. There were like fifty of them lined up in a row right here on the tarmac.

Yeah, it's a big airport for a regional airport. The runway is really long.

But not long enough for a big plane.

I mean we saw a United regional jet taking off.

How long have you been a pilot?

About almost two years. Actually, more like a year and a half, but I had been flying before to get my license. Last August, that's when I passed the ride check. I'm official now. I'm working on my instrument writing.

What do you all do professionally?

We do a lot of things. I work at a bar, and I'm starting to get into event stuff in the space we have in Denver. This one is a server now, a barista.

If I get my commercial pilot's license, I will be flying.

I don't know. I think it's time we moved to helicopters.

Helicopters?

I would vote for drones.

You would need a big drone!

The Chinese have a big drone to pick people up.

Yeah, I saw that. Honestly, I wouldn't trust any kind of aircraft that doesn't have a human pilot. It's not warm and fuzzy.

I think eventually they will be safer, because they are going to have sensors. They won't let anything...

Yeah, but if something goes wrong, you just have no ability to take over.

Yeah, like I feel machines only work about 62% of the time. I don't know, maybe it's just me.

And with things like aviation they tend to change very, very, very slowly, so I can't picture the government ever allowing only autonomous flights. It takes people.

One of my riders, he started six Silicon Valley start-ups and sold six of them. His latest investments are in flying cars. He says the infrastructure is already there. They are just going to follow the roads.

I don't want to fly a car. It would be cheaper to just learn to astral project, but a flying car...

His other investment these days is in this app for a doctor on video call. It's an app on your phone, and you have instant access to a doctor anywhere on the planet. They are wired into all the pharmacies worldwide, so you can get a prescription instantly.

That you just talk to?

Yeah, by video. They are wired into all the pharmacies, so you can get a prescription instantly.

That's dope! There's one for massage that my friend developed.

Oh, is there one for massage?

Yeah, you just set it up, and they come over in a few minutes.

My cousin started an app for dog walking. It's kind of like their tag line is "It's the Uber for dog walking." I use it. You go on and they have a bunch of different walkers.

"Uber for dog walking," that's a good one!

You just go on - I need a dog walker. I just want someone to walk my dog today, or like right now, and he will match you with somebody near your house. He's doing really well. They are live in like 10 cities. San Francisco, L.A., Denver, Chicago ...

Oh, who started that?

My cousin. You never met him. He hasn't visited Denver in a few years, but he started Wag. Look up Wag.

Wag - that's a good name. It's all about the name and the market.

I've only met your mother. I feel like I should know all this.

You met my dad.

Yeah, definitely your dad.

My mom has only been to Denver once. She doesn't like it very much. The altitude makes her sick. She is not in the best physical shape, so...

Yeah, my parents don't ever want to be anywhere where they are not surrounded by conservative Christians who believe everything they believe. So, it's like a little scary. I ask them, "Why don't you guys move here?" And my mom is like, "Oh, no!" Their bubble is so fragile and delicate. Indianapolis is a town; it's a large city. It's a large city of people who have given up their dreams.

It's like The Matrix. When you go there I mean the sky is legitimately lower. The clouds are not so silky. Who wants to be where its sunny like maybe 30 days out of the year? It's pretty brutal. That's the way Syracuse is too.

I feel that layer that you see in people's eyes, that spark, like that mischievousness, it's so rare in Indianapolis. No one will play with you. Everybody is just so bottom-line. Except the race is great.

When I was nine or ten I used to track racing and the Indianapolis 500 on the radio. My friend Billy and I would line up the cars around his swimming pool, turn up the radio real loud, and move the cars around the swimming pool based on their actual positions in the race. We'd do this for hours. I used to dream about being an Indianapolis 500 race car driver. Once when I was back in Indianapolis for a trade show I went to the track and got to go around the track a few times it in a special vehicle. To this day I track all car racing. After the race, we'd cross his wash and go play up on Indian Hill and find pottery shards, beads and arrowheads. Then we'd go pick the most incredible blackberries and his mom, Betty, would make delicious pies out of them.

I've been to the race. Yeah, I love racing and pies.

Wow. What time did Meow Wolf close?

They closed at eight. Time just flies when we are in there, just like reading all the stuff. I was looking at it all, trying to figure out the puzzles.

Did you figure it all out?

No, but they ...

What's your analysis of what Meow Wolf is all about?

Well, they are talking about singularity. They are trying to show you and the world what's happening behind, or under or pervasive with your world all the time, and that it's all pervasive magic. That's what's happening.

Pervasive magic. Thank you.

Magic is real. Thanks for the ride.

∞

— LADY IN COAT —

What do you want to know for your book? Do you want to know why I came? Why I'm here?

I would love to know.

My first best friend from the third grade passed away in January, so I came for the memorial service, which was Saturday and today is Monday. I have been here a week, Monday to Monday. But my first few days were kind of challenging. I didn't get off to a good start.

What happened?

The television in my room kept spontaneously going on and off, and it kept me awake and I lost many hours of sleep. They sent people three times to fix it. They never did fix it. They finally had to replace the TV, which they should have done in the first place, because my upper respiratory condition got worse the first two days, Tuesday and Wednesday. I was coughing all day long and all night long, and then when I finally got a good night sleep, I didn't cough at all from then on.

That's good.

So, of course I blame it all on not getting any sleep the first two nights. So, I wasn't feeling real well, so I didn't get up and about and I missed a lot of museuming that I wanted to do.

Did you get back here to see her very often?

This is the first time, so the answer is no.

Where are you from?

San Francisco. I was here once in the year 2004 for a day and a half. It barely counts. It counts a little bit, but it's not like being here. So, are we on the Santa Fe Trail right now?

No, this is Old Pecos Trail. Old Santa Fe Trail is right down there.

Okay. So yesterday I went to Abiquiú with a friend.

Did you see the Georgia O'Keefe House?

I saw everything. It was absolutely fabulous, absolutely fabulous. I have never seen anything like that in my life.

My friend used to own a woman's clothing store on the corner of the Plaza.

Is that the fancy one that is there now?

No.

You know the fancy one that is there now?

Santa Fe Dry Goods and The Workshop next door. It's my lady's favorite store.

Well, yes, I bought a jacket there. I also bought a skirt there.

Before Santa Fe Dry Goods, it was called The Guarantee on the Plaza, a very upscale women's clothing store co-owned by Abe and Marion Silver with her sister and husband Jane and Gene Petchesky. Before that it was called The White House. Abe would tell stories of Georgia O'Keefe coming into his store in late afternoon, and how he would lock the door to give her privacy.

Oh, she didn't want everyone watching her undress

And he sold undergarments to her for like years. He had more Georgia O'Keefe stories than you could shake a stick at.

I can imagine.

She was a character around town.

Yes. My friend who passed away in January was also an artist of note. She had six paintings up in the Santa Fe Museum of Art in the alcove. You are familiar with the alcove collection? It changes every six weeks. She has six up there now. I think it closed yesterday or it is closing today, one or the other. Her name is Ciel Bergman. It's worth sneaking in there to see the six. I think today is the last day.

It's in the fine art museum?

Yeah, or is that the main big museum just downtown and around the corner from the...?

Downtown, yeah.

The one that has the alcove exhibit, the one that they are redoing for its hundredth anniversary, that one. Ciel Berman, I think she is a little bit famous; someday she is going to be very famous. Six of her paintings are in the alcove collection exhibit that is closing either yesterday or today.

And was she your childhood friend?

Yes.

Where did you all grow up?

Berkeley, California.

You grew up in Berkeley? Was this in the fifties, Berkeley in the fifties?

Yes, and the forties. We met in the forties. We are really old. In fact, we met in the early forties during World War II - middle forties.

What was Berkeley like in those days?

Different from now but always unique, but it was not as radical as it became in the sixties. I was the last of the Silent Generation.

Did you live there in the sixties?

No. But my father and mother did and my father died in the family home, and one of my daughters lives in that home now. But Berkeley was always individual. It was always innovative. It was always ahead of its time, but it was not always as kooky and leftist as it is now. I do not consider leftist and liberal to be the same.

What's the difference?

Liberal means tolerant; Leftist can be holier than thou rigid. That is not liberal. They think they are liberal because they are leftist, but they are not. They are rigid, and everybody who is rigid and judgmental is not liberal. I am a true liberal. I am tolerant, accepting of differences and respectful of different points of view. The leftist fanatics are not.

What do you think Jerry Brown is?

He is a mixture as am I.

He is a mixture? During his first term, my lady had a children's issue she was passionately dealing with and she drove from San Jose to Sacramento, walked into the Governor's Office and requested to meet with the Governor. The Governor just happened to be walking out at that time and told her sure, let's talk, and they spoke for the next hour. He helped her with her project.

He is an interesting character. I used to carpool with Nancy Pelosi. We had our babies together and we were neighbors.
I like Nancy.

She is a great person and a hard worker. She is very genuine and very hard working. I used to see her on the weekends.

We'd go to the same swim club. Her husband would be watching the five kids, and she'd be reading the New York Times cover to cover. She had five babies. I had three, all 17 months apart. She was a very hardworking mother, hands-on. She didn't turn over the raising of her five children...

She has five kids?

Yes. I have three, she has five. She worked very hard. Every night she cooked their dinner and she sat down at the table and read to them. And Dianne Feinstein as well, hardworking and honest. She was a classmate of my sister-in-law in school.

Where did they go to school?

That was at Lowell High School in San Francisco. She was a neighbor. She lived half a block away as did Nancy in those days. They are both very good, hardworking people. Not full of themselves at all. What is the museum called that I was referring to, that my friend's art is in? Is it the Fine Arts Museum?

Yeah, Museum of Fine Arts.

Museum of Fine Arts, okay. So, your wife is a shopper and likes pretty clothes?

My lady, among other things she does, is a fashion designer. She goes through all these fashion magazines at night and pulls out stuff. She designs a line of coats and pants.

For women or men or both?

Women.

Well, I just bought a full-length fur coat at a garage sale yesterday on the way to Abiquiú.

You think you got a good deal on it?

I know I got a good deal on it.

What kind of coat is it?

It is Persian lamb, and it was made in Spain. I will model it for you.

Great.

It is really hard to wear fur coats these days. It gets spat on, or you get tomatoes thrown at you. You have to be very careful when you wear them. I don't know why I bought it. I have a full-length fur coat that I bought in Helsinki with mink scraps.

With mink scraps?

Mink scraps and it is reversible; and it is unstructured, so there are no shoulder pads. This one has big square shoulder pads in it. It's probably from the forties, but it's in really good shape. It has hardly been worn.

Where was the sale?

It was on somebody's lawn, halfway to Abiquiú, three quarters of the way up to Abiquiú. But the person who was doing it is a well-known photographer in town. Her name is Jennifer...

Esperanza?

Yes, Jennifer Esperanza, you know her? I bought it from her. You can tell her you took me to the airport.

She is a classic herself. Quite the photographer.

Yes, she is. Well, she liked me and I bought this coat from her, and then she gave me this sweater. I didn't buy it. She just gave it to me.

She did a book of characters around Santa Fe, and my lady was one of her characters.

Really? I'd love to get that book.

It's probably on Amazon. I heard she was moving.

She is, to California. I have a daughter who does tintypes. She is a caterer and a chef and a fine art photographer. I got her some really great tintypes there too. She does her own, but she collects old ones from other people.

You have grand kids?

I do, five. Two in Arlington, Virginia and three who have been born and raised in London, except that two of them with their mother, my daughter, moved back to San Francisco last year and one remained at Eton as a boarding student. So, my first-born grandson is a boarding student at Eton.

Oh, boy. My grandkids are going into college now.

Aren't you lucky?

They are seniors in high school. One has been interviewing at Brown and other schools, and the other is going to the University of Arizona.

You know, the cream rises to the top. It doesn't matter what your grades are or where you go to school, the cream rises to the top.

I know, amazing! Okay, this car is going to pull out. I am going to pull up here and get your stuff out.

You want to see the coat on me?

Yes, I would love to. Oh, it's beautiful!

Ok, thanks. Bye.

— HORSEMAN'S HAVEN —

You know, I am doing a book of my Uber riders.

Oh, really?

And I am recording my conversations with Uber riders. Are you okay with that?

Yeah, sure. Absolutely. Feel free.

I never know what's going to come up. This woman I just picked up had a beautiful coat that she wanted to show me when she...

I saw her put it on. The black coat?

Yeah. She was so proud of that coat. She had just bought it at a garage sale. Where are you from?

Corvallis in central Oregon.

What brings you to Santa Fe?

I've never been here but I've always wanted to come. And everybody I spoke to as I was planning my trip told me it was crazy, but "that's where I want to go," I said.

So, you are just here to see Santa Fe?

Yes, just as a tourist. What do I need to do? What can't I miss while I'm here?

So, you are going to be in town until when?

I'll be here until Friday, but we are staying... In the middle of the week, we are staying at the Hyatt Regency Tamaya, so we will be 40 minutes away.

It is down near Albuquerque. It is the big one on the Indian reservation.

Is it?

When do you go down there?

Tomorrow. And then, we are back at the end. So, it is Santa Fe bookended by that.

I see.

Yeah. I did not do the preparation I should have done. Usually, if I am going to travel, I read a guide book at least, and this time I just didn't have a chance so I will see what there is to see. Everybody talked to me about the peace and serenity of the place; that it is a calming sort of place.

You might want to try 10,000 Waves or Sunrise Springs.
Somebody said that, yes. Are those spas?

Yes. But if you really want to experience northern New Mexico, you might want to go to Ojo Caliente.

Is that a hot spring?

Yeah. It is a natural hot spring. Or hike up in Bandelier or up above Santa Fe.

Yeah, maybe. We might. We'll see. I am meeting my friend. She is coming from the other end of the country. We are meeting in the middleish.

How far back do you and your friend go?

My gosh, we have been friends for 34 years.

Thirty-four years?
Yes.

You are not that old!

I am that old. I am 46. We met when I was...

Are you 46? You don't look 46.

Yeah. We met when we were freshman in high school, the very first day of high school. My best friend to this day... I mean, I have others but many of my best friends to this day are the women I went to high school with. They are just great.

There is a special bond there.

Yeah, and there is such a shorthand for somebody you know that long. Do you know what I mean? And we live across the country from each other, so I don't get to see her very often. But we get to do these adventures every once in a while, and it is such a treat.

My best buddies are from Sedona, where I grew up. Sedona, Arizona. They are still some of my closest friends, Tim and Bill.

Yeah! Sedona is supposed to be another incredibly gorgeous place.

That's where I grew up. Some of the girls from Sedona are having a potluck get together real soon, Jannie Mae, Mary Lou and Nancy among others. Yeah, reminds me of when we were eleven or twelve, we'd have dances on a warm summer evening outside on the porch at Timmy's house, six or seven girls with six or seven guys. I remember the first time I got up enough nerve to ask Jannie Mae to dance cheek to cheek. I think it was the summer between seventh and eighth grade. One of the more romantic times in my life. Just tingling with excitement.

Oh, really?

Some of the guys are going but I can't make this one. We actually have had formal elementary grade school reunions. We are all in our early 70's now. At one of the reunions I was reminded by Chuck how he and Nicky had saved my life one day down at The Point in Sedona. We were playing in the creek and throwing mud at each other, romping across the creek and I stepped on a piece of glass that completely ripped open the heal of my right foot in about a ten-inch gash bleeding profusely. Chuck and Nick carried me up the 200-foot embankment, we all got on his Vespa motor scooter and they took me to Doctor Schnur's office. My parents were out of town so the doctor couldn't get any parental consent, but he sewed me up anyway, thank God. There were benefits in growing up in a small town. All the mother's watched after all us kids.

And you still have reunions? That's lovely.

Well, we all went from first through eighth grade together. Plus, a lot of us went to church together to the Wayside Chapel. We had Reverend Bennett holding both the lapels on his suit coat with his stomach sticking out and lecturing us about the ways of the Lord. Us kids, for the most part, tried to get isolated in some back room where we'd play spin the bottle with the girls, especially for Wednesday night social events. Except we'd all want to come out when Mrs. Etter sang, because we wanted to watch the turkey wattle of her throat go crazy.

Oh, my gosh! First grade? Church? Goodness. That's a bond for sure! How often do your reunions happen?

Oh, every five years or so.

That's so nice! And are they always in Sedona?

Yeah. Some of the kids I grew up with, they still have their family homes there. Tim Fuller's mom Faith, who just recently died, had her home there all these years and we had a reunion down at her place a while ago. When we were ten or so, I remember going down to Faith's house with six or seven other kids and she would read The Hobbit and other books like that to us. We'd all be sitting around anxious to hear the next escapade of Bilbo Baggins. Also, we all became very adept ping-pong players. Nicky Fuller and Chuck Burrus were the older brothers by two or three years and they would pound us relentlessly at ping-pong.

We all sort of stayed together as a gang until we started high school. Many of us took the bus every day to school. We had the Wolschagel girls who lived way up in Oak Creek Canyon at Mayhew's Lodge, and then the Anderson kids at

Junipine, then the Todd girls from Todd's Lodge and then they picked up kids from Indian Gardens and then us from Bedside Manor. We lived about three miles up in Oak Creek Canyon.

Then when we went to high school everything changed. Jannie Mae, Mary Lou and I went to Flagstaff High School, Nancy and others who lived in Yavapai County went to Mingus High and Billy, Chuck and Nicky went to Verde Valley. Tim went to Middlesex School in Concord, Massachusetts were, as it turns out, he was Bill Richardson's catcher, who later became Governor of New Mexico. Tim's mom had some kind of affiliation with Verde Valley School. She had grown up in Pecos, New Mexico with her father, A.V. Kidder, who was the lead archeologist at Pecos National Monument and worked at Mesa Verde National Park.

Yes. What a great thing! So, do you have any recommendations? Where should we go for dinner tonight? Is there somewhere around the hotel that is fabulous?

Around the hotel? I think one of the best places on the southside of town here is the Blue Corn Café right here.

Blue Corn?

Yeah, it is right here on the corner, as far as around this area.

Okay.

But there's, like, other local places, too, you know? Like, Tune Up, but that is closer to downtown. Blue Corn is right over here.

Oh, okay. How far is the hotel from downtown?

Okay, you are about 4 miles.

Oh, okay.

Right down this road, Cerrillos.

Got it.

Now, a real local place close to your hotel is Horseman's Haven.

Is it? I was just looking at it, wondering if it was any good. It's got a lot of cars.

Well, let me tell ya! I used to eat there every day when my office was down here on this side of town.

Really. I may have to walk myself over and eat lunch over there.

Yeah, well, it's not bad. Lunch is very good. The chili can get hot too.

Alright! Well, that's good to know.

But it is right behind your place.

Yeah, really. It is right here.

I am sure your hotel will say, "Hey, that's the place to eat." They also serve very good breakfast.

Okay, good to know. All right, John, thank you so much!

Thank you.

— CASE DISMISSED —

Okay so this is the interesting part?

Yeah, I'm on a hangover. So, I was going to say -- I'm from California. I have been here about 15 years and I've never had any problems at all and about a year ago, almost a year ago, I got a DWI, and it sucked because I wasn't even drunk or anything.

What were you doing?

I was driving. This officer pulled me over late at night, and asked me if I was drinking. "Yeah, I had about two beers," I told him. He was just getting really close to me and stuff so I basically just tell him, "Listen, just so you know, yeah, I have been drinking." And he said, "Oh, how much?" I said, "About two beers. Maybe even a little under two beers." He said, "About how long ago did this happen?" I told him, I said, "It happened, I don't know, maybe a few hours ago I had them." And he said, "Okay, wait right here." He calls his lieutenant and the lieutenant comes over. He pulls me out of the car, and asks me to take a field sobriety test, and they have to...

Did he just request that you get out of the car?

Yeah, and so he requested that I get out of the car, and he asked me to take a field sobriety test. Before you actually get somebody to take a field sobriety test you have to ask them using what's called the implied consent act. So, they literally have to read this piece of paper, and I thought he must be kind of a rookie, because he was holding a piece of paper up. And I was, well policemen should know this already, whatever. So, he asked me to take the implied consent thing, and he reads this paper. And I said, "Sir, can I ask you a question?" He said, "Sure."

And I said, "If I take this test, and I pass it, and every other test you're about to give me whatever it is, and I pass those, am I still, are you going to let me go, or am I still going to be taken to jail?" Which legally is at his discretion still, because I did already admit to drinking and driving. "I told you I was, and I know the law, and I know even after all this, you can still take me to jail," I said. Yeah, so I told him. I said everything just like completely respectful, and then he doesn't say anything. He ignores me, and reads the implied consent act again after he's done. Blah, blah, blah!

Oh, he read it to you?

Yeah, and then after he reads it again, I tell him the same exact thing. I said, "Sir, can I ask you a question?" He said, "Sure." "If I pass this test, and every other test you are about to give me, will I be able to go home, or will you still be taking me to jail, because it is at your discretion? I just admitted to you that I was drinking and driving."

And so he ignores me again, and he reads the implied consent act again. And at that time, I just got really frustrated, and I just told them, I said, "You know what man, I'll just get real candid with you." Then I said, "You know man, listen, I think this is bull shit! I think that you should probably just take me to jail right now, and charge me with whatever you're going to charge me with, and I will get out. I'll see you in court, because I don't really think this is fair. I'm more than sure you're probably just going to take me to jail even if I pass all these tests. I have to go to work. I have to go to work in the morning, and I would really appreciate it, if you wouldn't mind, just taking me to jail right now, so I can get through all this stuff and hopefully be back to work in the morning."

And so he puts the handcuffs on me, and he starts reading me my Miranda rights or whatever. And I told them, I said, "I can just make my request there." So, I'm just sitting there. "I've never been to jail before. Would you mind just trying to make this as smooth as possible for me, as quick as possible for me?" I said. "I will do whatever you need me to do. I'll show you all the respect you need, but in turn I'd like yours as well." So that's it. They just put the handcuffs on.

They took you to the court?

Oh, yeah, this was a year ago. So almost a year ago. Yeah, actually it was a year ago in February.

So, what happened in court?

Man, I got so lucky. I kind of like paid $5000 to a lawyer, and maybe in the end I didn't need to, but it's better to have a law-yer whether you need one or not.

And, how did that work out?

I went to court, and they dismissed it actually. They dismissed the whole case.

Because ...

Because the police officer lost the recordings from his lapel camera and from his dash cam. It was just completely gone, like as if he never stopped me.

Was he recording at the time?

Yeah, they always do. They have 24-hour surveillance on them all the time now. Police are fitted with a lapel camera, and they are also fitted with a mike on them. So everything is being recorded and ...

So, the case, they lost it? Your case was dismissed?

Yeah, well there was no evidence to try to convict me of any-thing. I went to court three times, and then finally the lawyer said, "You know what, let me ask the judge to dismiss this, because you have been in court three times, and they still don't have any evidence. They said they lost the evidence." But the DA didn't want to let me get off that clean. He wanted me to plead guilty to careless driving, which was 24 hours of community service, and speeding, which was like a $10 fine, and that was it.

So, you got off?

I got off, but here's the kicker.

Now you don't have to report it to your insurance as a DUI.

Exactly, but, well here is the thing that sucks in New Mexico. The DMV still has my arrest on my driving record for life.

That's what you were arrested for?

Yes, exactly.

So, it's on your record for life that you were arrested, even though you weren't convicted. Is that correct?

Exactly. It's on my driving record. So, I still get shitty insurance rates, but I've never been convicted of anything before so...

What do you do in town?

I'm a server at Del Charro and Santacafé.

Let me tell you a story about Santacafé.

Okay, go for it.

My son, his first job was there as a busser. My son is 31 now, but when he was like 15 and 16 there was this girl around town, her name was Zoe. She'd come over to the house once in a while. They were both bussers. Well, my lady put on a fashion show down at the Museo de Cultural, and this girl, this girl that my son worked with, Zoe, she was one of the models. I think she was 14 or 15 at the time. But she pomped around the stage in such an interesting fashion that day. Anyway, she grew up in Santa Fe. She was born in Arizona, and her real name is Arizona Muse. She has become one of the world's top models.

Oh, really?

Yes.

Oh, wait, Zoe. Do you know what? It's so funny? My wife was at Santacafé around that time too; my wife is a little bit older than I am. I'm 30, and my wife is 34. She was working at Santacafé a very long time ago too. Zoe was a busser. She was the same girl actually, who was here in Santacafé. My wife knew her too, and it was Zoe, because I remember one day we were walking into, I think it was the Coronado or Cottonwood Mall down in Albuquerque, and she sees this girl on the front of, it was in Macy's, and she was on the front of one of these like perfume things or whatever.

That's called Muse. Yes, that's Zoe. That's Arizona Muse.

Yeah, okay, yeah.

My son's name is David Bishop.

David Bishop, that sounds familiar now.

He worked for a while at Santacafé, then he went to New York for a while, but then he got a job with the Compound for three or four years. Recently he worked at Coyote Café for about four, five years. But now he just moved to Sonoma County to be with his girlfriend. They both met here.

Oh, that's cool.

But he's 30.

I have always thought my wife should be a model too. She's actually, really, really gorgeous. Here's a photo of my wife.

She's beautiful.

Yeah, I'm always telling her that you are so pretty, you are prettier than most of these girls I see on TV.

How many kids you got?

Three boys, they are 14, 13 and 9. Julian is our biggest one.

Where does the 14-year-old go to school?

DeVargas. He's finishing off the last year before they do the merger with Capshaw, and then they are going to call it Milagro Middle School and remodel the DeVargas building.

All right. I started a high school here in town, The MASTERS Program. It's at Santa Fe Community College. It's an early college charter high school.

That's what I was really wanting to get my boys into, something like that.

It's for 10th, 11th and 12th grade. You have to do it with a lottery. But kids who pursue it, usually they get in, even if they don't make it on the first round. Or they get on the waiting list. We have kids who drop out.

Yeah, maybe I'll try to get him on that. Well he's going to 9th grade next year.

Yeah, well, the following year.

Maybe. Maybe I'll see if I can get on the waiting list. Am I allowed to get on the waiting list even though I --

No, no, you have to do the lottery in March of next year.

Okay, and of course lots of kids apply.

You see where things lie.

Anyway, back to what I was going to say. The reason I'm Ubering is because my red Chrysler 200, I can't drive it, because I still have alcohol on my breath from last night. I don't really get time with my wife. The kids are so demanding. I don't get to see her a lot, because I work so much, and she works a lot too. So maybe twice a week we get together at night. We drink and have a good time and talk, and we just stayed up so late, because we are trying to catch up on things. We didn't really realize what time it was. We got so drunk last night. We were dancing in the living room, just us, because the boys were sleeping. That's all we, we don't go out anywhere anymore.

I call our living room, Sala. Sala is the Spanish word for living room. My wife, she's Latin. She speaks Spanish, so I call it Club Sala. It's like Club Living Room. We don't go out and do anything else, and I'm never really drinking and driving either. Even that night when I got my stupid DWI, I really feel like if the cop would have tested me, I probably wouldn't have had any alcohol in my system, little to none. But it's all right.

So that's what's up. That's why I can't drive, because the MVD charged me with aggravated DWI. Even though the court of law, the magistrate court, says that they don't have any evidence to charge me or convict me.

So, they charged me with that, and they found me guilty in their little hearing system, so basically, through the MVD, I have to have an interlock in my car for a year, which is stupid. I've been paying all this money, really inconvenient, because sometimes the damn thing just defaults and messes up. Then I have to take it in, and they charge me like a $100 when I'm like, this is your machine, and it's broken. It's just wasted money. But it still just sucks, because I don't really feel like I should have ever gotten it in the first place.

I find that with drinking and marijuana that if you have a little alcohol or a little pot or something, it does alter the space a little bit. But it's the same space that you can be in with drinking or without drinking. Because I quit everything, and I don't notice any difference.

Yeah, I guess it just depends on the person, and where you're at in life. For me I don't ever use it as a crutch. I do it for enjoyment, and it's the thing that my wife and I like to come together and enjoy because we are young parents and we have so many stresses from life that we try to just enjoy that one thing together.

It's a sacred time for you.

Pretty much, yeah. We don't always have to have booze on hand. I'll start for something, and then she starts for something, and we drink together and have a good time.

The major thing is to love your kids. Just every minute be in that space of love.

Yeah, that's true. We definitely do. I was actually just playing with my boy, my youngest one. My two older ones, they're out with other family members today.

We are in the great-grandbaby business.

Oh, yeah?

My lady has two great-grand kids. Seven and three.

Oh, that's nice. I really wish that my boys were that young again, you know what I mean?

I will show you this photo. Right there, it's her. That's Aliyah.

Oh, wow! What a cutie. And that hair! It's amazing man. Oh, I'll tell you, I wish so badly that my boys were young again, really young. I look back on these old videos of them, and can't believe it. So maybe we will see you sometime at Santacafé or even Del Charro.

You never know. Right here?

Stop light, yeah. That would be great. I do have a headache. So, I have 15 minutes. I'm actually going to grab a beer in here really quick, and then head to work, so I don't have a splitting headache. All right, thanks a lot!

Okay. Adios.

∞

— ALL GOOD THINGS —

Do you all live down on Marquez?

I do.

Oh, you do? Where did you get that scar?

In my lip? 15 stitches.

Oh, my Lord.

Yeah, my sister kicked me off a hammock by accident.

How old were you?

Four or five.

Accidents! I cut off my brother's finger by accident.

Oh, my god.

It happens kind of often.

I slammed it in the door and cut off the tip.

Does he have a thumb?

Well, it's a little bit shorter than the other now. It's plastic surgery, but like, it's still a little funny looking.

That girl in my class in the 4ᵗʰ grade gave me seizures. She pushed me off a chair and my head hit the floor. Then I had a seizure, and I've had them every couple of years afterwards. If it was some type of subdural hygroma, I'm surprised I'm not more brain damaged.

From being pushed as a child?

Yeah, she pushed me off a chair, and I fell backwards and my head hit on a concrete floor.

Oh, boy.

In 4ᵗʰ grade. I did get a stitch in my eyelid.

That sounds painful.

Yeah, it was terrible. I was just being a novice though. So, it was like 4ᵗʰ grade, and you know how they line up desks in 4ᵗʰ grade?

Yeah.

All of the chairs were pulled back, and we went out to recess, or whatever we were doing, and when recess was over, I was the first one back in the room. So, I was walking on top of the chairs to get to my desk and I missed the last chair, so I just fell, and this eye just rammed into the chair and then it was split open. And there was a time I fell while running and just broke my face, I just broke it. My nose is still broken from that and I broke both arms at the same time. Just how many stupid memories. I got a nail through my...

I stepped on a chainsaw.

You stepped on a chainsaw? At least it wasn't running.

True.

Then you would not have had a foot.

My daughter fell down a flight of stairs when she was two. I remember picking her up. Her whole face was covered with blood.

Yeah, we just had a similar stair incident. She fell down and broke her neck in three places.

Oh, my god. Have you ever been at the store right here, Look What the Cat Dragged In?

No.

This is my lady's favorite shop. Random clothes, random kitchen stuff, random everything.

That sounds like...pretty random.

It's the least expensive used shop in Santa Fe. But there's pretty good stuff in there.

I can get her something in a nice store.

Are you sure? My friend Victoria just had a baby.

How old is she?

19.

That's like me having a baby! When I was home for break, she got married. I was like, "Wouldn't it be weird if I got married right now, mom?" She was like, "I got married when I was 19."

I did too.

Times are changing.

I had two kids by the time I was 22.

My grandma had three kids by the time she was 21.

I can barely put on two of the same colored shoes. I'm just trying to get my math homework done, like, look at the clouds...

Have you seen the movie All Good Things with Jake Gyllenhaal? You would like it. "Ritz crackers or saltines? Saltines you only eat when you have your stomach full." I think sophomore year I ate an entire tin of Ritz crackers every time I went to school. That was what I ate during the day. I also liked the mini ones, just because I think they taste better.

Any particular place up here? Ok. Thanks.

Just the lofts. Thank you.

∞

— LACROSSE —

Maybe you can talk a little bit about lacrosse as far as the spiritual aspects and what it means to the Iroquois.

Okay. Well it requires what we call our self - Kanonsionni. We refer to it as the Creator's game. Sometimes you hear that it's called, "little brother of the lord," but that's not what it's supposed to be. So, that's not a medicine game. You play it for the enjoyment of the Creator. When you're playing, it's the highest honor. When you're playing, you're not playing for yourself, you're playing for a higher, greater purpose, and you're supposed to carry yourself in the best way. It's to teach you how to be a good human being essentially.

Now how long has lacrosse been played by the Iroquois?

We have this saying, a lot of indigenous people have this saying, "since time immemorial," thousands, thousands of years at least.

Where is lacrosse played now? Is it played all over the world or primarily in the United States?

It's primarily U.S. and Canada, but there are over 60 international teams recognized by the International Lacrosse Federation. It's played all over the world, and especially within the U.S. it's spreading, like out here in Santa Fe. It's spreading to California, Florida. The hotbeds for the longest time were in Baltimore, that area, and Long Island, and then upstate and central and western New York.

Are you exclusively with Santa Fe Prep or could you ever help another high school?

I actually work with the youth program right now. I'm not working with the high school yet.

Working with the youth program up here?

Yes, the youth. We just practice at Prep and it's kind of like their feeder system, their development system.

I see. I started a school, a high school here in town called The MASTERS Program.

Yes, I've heard of it.

It's at Santa Fe Community College, and they've been looking for a sport. They have 210 students.

Yes.

I was wondering, maybe you could be there ... you could come up to the school and talk to the students at some point in time.

Yes, that would be great. I mean I'm kind of a younger guy. I don't have experience.

It doesn't matter. It's the energy.

Okay, yes. I get you. I get you. Cool.

I'll talk to the principal at The MASTERS Program and see if she has an interest in this. She may not.

Yes, I know. I understand.

Do I turn in there?

Yes. There's my boys.

∞

— NASHVILLE —

Where are you heading today?

I have a training I'm running in Nashville.

What kind of training do you run?

I do the logistics for my company, and we're having a financial management training. I've never been to Nashville. I'm looking forward to it.

Nashville. I've never been to Nashville either. How long have you lived in Santa Fe?

Not very long. I moved down last summer from Seattle. Yeah, I grew up there. My husband and I have been living up there for a while where he did his residency in medical physics. He got a job down here.

Is he a doctor?

He's a medical physicist. He works with cancer treatment machines, working on plans for treatment processes.

Does he work at Los Alamos or at one of the cancer clinics?

He usually just works for a department at the cancer center – St. Vincent's Cancer Center. He's been liking that a lot. There are a couple of different sides to it. You can go into diagnostics, which is working with things like MRI and ultrasound. You can go into research, which would probably be more like what they do in labs.

Does he fine tune the machines, or does he actually work with the machines and the patients?

So it's kind of an interesting field. I had no idea what it was until I met him. The radiologists or oncologists will prescribe a certain dose. That goes...

Of chemotherapy?

Radiation therapy. And then that will go to the medical physicist to program it into the machine to make sure, because each person is different, all of their – everybody's organs are in a slightly different place. Everybody's body has certain densities. So, they conduct a few test runs with the patient's measurements to make sure it will be delivered at the right location. And then if there's a problem, he can kind of work with the software if there are small problems. But if there are larger problems, they call an actual machine tech.

I see.

He describes his work as kind of like being a pharmacist.

And what kind of a business does your company do?

I work for the league of conservation voters and environmental groups. My organization is based in D.C., but I'm able to work remotely, which is great. I work in the same office as the Conservation Voters of New Mexico.

Where is that?

It's under DeVargas, right up off Sandoval. I've been doing that for about three, three and a half years. It's been fun. It's a good group of people. We have 29 partner states across the country, and New Mexico is actually one of our more active groups. They're doing a lot of work in land conservation. I'm working right now out in McKinley County on iridium mining. And we were just – so we do political work as well. We were pretty active in the recent legislative session. Unfortunately, there's a lot of work to be done, probably never be out of a job.

Well thank you for the work you do. Here we are.

Thank you.

∞

— BRAZIL —

Where are you from?

I am from Brazil. Yeah, from Rio.

You speak Portuguese?

Yes. Brazilian Portuguese. That's different.

Oh, it's different than regular Portuguese?

Yes, some differences. It is quite similar, but sometimes you get in trouble.

What brings you to Santa Fe?

It's an academic meeting.

Academic?

Yeah.

Are you a professor?

Yes. I am a nursing professor.

My lady has a nonprofit here that provides free homecare for people. She works with all the nursing students at the college. A lot of those students like to go out with her and do volunteer work, hands-on...

Yeah, that's nice. It is necessary.

And is there a conference here in Santa Fe?

Yes, it is a meeting. It is on applied anthropology. Inside the meeting there is another meeting of the nursing council of applied anthropology. And we have research and results to present.

Well, we've had pretty good weather up to now. But today and tomorrow it is supposed to rain and snow. You don't get very much snow down in Rio, do you?

No. No snow at all. Sometimes, it is very rare nowadays, but sometimes in the mountains. There is a mountain area in Rio. It is not as high as up here. I think it is 2,500 feet, 800 meters.

Right. And you've had snow there?

Yes, sometimes, it is very rare, in winter. It's more like sleet. You can have some ice in the morning on the grass, but not snow really. At the south of Brazil, yes, you can get snow. But not more than two inches.

Wasn't the president of Brazil recently impeached?

Yes. She was. Unfortunately.

How long was she president?

It was her second mandate. She has been president for five years.

What was her offense?

Political issues. She was continuing President Lula's policy towards social policies, minimum wage policies and minimum income policies. I think right-wing parties didn't... weren't satisfied. And also, the crisis, the economic crisis. She could not...

So, was it a political impeachment or was there something else?

Yes, it was a political impeachment. She committed no crime, no crime. They can't find anything against her or against Lula. They keep searching, but they can't find anything. It is political. And now, Brazil is a mess.

And now Brazil is a mess?

Everything is a mess: Social, ethical, political and economic. And the state of Rio de Janeiro is twice a mess. My university is being attacked by the government. We've had our funding cut, our scholarships, all that. They have all been cut. Our wages, our salaries are being...

Have been cut?

Delayed, yes. I have been two months without a salary.

Really? How long will it continue?

We don't know. We keep talking all the time here. Sometimes they just release the money here and there, but it is not sufficient. We could not start our university classes yet this year, because we don't have any elevators or cleaning.

How many students go to your school?

Thirty thousand. It's a big university. It is a 70-year university in Rio. But anyway, I came because I have a scholarship, a federal scholarship, a research scholarship. They gave me a small one, and helped me to buy tickets for the hotel and so on. I need to do this. It is my job to go to meetings and present papers, and so on. But as we use it to travel and go just to participate, that is not possible if you don't have funding. It is hard times. And the problem, the biggest problem is that the judiciary system, the legal system, the judges, they all have a political agenda today. They protect themselves and they protect politics. It used to be an independent power. Our judiciary system is no longer independent.

No longer independent?

No, no. We cannot any more trust judgments. It's very difficult. Our constitution is being changed.

Did the judiciary used to be independent?

Well, more independent than now. It always had some political involvement. I don't know. But now, everything is changing very quickly.

Yeah, right.

In a very bad way.

You are going to end up at Jo-Ann's Fabric, right?

Jo-Ann's, yes, the fabric store. They have some very good fabrics.

It's not that far. Are you a fabric person? Do you like fabrics?

Yes. I like to sew and to weave.

You like to sew and do what? And weave?

Weaving. And how do you call it? Style design?

Yeah.

But this summer was impossible both to sew and weave, because it took too long.

My lady liked to sew and to weave. Her hands got so bad though that she can't do it anymore.

That's too bad.

So, she's sort of a coat and pants designer. She has a certain classic style, and she sells them to different people who know her. At night, she goes through all these fashion magazines like Vogue and Elle, and she tears out pages. She loves it. It's very relaxing for her to do that at night in bed after her busy day. She loves to look at fashion magazines.

I like to sew, and Jo-Ann's has some fabric stuff you just can't find in Brazil. Sometimes you can find some but it's way too expensive.

Yeah.

And also, some tools.

Well, she goes to Los Angeles and New York to buy her fabrics.

Oh, they have great shops there. Like...exclusive fabric stores.

Yep. There was a fantastic fabric store up in Taos for a long time. I think they've closed.

I just like to sew stuff for the babies, the grandkids. I was complaining all the time my kids are very close to 30's and no babies at all. But now we finally have babies.

Oh, boy. What about the babies?

So, when they started all of them have one baby now.

So, you're a grandparent now?

Yes. I have three grandsons.

I have three granddaughters.

That's wonderful. Now, I have three grandsons. One is two years, the other one is eight months, and the youngest is three months.

Oh, boy.

Beautiful boys.

See we're in the great grand baby business now. We have-

That's an industry?

Yes. A wonderful industry.

My husband has fifteen grand-kids.

Really? Holy moly.

Yeah. He married a lot. And between there are stepsons and real sons and daughters. He has fifteen and also mine.

Grand-kids are great. Now we've got two of my grand-kids who are seniors in high school going to college next year.

That's great. I think the relationship with the grand-kids is so different. They're so much better. Last week my two year old grandson didn't want to go back to his house and I tell him, "Let's go to see your father and your mother." "No, no daddy. No daddy. Papa no. Papa. Papa no." He is in the terrible twos, and he went to school and was crying.

I see. Jo-Ann's is right there. Okay?
Okay, okay.

Are you going to walk, or you want me to wait for you?

If you stay, I think I will be 15 minutes for the most, 10 minutes.
I'll wait for you.

Okay. But in Jo-Ann's, I'm going to stay.

Yeah. I know. Okay, you go in right here and I'll be right parked back there.

All baby stuff; zinc ointment for baby rash. They're so much better here.

Ok, you're back. So, you want to go to Jo-Ann's now?

Yes, please.

Are your babies, granddaughter, are they here? Or are you taking it back to Brazil?

No, no. Yes.

Oh, yeah. Because you can't get it down there.

My baggage is going to be full of baby stuff, basically. I have one daughter who lives one hour from Rio de Janeiro.

From Rio De Janeiro?

Yes, yes. Probably one hour. And another one who lives in northeast Brazil. That's far away. I only stay with her when she had the baby in January, and now I am going back the end of April for first of May vacation.

Are you sure they're open?

I saw it on internet that they're open at nine. It's not 10 o' clock yet. It's almost-

Okay, here we are.

Thank you.

Thank you. You've got to enter this door. Oops, you forgot your cell phone and wallet.

Thank you so much. What a Papaya Head!!!

AS SHE LEFT, I COULDN'T HELP BUT WONDER IF THE COURT SYSTEM IN THE UNITED STATES COULD BECOME POLITICALIZED LIKE BRAZIL.

∞

— AVOCADO MAN —

Welcome. Say, I'm doing a book on my Uber riders. Are you ok if I record this conversation?

Sure. This should be interesting. Well, first of all, my name is Lyndon Johnson.

Lyndon Johnson, there you go.

Maybe I'll make the book - under the chapter "Famous Names.".

Is that your real name?

It's my real name. They call me LBJ.

I actually knew him.

Did you?

Yeah.

LBJ. I've read and watched all his bios. They say he was a tough SOB.

Well, I didn't know him well, you know. I was a Page in the U.S. Senate.

Fantastic.

When I was 14, 15 and 16, right there when Johnson was Vice President. We used to sit on the rostrum, and he'd snap his fingers and say, "Sonny,", do this or that."

In that Texas twang, I'll bet.

Oh yeah.

"Say, Sonny." That's LBJ.

I was on the Capitol Page School basketball team, and after the first game I played, a bunch of guys and girls got in this car. We're driving down the street. Then one of the girls said, "There's where J. Edgar Hoover lives." Then we drove a couple more blocks down and stopped at this house. There's a couple of guys standing outside. We go down to the basement, and there was a picture of Lyndon Johnson on the mantle. I said, "What's his picture doing here?" She said, "That's my daddy.". "Is that right? Is that right?"

Lucy?

Yeah Lucy. She's a year younger than me. And her sister is older, maybe two years older. But we used to go over to their house.

It's quite interesting. I go to Austin on business sometimes, and the Johnson ranch is 20 miles outside Austin. And, you know, I go to pay my bar bill, or what not, and all of a sudden they go, "We have Lyndon Johnson here,", and about twelve drinks show up. And it's like, good Lord, I wasn't planning on getting drunk or anything.

Were you named after him?

No, no.

It was just...?

Lyndon is a family name. I was born in Salt Lake City, Utah to conservative parents.

So, you live in Phoenix now?

Yes, I live in Phoenix, well, really Mesa. You know Phoenix is made up with a lot of adjoining cities, right? So, we call it like the metro area, because they're all adjoined. We have about six million people now in the Phoenix valley.

My daughters live in Avondale and Chandler.

Is that right? Chandler is pretty close to Mesa. Avondale is a little further west. I have a daughter in a place even further west than Avondale called Buckeye.

Yeah, I know Buckeye. I grew up Sedona.

Did you really? What a great, great area, eclectic, avant-garde. I love the artistry. I love the vibe. I like Santa Fe. Santa Fe has just a tremendous aura, you know, of peace. You are who you are, and we accept you for that. Nice feeling here.

What brought you to Santa Fe?

Business. We actually had to meet somewhere for meetings. So, it was like, let's go to Santa Fe. It's such a chill town, you know. So, we all just met here. Wish the weather was a little like yesterday. We wanted to go hiking this morning, but it was snowing. Say, someone left their wallet and phone back here.

Thanks for noticing this! The person that... Lord, I've got to take, I've got to go back down now to ... I dropped her off at a fabric shop. She's from Brazil. I'll take it back to her after I drop you off. ???

She will be thrilled to see you.

I know. What kind of work are you in?

I sell flaxseed, avocado oil, whole avocados from Mexico, chia seed to big box retailers like Costco, Sam's Club.

I think that's a great ad and song they sing, you know, "Avocados from Mexico".

I'd say it has grown almost threefold just in the last three years, the supply and demand ...

The avocado side?

Yeah. If you've been watching, you'll see the prices have really gone up. Supply and demand is short now, and it takes five years to grow a tree.

It takes five years to grow a tree?

That can bear a good fruit that's edible.

Yeah.

And that's a small tree. It might be 12 feet. I mean the best trees are 20 to 35 years old. They'll be up to 60 feet.

How many avocados do you get off one tree?

Oh gosh, that's a great question.

100, 200?

Oh, yes. The bigger trees, yes. And there's two seasons by the way. So, you can cut the avocados. But what we do -- the longer the fruit hangs on the tree, it doesn't necessarily go bad. So, you cut it at different times, because we like to look at a season as six months. Between the last month of holding to cut it, and then putting it in cold storage, you get an extra 21 days before it ripens, if you have it in cold storage. So , we make it fit the season. And then of course the trees will grow a little differently at the lower elevations compared to the higher elevations. You can keep them longer, because it's cooler.

Are you a broker from the farms to the wholesaler?

No, it's my business. And basically it's...

Oh, you have the trees?

I have a partnership with the Mexicans. I'm very fortunate to have a good partnership relationship with them. So how long have you been here in Santa Fe?

Thirty-one years.

Okay. So, you were born in Sedona?

No, I was raised in Sedona. I was born in Los Angeles.

Okay.

LA County Hospital, and then we lived in LA and San
Bernardino. We moved to San Bernardino when I was like
three or something. And then when I was six, my father
got transferred. He was with the Boy Scouts of America.
He was in charge of scouting for Northern Arizona. And
we moved to Sedona when I was six. So, I moved there in
1952.

Gosh. Would have been sparse.

The road to Phoenix was a dirt road.

No I-17, huh?

No, it was paved from Phoenix to Black Canyon. I guess
Black Canyon is about 30, 40 miles outside of Phoenix.
And then we had to go from Black Canyon up through the
valley there, and cut over through Humboldt and Crown
Point to Prescott. And then Prescott to Sedona was paved.
But Prescott down to Black Canyon was all dirt road.

Interesting. So how long in Arizona, and then how did you
become a Page?

As a little boy, I'd go out and put up signs for politicians.
My mother had me read all these books about presidents
and generals, called the Landmark books. And I learned
all about politics, leadership and stuff like that through
those books. I was just intrigued by leaders and politics.
At our kitchen table, my parents would talk about politics.
I think one of my dad's friends ran for Congress at that
time in Arizona, and I put up signs for him. Later my dad
read an article that Senator Goldwater's former page had
graduated from high school, and that he'd been looking
for a new Page. So, we wrote a letter to him, and got some
people we knew to write letters of reference. I don't know
how many kids applied --

Quite a few, I'd bet.

I'm sure they did. I don't really know how many applied. Until this day, it's like a whole fraternity of guys, we all went to high school together. We were all supposed to be President of the United States.

Oh, yeah.

But one day in the Capitol, I was going up an elevator with this other Page. His name was Sid Kaplan. And when we got to the second floor, the elevator doors opened, and there was President John F. Kennedy.

Really!.

I stuck out my hand, and shook his. He said, "Who appointed you, Sonny?" I said, "Senator Goldwater.". "He's a good man. He's a good man," he said.

Very interesting to see what he could have accomplished had he lived.

It's fascinating, yeah.

It's just very -- it's like a magnet; you were drawn to him.

Many experiences in Washington D.C.

What a town!

We all get together for reunions every three or four years. Pages from the 40's, all the way through today, are members of an alumni group and we have reunions. There are still three or four people from the 1940's that are still ...

Alive.

Yeah, one of them is Johnson's protégé, Bobby Baker, who got in trouble when Johnson became President. He was Secretary of the Senate. He was a Page though in the 40's.

Before his political career?

Before his career of service in the Senate.

And your name is?

John Bishop.

John Bishop? Pleasure to meet you, John. Good luck with your book.

Thank you, Lyndon Johnson. Thank you so much.

— SPACECRAFT —

of L.A. you all from?

We live in La Cañada, which is up there near Pasadena. It's a tiny town.

So, were you born in Santa Fe?

I've been here 31 years. I was raised in Sedona, Arizona. I moved there when I was six, but I was born in Los Angeles.

Wow! What part of Los Angeles?

I believe I was born in L.A. County Hospital, which was down in the middle of L.A.

What I mean is, you lived there for a while, really lived there?

I lived there until I was 6, but when I was like three or four my parents moved to San Bernardino. Are you all from here?

Well, I'm from Pennsylvania. My husband is from the U.K.

From the U.K?

I was born in Pasadena.

My grandma used to live in Pasadena. We'd go over there for Christmas time, New Year's, and see the Rose Parade. How do you like Santa Fe so far?

I love it. I was here 12 years ago. I loved it. And I just had to come back.

What part of the UK are you from?

I was born in Colchester, which is a small town on the east coast sixty miles outside of London. I was brought up in Malta, Hong Kong and Bermuda. Way back when they were colonies.

My lady is from Wales.

Which part?

Well, she went to school in Cardiff, but she was often at her grandma's home in a little town called Dale, near St. David's, which is all the way on the southwest Pembrokeshire coast of Wales.

That's a beautiful part of Wales.

It really is! I've been down there. Little roads, very narrow, just for one car, and you got to pull over, if another car is coming toward you. It's literally one lane. They've experienced a huge population boom in Dale, having gone from 90 when she was growing up there to 190 today. There is a lot of wind surfing and sailing in Dale.

I used to spend a lot of time in the Brecon Beacons and South Wales back when I was young. It's a beautiful country. Does she speak Welsh?

She does – sort of.

So how did you meet her?

We're both dancers.

Dancers?

Here in Santa Fe.

Really?

We have a dance group that's called Embodydance that has been going on for about 16, 17 years. I've been a part of it since the beginning. She is very nimble on her feet. She's a good dancer. It's a group of about 600 or 800 people here in town. On any given Thursday night maybe 80 or 100 will dance down at the Railyard Performance Center. It's very intimate. You really get to know people through dance. How did you happen to travel around to all these different places, Bermuda, Hong Kong, when you were a kid growing up?

My dad was in the army back then, and he would get sent to various places where there were military prisons. He was a military prison officer. I was brought up in all the best prisons in the empire.

That's amazing!

There is a big prison in Colchester, a military prison, and one at Corradino in Malta. We were there for two years, and one on Stonecutters Island in Hong Kong.

All military?

All military. They were for bad soldiers. And the one in Hong Kong was on Stonecutters Island. Now Stonecutters has been connected to Kowloon. They cleaned all the land in the harbor once it got handed over, handed back to the Chinese in 1999. So, you can still see the island, but it's part of the Kowloon Peninsula now.

What's been your profession?

I'm an engineer. Nothing quite as exciting as my dad. Space-craft.

Yeah, right! Here in the U.S.?

I worked in Europe for a long time. I came here in 1990 to the U.S. to work in California, because there is a lot of work in California. I love it so much. I'm a native Californian now.

The European Space Agency contracted with me through a foundation here in America to send a nickel disk on the Rosetta Space Craft that the European Space Agency launched about 12 years ago. It landed on a comet about two years ago.

Yeah. Philae, the lander on the comet.

Well my disk is on that comet now.

Wow! That's awesome! That's a lot of fun.

We created that with a focused ion beam many years ago. It has different passages from the bible in seven different languages.

Well, that's a fascinating project to be involved in. How did you manage to get the contract for that?

Well, I had a technique of doing it at the time that was the only way to put that much data on a small disk. I work in focused ion beam technology. I did it for an organization called Long Now Foundation in San Francisco that is into archiving. Now we are working with putting very small mantras inside Buddhist prayer wheels.

You are the first guy I ever met who has a focused ion beam actually in your studio. That's pretty amazing.

It's in my lab near Portland, Oregon. Here's the bank. I'll drop you off here.

Thank you so much.

∞

— CLIMATE CHANGE —

I've done quite a few interviews so far.

You said you're writing a book?

Yes, just glimpses of people when they're riding around in Uber.

This is about the experience of it.

Yeah, well we get all kinds of interesting people here in Santa Fe.

I'm sure. It's a beautiful town. So, most of them visiting here?

Yeah, and locals.

Yeah, I'm very excited we'll check it out.

Where are you from?

I'm from Cincinnati.

What brought you here?

I'm in town for a conference at La Fonda. It's about applied anthropology. It's an international conference, people from all over the world that do really all kinds of stuff. Some people do like your basic ethnography, dealing with different cultural groups, and then some people do public health and others doing climate change. So, we got all kinds of stuff.

Climate change falls under anthropology?

Yeah, it's applied anthropology. But really, you can use it for any discipline, you can work for a non-profit, you can work in another industry or like in business. You can work in, I mean, really any direction that you want to take.

How did you know you wanted to go to this field?

Oh, I really didn't. I went into college, and I didn't know what I was going to do. So I figured out just take all my prereq's first, and then my second semester college I took an anthropology course and I just fell in love with it. So, I've been doing it ever since and doing lots of research and...

Follow your heart.

It's not going to make me a lot of money, but it's what I want to do. That's what important to me.

Mark Twain says make your vocation your vacation, and you'll never work a day in your life.

Oh, it is so. Well, I love all the research that I've been getting to do, and well last summer I was in Belize for a month working with...

What was Belize like?

Well, when people picture Belize, it's typically like the resorts, coastal area, beaches. That's not what we are doing in the villages. I was working with sugarcane farmers.

Really? In the interior?

It's about an hour outside of Belize City, so it was nice. It was really small where we were, but we did get a chance on the weekends to go on excursions. Once we went to the zoo, which was really cool. They have in their big cat exhibits, they had cages inside a big closure where we'd do tours. You can pay to go in the cage and then the cats come and mess around with you and play with you. And then we went to...

So, you're in the interior cage, and the cats were out of the cage?

Yeah, so it's like the cat enclosure is here, and then there's a cage inside of that. They take the cats out of the enclosure and let you go into the cage and then they bring the cats back out, so you're inside the enclosure. Unfortunately, they weren't doing it the day we went, so I didn't get to do that, but it was really cool. And then we got to see some of the Mayan ruins which were just incredible, so beautiful. And I got to eat lots of mangos, they're everywhere.

Mangos are fantastic, aren't they?

They have a rule there where if the tree is hanging and a fruit drops down on the street outside of somebody's property, it's fair game. So, there were mangos everywhere. We were walking around, pick up mangos and bringing them home with us.

You know some people are highly allergic to mango skins because it contains urushiol which is the same toxic substance that is in poison ivy. I've known people that get significant rashes around their mouth from eating a mango. Is this like an Airbnb place?

Yes. The Airbnb was a lot cheaper than the hotels since the conference is going on, and I mean, I got a full place instead of just a room. Ok, bye.

Thank you.

∞

— COLUMBIA —

People are awfully fascinating.

Yes, do you have like a specific goal that you are going to analyze?

I'm going to write a book.

That's great.

Just random conversations with Uber and Lyft riders in

Santa Fe.

That's good. You know, I can't say no, because I'm an anthropologist here for the convention. I'm recording people's conversations all the time.

You do? What do you do?

I'm an anthropologist, and I'm a social scientist, so I do qualitative research. Part of the method is recording conversations, sometimes formal interviews and sometimes informal conversations.

Where are you from?

I'm from Colombia

What town?

Manizales. Do you know Colombia? Have you visited?

No. But my daughter is married to a fellow who was born in Bogota and who has family in Cali and Medellin. My granddaughters are half Colombian.

Yes, that's great. So, they must be smart and nice and beautiful. Do they live here in the U.S.?

They live near Phoenix. Yes, how many of you are up for this convention?

I have no idea, but I guess a lot of people, because this is like the second largest conference in anthropology here in the U.S. They get together, and present what's new, and what they're doing. But this convention is specifically about applied anthropology, which is still huge, but not as huge as general anthropology.

Right, so what do you do with applied anthropology? And why anthropology?

I'm working with survivors of the Colombian war, and using some ethnographic methods, which is the main methodology in anthropology to kind of heal and talk about their experiences and try to project a new, better and more peaceful future. We've had more than five million people displaced by this civil war and more than 220,000 died, most of them children.

Wow. That's certainly an honorable thing to do.

Yes, it's hard. I'm just supporting the survivors of war, like very strong people.

All right.

They do all the work. I just support. I'm there to collaborate. How long have you been an Uber driver?

A little over a year.

So, I guess you have already collected some good material for your book?

I have. I've done over 3,000 rides.

Wow, that's a lot.

Some of the more interesting ones were riders I had before I started writing the book. For instance, I had this lady who has been a sock designer for her entire career. For 40 years she's been designing socks.

Wow.

She has a design facility here in Santa Fe and a factory someplace else.

You never think about that, but yes, someone has to design socks.

You never think about it, do you? I had an 85-year-old guy who had just received a patent. His dog was having breathing difficulties, so he invented a portable respiratory system for pets, and he had just received his patent that day.

How was he?

He was good, but he had lost his dog a while ago. Right here is the end of the road.

Okay. Thank you. I'd love to read that book.

Thank you.

— GIRL FROM NIGERIA —

Where are you from?

I'm British and American.

British and American?

Yeah. But you see my dad is Nigerian.

Your dad is Nigerian and your mother is from?

My mother is British, but I was born in New Orleans.

So, what's that make you? Are you a U.S. citizen?

Yes. My friends call me Nibrican.

They call you what?

Nibrican like a Nigerian, British and American in one word.

I see, that's funny.
What about you?

I'm Swedish.

Oh, that is so cool.

My mother is Swedish at least. So, I'm 50% Swedish and the other half is like Austrian and Scottish.

I love Austria.

My grandma's maiden name was Trapp, and there was always a saying in my family that on my father's side, that my family is related to the Von Trapp family of the <u>Sound of Music.</u>

Wow!

But I don't know if there is any truth to that.

I'd believe it.

Alright. Do you work at Taco Bell?

Oh, no. Me and my friends are having a get together. They ordered a few things and elected me to go get it.

I love the Taco Bell tostada.

Really?

Just bean tostada. That's the only fast-food I ever get.

Okay. Wait, what is it like?

Okay. It's just a corn tortilla.

Yes.

With beans and lettuce and tomatoes and salsa and stuff on top.

Oh!

And it's like a flat taco.

Oh! That is cool. That's amazing. I just started eating like American fast-food, because like college doesn't give you much of an option and it's been like when people – when I go to a fast-food restaurant, it's more like I don't know what to get.

So, you didn't grow up with fast-food?

No, my dad, his dad was a dictator. He had many cooks.

Your grandpa was a dictator?

Yeah. So, we had like people all around us.

Which country?

Nigeria. So, when I was growing up, we would have like cooks who would cook it from scratch.

Oh, my!

And I hated eating like anything that wasn't made from scratch. So now it's kind of like I don't know what I'm eating. I feel like sick inside, but it's good. And I can't cook here, because I have so much work to do. So, I'm just like...

How did you hear about St. John's?

I was – my fellow Johnny was at Oxford University...

A fellow Johnny?

Yeah, like someone...

Oh, from St. John's?

Yeah, he was at Oxford for a semester, and I was at Oxford, and I was like "What are you doing here?" And we had this conversation. I was like I love this school: I love to read. So, I made my transfer and it worked. I was just like okay, let's go to America. I mean, I have an American passport, but I've never thought of coming to America.

Do you only have a U.S. passport, or do you have multiple passports?

I have two, because I'm not allowed to have more than two.

Yeah. My lady has a – she kept her British passport.

Really! That's cool.

She's from Wales.

That's cool. And did she have an American passport as well?

No, but she has her American green card.

Oh, that's smart. Sometimes I go to the airport to confuse them, so I just like give them two passports like, "Just stamp whichever one you want."

And what do they say?

They're always like, "Ma'am, would you step aside please." I'm like sure. And we go over this whole process every single time, and they're like, "Well, when did you come to America?" And then I show them like the birth certificate and everything, and they're like, they think I'm a spy or something, so it's always like...

Has it gotten tougher?

It has. It's straight away harder. I came back from Nigeria with an American passport, because I didn't think like they were going to question me. But my American passport was in the bottom of my bag, and I just had like brought up the Nigerian passport. I didn't want to search for the other one, and they were like, they kept me there for an hour just verifying. And I was like wondering if something had expired somewhere, because I just had a visitor's stamp from when I had been here before from Nigeria. I haven't used that passport in a while.

I see.

Eventually I managed to find my American passport and they were like, "Oh, so you're American too? How did you acquire citizenship?" I was like, "Oh, this question is really unnecessary. The point is I can prove that I'm a citizen. I can prove that I'm legal. Can I just leave?" And they just – they're – it's a bit different now, because before I used to just walk into the country and walk out, and it took like a minute. They will just cut in and just leave. But this happened in January, and I didn't come like till three days later from there, so...

Oh, boy! So is your family still involved in politics and...

Yeah, my dad is running for President of Nigeria.

Oh, my. How many brothers and sisters do you have?

I have six brothers. I'm the only girl.

My lord! You must be treated like a queen.

Actually no, it's annoying. I hate it when people assume that you have that much protection.

Well, brothers. Where are you in the chain?

I'm like 6.

Are you the baby?

Yeah, I'm the baby. I'm the last one to come out.

So, your mother wanted a girl?

Yes. What?

Your mother wanted a girl? She...

Oh, no, my father wanted a girl.

Your father wanted a girl: someone wanted a girl?

Someone, yes. My mom was like I – because mothers and daughters growing up, it's not really as rosy as it looks. But my dad, it was more like, "I want a daughter, because I have too many boys in the house." And he didn't have a sister, so I think he just wanted a female that was related to him along the line somewhere. And that's when I came about. He was really excited. But he is still scared for some reason that I'm all alone in the U.S., so he will never stop.

Do you think you'll ever be involved in politics?

Oh, yeah. Right after law school I'm going to work for a while and then I want to run for President of Nigeria.

You're going to go to law school?

Yes. I want to...

You've got the drive.

Well, if I wanted to live in the U.S., it would have been easier, because you guys are more liberal. There was a survey that was taken in Nigeria about a female president, and everyone was like no, even the women, they were just like, oh boy, we can't have a female president.

I think a lot of women have that view here in the United States too.

Yeah, but they had reasons. But the women back home, the reason was that women were supposed to be a second like property of men. But the women here had valid reasons in a sense that maybe she is not stable enough, maybe she – but the whole thing, the whole point back home was, "We can wrestle and they cannot." If a man can do it, a woman cannot, that was their view...and I was like you guys are crazy.

And let's say you can be a leader for women. You can be a leader for everybody.

I wish. I hope. I really hope, because I want to do good in the world.

Just serve the people.

Yes, I want to...

Always do good.

Exactly. I want to have an impact, so I mean my granddad was pretty much – he was a colorful character.

Who is that?

My granddad, so it's kind of like I want to rewrite it in a sense that I want them to see another side of the fact, not like he was – I mean every dictator wove a colorful path.

What was your grandpa's name?

Abacha.

Abacha?

Yes, so he – when people in Nigeria see me, they're – it's like I do not reflect that part of my grandpa. So, it's more like, I mean, I'm a nice person. I'm like two generations away from him, so – but I admit that.

So, are we just going to drive through and you know what you're going to order?

Yeah, you just say the name of the order, and they will give it to you. Order for Victoria.

All right, one second. Ok here.

Have you gone back to Sweden?

Yes and one of my daughter has too.

Did she like it?

She loved it. She loved seeing all of our relatives with my mother. She took each of my granddaughters on a special trip after they graduated from high school.

That is amazing. It's hard to see young people who're interested in knowing the good stuff, just good.

What is it you talk about at St. John's?

We have really grown our discussions. You wouldn't believe these are such young people. We have discussions, like it's just simple marketing. It's the same thing. We argue about politics and Socrates and Plato all the times. It's a basic argument in St. John's. It's really hard.

You got everything?

Yeah. This is crazy. They've sent me out to get the food orders, and I forgot half of the orders.

Oh, my god! So, they just ordered in the hotel, and you can't go wrong?

Yeah, because I don't – like I'm the one who doesn't talk much in the group, I just do stuff. They order, and I go and get it, and then I'm the organizer. So, when I forgot half a menu from Papa John's before, I mean Domino's before, and I came with two pizzas instead of like eight, and I was like I didn't know that. Like the guy was too fast for me, so I didn't ask. So, this time they had to order online where they know it will be shown on the screen.

I didn't know that you can do that online.

I didn't know that either. It's amazing what people find out when they're desperate to not go out.

Are you in your first year or second year?

Second. I like the setting. It's like in America, but not America. It's too technology forward, and too rational that New Mexico stands out. I like that gap.

What do your brothers do?

One is an engineer. One is a business guy. He imports and exports stuff. And – well, the other two have – it's an oil company, and they're both like CEOs in it. It's – I don't know how that happened. And the last one is an engineer, even though he doesn't like it, so.

And you're going to be the lawyer?

Yeah. I'm going to be the one to bail them out in situations, because I've always been the one who gets them out of situations from my dad.

Oh!

So, they always make the show, but I'm like if you ever need a lawyer, it's like my life ordained job to get everybody out of trouble at some point, so it makes sense. What do your daughters do, or what did they study?

My older daughter is a teacher for the blind. She is married to a guy from the upper portion of Namibia.

Oh, super.

So, she's married to a black guy. Their daughter is 18.

Wow!

She just is graduating from Xavier High School in Phoenix, and she is a soccer player. Her team won the Arizona State Championship this past season. I'm so proud of my kids and grandkids. You know and the work – and the remarkable parents they are to their children.

So how does it feel?

It feels fantastic – you want to be content? One of the ways to be content is to not owe any money to anybody, including credit cards, mortgages on houses, cars, just live within your means, and keep saving, save through property, save through inheritance.

Yeah. You reminded me of a quote from Socrates in Plato's books.

What's that?

He said like, "There is nothing as incredible in a man's life as he grows old then contentment with his kid's success."

There you go.

Which another man was arguing with him saying, "As for me I don't have – I don't owe any debt, so I think that's what virtue is." I mean they're arguing about wealth here. So, you just confirmed everything.

Well, that's good.

You have reached the highest point of virtue for a person, so I would go to school and say to everyone I've met you, yeah. Is your book like a memoir?

Yes. It's going to be about me and the riders.

Oh! That is a cool book. I would read that. It's like a very pure – there is no retransformation. It's just straightforward from the source. It's incredible. Thank you.

Bye-bye. Thank you.

— ROSE PARADE —

I won't say anything incriminating. That'll be a good line for your book.

Oh, yeah, right. Well, you guys have a big ride there, don't you?

Yeah, we do. It's comfy; it's comfy.

We've been on a grand learning curve, driving thousands of miles learning how to drive it.

What do you call it, a fifth wheel?

It's a fifth wheel, yeah. We've been through a lot of states.

What's the cost per night to park usually at a place like this?

Anywhere between – a low-end place is about $30. That's like a real rough, kind of no real amenities, meth heads. And then really high-end is about $60. So, kind of in between, but normally it's between $40 and $50 a night.

Yeah. Where have you been traveling?

Well, we came from Oregon, and we came down from Utah, went to Vegas.

No, Idaho first.

Yeah. Then we went to Vegas, then we went out to Tucson and then southern New Mexico. And then we went back to Vegas to see a show that we really didn't see, because I bought tickets for the show, and it was actually in Maryland. So, I had to sell them while we were in Vegas. We made reservations, so we stayed and had fun there the second time around. Then we came here. And now we're going to start heading north, and then spring is arriving.

I've never been to Santa Fe. He had never been to the southwest portion of New Mexico, so I showed him around. And now he insisted to show me Santa Fe.

Cool. That's a pretty good place to eat when they're open, Café Fina.

Which one? Café Fina?

Yeah.

Yeah. I saw a lot of people parked there yesterday. So where is a good place for some really hot chile?

Really hot chile. Listen, I like the chile at a place called The Pantry. It's the number one breakfast spot in Santa Fe. Their chile and their salsa are exceptional.

Okay. I like to hear that.

They've been around since the '40s.

Are they downtown, or...?

No, they're down on Cerrillos Road. About a mile and a half from the Plaza.

Okay. Pantry, that's easy to remember. What about downtown, where's a good place to eat while we're on foot? Any recommendations?

Downtown I think I'd do the Shed.

That's where we're going.

I'll drive you by it, and show you where it's at.

Thank you. Oh, is there a post office downtown?

There is.

Okay. Do you know like approximately where it's located, so I can...?

Well, I know exactly where it's located.

Okay. Maybe we should have you show us where that is, drop us off at the post office, and just go on foot from there.

Yeah. The post office is just like two blocks from the Plaza.

Okay.

I figured it had to be down here.

Yeah. Oh, that's another question. Do you know any place that I can go horseback riding that's not just super touristy though? I can actually gallop a horse.

Yeah, right. I have to look into that, but I think you can just Google it. There's a ranch down on Hwy. 14 that a lot of people go to.

Okay. I mean, I don't mind going on a tour, but I don't want to go with people that are inexperienced and can't do anything.

I'll tell you. This ranch is right here on 14, I think you can Google it, you know, "Horse ranch on Hwy. 14," something will come up. They train all the movie people that come into town how to handle and be with horses. So, I know they're pretty adept with horses.

My family is from San Lorenzo, which is this little, not even quite a town, up in the mountains, about a twenty-minute drive.

Is that where you grew up?

No, my mother did. So, we try to go often. In August they have San Lorenzo Day which is the patron saint of the town. They have a procession through town carrying a cross and the saint, and then they have a mass at dawn, and then it's just a big party with music and food. It's fun. So, I kind of took them through that whole thing. That happens in August. I'm from Los Angeles originally.

What part?

South Pasadena, it's right south of Pasadena, but it's also right next to the Rose Bowl.

My grandma had a house in Pasadena.

Where? Do you know?

I'm not sure. It's about three or four blocks from the Rose Parade.

Well, that's a long stretch of possibilities. Now we've decided to try something new in Oregon. Now we live in a log cabin, 17 miles out of town near Ashland. It is right over the border of California. It's super beautiful, but it's under a lot of snow right now.

It was. I'm sure it's better now.

Yeah, now it's probably better. But when we decided to leave, I went to get extra supplies for our cabin, and he was sick. So I went by myself, I drove from Portland, which is like five hours north, and I was up to my thighs in snow in our driveway.

Are you retired?

No. We need to get back there. Start a life.

I'm a contractor, so I wasn't planning on doing much work between October and now anyway. So I'm going to get everything up and running.

What do you build?

Well, I'm a drywall painter, so a lot of interiors. I do exteriors too. But basically, I'm a specialty guy. I flipped the house before. I'd do that again, but I don't know if I want to get into full on building again, especially in a place like Oregon. So many -- it was not as bad as California but it's almost as bad as California, so many regulations and they're up your ass. And they target little guys, because the big guys just pay them off.

They pay them off?

Oh, yeah. Pay off the government; pay off the politicians.

The zoning people and local people, you mean?

Yeah. Oh, yeah. Corrupt, corrupt. I mean, the things I've found out the last few years, make your toes curl.

Really?

Oh, yeah, I mean, it's so bad. They're all Democrats too, most of them, not all of them, but most of them are.

I was in the construction industry in southern California, and it ended up killing our company.

Yeah.

The permitting would take so long that they couldn't get steady --

And then you've got all these environmentalists, and every little thing they fight. "Oh, there's a glassy link slung over here." And they're so full of it, because half the time it doesn't even affect them. I grew really tired of California. It's nonsense, especially where I was. I was up in northern California. It's just, you know, either they're --

Well, isn't Ashland the same thing as northern California?
It is. The reason we went there is I own the place. So the price was right to live there.

Oh, you're right. It's always the price. When you have something paid off you might as well live there.
That's what I figured, that outweighed anything else. It's not as bad, because we live up in the mountains, so it's not quite as bad. But there's a lot of transplanted Californians there and a lot of PCers, politically correct types. They make up their own little language, and I'm just done with it. And I never want to be censored. You try to censor me; I'm an old punk rocker.

A punk rocker?

Yeah. I'd be like, "Hey, you know what? You're going to tell me what to do and what to say? Oh, you've got another thing coming."

But we want to end up on the coast.

What does a punk rocker mean?

Well, it's just an aesthetic of, you know, more than a music, it's more of an aesthetic. Just that you just don't take any crap from anybody.

I see.

If it's justified, you stick to – but they're highly principled people, actually. And they don't go in for dogma and nonsense, and they do it themselves. They don't believe in experts. You know what I mean?

Yeah.

It's like, "Oh, what do you mean this isn't good music?" Of course, some of the best music in the world was punk rock music. So, guys who really couldn't play very well in the beginning, but they learned, and they honed out their own little niche, and it's returned to rock music. It's returned to the real formula of rock and roll, you know, four or five people in a garage, or three people in a garage banging it out right from the heart, making their own music. It's emotional as opposed to a bunch of studio guys in suits and their big bombastic stage nonsense. The band is away from the audience. They're separate. They're not a part of a community. And that's another big thing. Even the big-time people I like, they tend to be younger, a little more accessible. And when you go see them play they're engaged with the audience, not just standing up there playing their songs and walking on stage.

Were you involved in the music?

Yeah, I still am. Now, I haven't done anything in about a year. I had a band for 20 years, same guys, played all over. I know a lot of people-

Is it punk rock music?

No, not now, it's more mainstream classic rock. It has an edge to it.

Blues.

Yeah, we like the blues, you know. I like jazz too and all kinds. But we have our wheelhouse that we kind of play in, and that's what I learned over the years, just to play to your strength. Don't try to do something you're not so good at just to appease some segment of an audience. That doesn't work. It never works. Don't listen to the experts. The bands that I know that made it, the experts all told them they were terrible, that they'd never amount to a hill of beans. And two of the guys, two of the bands are world famous, massive, have made millions and millions and millions of dollars, play stadiums all over the world. So much for the experts. But then again, the experts told the Beatles, every record company in England told the Beatles they couldn't play, that they were terrible, couldn't sing, and that the guitar music was done by others, and they were silly and stupid.

I was in the music business in L.A. for quite a while.

What'd you do? Did you play or...?

No. I mean, I play guitar. I have a Gibson J-200 from the early seventies with an excellent action, but I was in the music business - the business side. I started a thing called The Recording Workshop in Chillicothe, Ohio with a guy name Joe Waters. In the first year, we taught about 80 students all about the music business and the art of being a recording studio engineer. Then I moved to L.A., and I ran a recording studio, production company and a publishing company for a guy who had signed Billy Joel.

All right.

His name was Artie Ripp. And he's an old-time music guy, partnered with Neil Bogart in Buddha Kama Sutra Records and different old classic guys from the early '50s. He produced acts like Jay and The Americans, Shangri-Las and many others. I met the producers of Woodstock, Artie Kornfeld and Michael Lang, while working for Artie. Michael had referred Billy Joel to Artie, but Michael retained a royalty interest in Billy for years. My claim to fame is that

I gave Mitchell Leib his first job when he was nineteen. Today he's President of Disney Music. Now, a lot of women go into that shop right there, Ooh La La.

Oh, a consignment store, I love that kind of stuff.

And they have phenomenal taste.

And I have phenomenal taste too. I'm a collector of pretty things, especially accessories. Very cool!

Now, I'm going to show you where the Shed is. It's right back here off of Palace.

Okay. Let me tell you, Oregon lacks Mexican food so badly.

You can't even get a good burrito there.

I might start a food truck industry with a lot of Mexican --

Yeah.

Well, that's cool. We're here for a few days, so if I can't get in today. I hate window shopping but I will here.

So, I'm going to take you now to the post office.

The thing about Ashland is it's quiet when it's cold and we both love music. So, imagine being from California, we're spoiled with entertainment.

Yeah. I'm from San Francisco, so it's like – yeah.

So, we like the Portland area better, although I would never live in Portland. But we're looking at maybe living on the coast a few hours south of there. And that way we can still have the music scene and the view of the ocean.

I lived in San Francisco during the early seventies in a communal house around Height and Masonic. I used to go to these SDS meetings, but didn't really know what they were about at the time. I once went downtown to Civic Square for a May Day celebration, thousands of people, with the cops charging into the crowd on their horses swinging their clubs.

Wow.

But listen to this. Someone in the communal house once held me up at gun point and demanded all my money. I told him I didn't have any, so he called my father, and demanded that my dad wire money to Western Union. Instead my dad called the FBI. We drove around San Francisco waiting for the money to be wired. At one point we had a flat tire, so we stopped at a gas station to change the tire. He turns to buy a Coke out of a machine, and when he turned his back to get the Coke, I ran into the street, waved down a van and made my escape. I called my dad to tell him I was safe, and the FBI came and picked me up and interviewed me. Oddly enough, several years later I was picking up some money that had been wired to me at the San Francisco Western Union. The person in front of me stepped to the counter and asked for a money transfer for Mr. Smith or somebody, and as soon as he did that these two or three bum looking like people jumped up, drew their guns, put handcuffs on him, and placed him under arrest. That's what would have happened with my incident.

That's amazing! Look at all these old doors. Can you recommend a place that has a lot of copper kitchen stuff? I'm looking for a copper pepper grinder to be exact, but I can't believe in the southwest I can't find any stores with copper jewelry and copper kitchenware.

There's a really good kitchen shop over in DeVargas Mall, right over here. That is pretty good. Okay. So that's the Plaza. But Seret's with those old doors might have some old copper kitchenware.

Right here.

Okay, I figured.

This is the federal building right in front of you. To the left of that is the post office. So it's a two-block walk.

They've got all these little shops and stuff here to keep us entertained, plus you're the Capital of the State.

Right. Ok folks, here you go.

Thank you, John.

— EAST TEXAS —

Yeah. It's our first time here, and I'll tell you what, it's beautiful!

Where you all from?

We're from East Texas. It's about 90 miles east of Dallas. It's a small town – 4,400 people. Yeah, but we live out in the country pretty much.

Farming?

We don't farm, but we have a little bit of land, but...

But then we have farms to the east and the south of us, so it's not like – we're not out there by ourselves.

You're just in Santa Fe for vacation?

It was his 50th birthday yesterday and it's our anniversary Saturday, so...

Well, that's a good time to do it then? You don't look 50.

Don't give him a big hand now.

Hotel Santa Fe?

Yes.

Yes. You dress super snazzy for driving around doing Uber. I like the hat.

Well, thank you. Where did you hike today? Did you do Atalaya?

Yes.

You did the whole trail?

No.

We didn't do the whole trail. We did about five miles of it.

Oh!

We haven't done the Dorothy Stewart Trail yet.

Yeah, that's back up there?

Yeah, very nice trail. We need to see all the mountains, because we're from the flat lands.

Flat?

Yeah. We got to see some hill, I guess. I don't know if you call them hills.

What do most people do out there? Oil?

Some do oil, yeah. There are a few active oil routes or...

They're – that was big for years, people did – did it on the wells, but last year, the year before, there was a time – when the gas prices shot down, and over 100,000 people got laid off in Texas. They had to stop working wells.

So then in the summer time, I guess it's kind of hot and dry here?

It's kind of mild and dry. It's not – it gets to about 90, sometimes a little higher, most of the time a little lower, but no

humidity to speak of.

Where would you recommend we eat for anniversary dinner on Saturday?

Okay. I would recommend Sazon.

Is it all New Mexican food, or is it...

It's not New Mexican food.

Okay. So, like steak and...

Yeah.

Okay.

Okay, and then wines?

That's what we want - steak. Sazon.

You should go on line and check their menu out.

Okay.

So, it's right downtown, but you got to make reservations.

Okay, good to know. What about other places to eat?

Well, you want local places, or like places where people go to for fancy dinners?

Just like the hotspots.

For fancy, there're places like Geronimo's, Coyote Café, Santacafe and the Compound. They say the best view of the sunset is from Coyote Cantina.

Okay.

And then local places are like Tune Up and Tia Sophia's. The best place for breakfast is The Pantry. It's very good.

Yeah. I saw The Pantry there, I think.

Yeah.

You were down on Cerrillos Road earlier?

No, you know when we were trying to search the Internet for places to eat, eat breakfast.

I see.

Yeah. We saw The Pantry.

Right here is our State Capitol called the Roundhouse. Now my lady and I, we eat a lot at a little place near your hotel called Saveur, S-A-V-E-U-R.

I haven't seen that one yet online.

It's very good.

What type of food do they have?

Okay. They're only open until 3:30 okay, so they're there for breakfast and lunch. And they have...

S-A-V-E-U-R?

Yeah, Saveur Bistro. They have great soups. They have a buffet type of thing, but they also have a kitchen that you can order from. Very standard fare in sort of a French way, Saveur.

Okay.

We eat there probably three times a week for lunch.

Oh, really! That's good then.

Well, it's very like safe food, good food. They're into my gluten free stuff. But they have vegetarian, as well as fish, chicken, sometimes beef or pork.

Okay.

They have good soups. They have specialty stuff that you can order, all kinds of different things.

Now, what about Vivian's Piano Bar?

What's the name of it?

I think it was Vivian's.

No, it's not Vivian's. It's Vanessie's.

Yeah, that's it. Have you been there?

Oh, yeah. You know, it's just right over here.

Is it – would you recommend going there?

Well, it's pretty nice. I used to go there a lot, and it was really, really nice. I don't know what the new owner is like. I haven't been there since it was sold several years ago. So, I can't really attest. But Vanessie's is known for having a great piano player. I used to get these large big huge baked potatoes from Vanessie's, and I'd get one baked potato to go. Now you all enjoy Santa Fe. Okay. Thank you.

Okay. Thank you so much.

— BOB MARLEY DISCUSSION —

What field of anthropology are you involved in?
Oh, well, I do research on disaster preparedness and management and kind of how people receive information from emergency management organizations in Florida. Yeah, it's still in the very preliminary stages.

Well, I have a fascination with emergency stuff, because of drones. You can send drones out immediately into places, instead of humans, and quickly assess natural disasters, stuff like that.

I wonder how that would work. I know one of the things in disaster management as a whole, like beforehand they weren't taking into consideration, we call it social vulnerabilities and the cultures of a population, so pretty much what makes a community a community. Like one of the things that they found is that they need human interaction with survivors, so I wonder what would happen if they did start to utilize drones. Yeah, how that would work, would there be kind of like a shift between it? That'd be cool to find out.

Well, I was told in the insurance business, drones are going to have a major impact.

I could see that, especially when it comes to things like wildfires or flooding, where it won't be safe for actual humans to go there. They could send in these drones, and kind of limit the mortality and death rate.

Yeah.

Oh, very fascinating!

What college did you go to?

It's called the University of South Florida.

I've heard of it. They are a big school, right?

Yeah, really huge. We have a couple of different campuses throughout the state. Florida is definitely different than Santa Fe. My body is not used to the high altitude, dryness and everything, because we are pretty much flat.

Right. A lot of people don't recognize Santa Fe's 7,000 altitude and the effects of it.

And I've definitely been feeling it, especially with my nose, because your air is drier than ours.

You have brothers and sisters?

Yeah, I have a pretty great family. They are kind of scattered all over.

What do they think about you getting into anthropology?

I don't know. I don't think I've ever asked them. I mean, I know that, because I'm Jamaican so...

Oh, you're Jamaican?

Yeah. So, kind of like having two cultures growing up, it was always something that fascinated me, looking at the similarities and things like that between nations. I'm pretty sure my family has gotten used to it.

Have you been to Jamaica?

Yeah. I was born and raised there. I came up here when I was pretty young with my family when we immigrated here.

But you remember Jamaica?

Oh, yeah, I mean, I go back often, because I have family there. So I think the biggest thing about me being in anthropology is how much I can travel. One, I just like to travel, and, two, my parents are like, "Oh, where are you now?" It's pretty fun! It's a nice feel. It's exactly what I wanted to study and spend my life doing.

I've been a Bob Marley student for many years. I saw him in the last couple of years of his life several times in Los Angeles, once at the five hundred seat Roxy. The night I saw him at the Roxy, Mick Fleetwood was sitting right in front of us and I saw him play drums on his glass all night long with two straws. Also, I met the boxer Sugar Ray Robinson that night.

Oh, wow. What's your favorite song?

I don't know the name of it, but the one line in it is, "Always climbing Mt. Zion." Now to me, what that means from Bob Marley is, always be striving to do your best. That's what I think his communication is, and that's what I think the Rasta communication is.

Yeah, because I know Rastafarianism as a whole, like as a religion, is pretty much about being the best that you can be.

That's right, and that's what I think this phrase, "Always be climbing Mt. Zion," means.

Yeah, I could see that. So, do you know much about the Rastafarian community, or is it primarily just what you've seen like in the media and things along that line?

Yeah, I've read a lot about Bob, and played him nonstop one year at Burning Man.

Way to rave! Yeah, that's kind of awesome.

No, I've definitely been into Bob. A couple of years after he died, I was in an elevator in the Mayflower Hotel in New York City. I got into the elevator, and there was this rather buxom lady with an older teenager, just knockdown gorgeous, beautiful girl, and we get down to the bottom. The doors opened, and there's like three or four more of these kids. I said, "Are these all yours?" She said, "Well, they're mine and Bob's."

Oh, wow!

It was Rita Marley.

Oh, it's kind of awesome that you got to meet her.

They were there to accept a posthumous award for Bob Marley, honoring him in the music industry or something. I'm not sure what. Other than the Haile Selassie stuff, I'm

pretty much a Rasta. I don't have the hair. I mean I don't do anything like that, but as far as Bob's philosophy, I think it's right on.

That makes sense. Yeah, I mean it's just about being peaceful, and loving your neighbor, and just being pure. Sounds good. That's cool.

Sometimes I'll ask a person with dreads, "Are you a Rasta, or are you just into dreads as a fashion statement?"

Oh, yeah, because, I mean, it's meant for two different purposes. I don't know, I find like the majority of people in America with dreads, they are not Rastafarian. They are just like it's a fashion thing. It has increasingly become a fashion statement. Are there a lot of people in Santa Fe with dreads? I mean, I haven't seen any so far.

There are some.

I learned yesterday that apparently there are a lot of films and movies that are filmed here in Santa Fe.

There are.

I didn't know this is like a film town too. That was a really good fun fact. Is it more of like a seasonal thing, or is it just constantly throughout the year?

Constantly throughout the year.

Have you picked up anyone famous yet?

Not really. I pick up a lot of people associated with Longmire. It's a TV program that's in its 7th season.

Oh, it's called Longmire?

Yes, Longmire. It's a pretty good series about a western sheriff in today's world in a small rural town that has to take care of business.

Apparently, it's good, if it's on season seven.

Yeah. Right. Okay, thank you.

No, thank you. This is definitely the most interesting Lyft I've had. Good luck with your book.

— SKI LIFT OPERATOR —

What do you do here in town?

I'm a ski lift operator. I'm actually headed to work. A little bit late but...

Do you take a bus up there?

No, I am just going to hitchhike.

Oh, that's where I am dropping you off is where you hitch-hike from?

Yes, it is called The Hitching Post.

Oh, yeah. I know where it is. Where are you from?

Silver City originally. Down by the Gila.

How many people live in Silver City?

About 10,000.

And does skiing bring you to Santa Fe?

Yes. I started working at Sandia last year because I was living in Albuquerque. I dropped out of school. So, they are owned by the same people.

Oh, they are owned by the same people?

Ski Sandia. Yes, so I transferred up here once Sandia's season was over.

How is the snow up there right now?

Dude, it is actually amazing. Yeah, this is the best snow we've had all year.

You guys had twenty inches the other day, right?

Yeah. It was insane and that snow was heavy. I had never seen snow like that, actually. I am used to the Mohave Desert. It was really dense, wet snow. And we got another four inches on Monday and another four on Tuesday. Yes. Those are both my days off, so that was great.

Are you a skier?

I am a skier, yes.

My son is a snowboarder. He skis, too, but sometimes he likes snowboarding, sometimes he likes skiing.

Yes. Yes, I want to try snowboarding. You know, I am a skate boarder and long boarder competitively for a couple of years. So, I do want to try snowboarding but I have been skiing since I was three so it is kind of hard to switch.

Right. My son was a rollerblader/skateboarder. I mean, you know, how the rollerblade... It used to be competitive between the two but not anymore.

Yeah, I was never very good at rollerblading.

I think it is an amazing sport.

Where are you from originally?

Sedona, Arizona.

Oh, really? That's a cool place. It's gentrified now, but back in the day, it was pretty cool.

I grew up there in the early 1950s. I moved there when I was six years old in 1952. Started first grade. Went through first through eighth grade there. My father loved watching

movies being made. In Sedona, at that point in time, most of the westerns were filmed there.

I've heard that. That's interesting, pretty cool. What was the population then?

There were less than 1,000 in the whole valley. Now there's over 10,000. I heard the 1955 Sedona phone book had 155 names. When I first moved to Sedona the only phone was at Oak Creek Store. The first phone we had was a party line. Different number of rings indicated whose call it was. Sometimes we'd go to Slide Rock and it was only us local kids that were there, no tourists like there are today. Yeah, everybody hitchhikes from this particular spot, don't they?

Yes. That is why it is called The Hitching Post. It is pretty easy to get a ride, usually 5 to 10 minutes.

We had a restaurant in Sedona called The Hitching Post. Now I think they call it HP Cafe. Right down the road was Oak Creek Tavern. They both literally had hitching posts for folks to tie their horses. I remember Doc Woodcock and Red and Willy riding their horses into town, hitching them up, and then spending the next couple of hours in the bar. One night my mom got a call from Doc Woodcock to come over the next morning. When she got there, she found him in a pine coffin he had made. He'd got into the coffin and shot himself.

Wow, that's quite a story. I was kind of out of it last night. Usually, I just carpool up with my co-workers. Today will just take a couple of minutes. Sweet. Thanks, John

Right. Okay man. Thank you.

∞

— DENTIST WIFE —

Around my house it seems like I really do need a crutch. It just gets more and more sore.

I'm doing a book on my Uber riders, and I record conversations. Are you okay with that?

Sure.

Pretty interesting people get into my car.

Oh, I'm sure. My son drives Uber.

He's an Uber driver?

In Nashville.

How's he like it in Nashville? He must meet all kinds of people.

He's leaving in May, because he's finishing school, but he mostly has been driving around the university. He's enjoying it a lot, because he can study and then drive when he wants.

Right, this is sure a nice neighborhood.

Oh, I love it! So, you're a writer?

I'm an observationalist. I just observe.

Have you written before?

No. Well, that's not true. I did one time. I'm a poet and member of an organization here in town called The Live Poet Society.

Oh, really, as opposed to the Dead Poet's Society?

Yeah, right. We get together every two or three months, read our stuff.

I just started reading a book this morning that someone gave me, and there was a poem in the front of it that I sent my friend and my husband who are fishermen.

Fishermen?

And the poem is cool, because it's like from the fish's perspective, is how I looked at it.

All right.

It said, "Cedar wax wings, dark among the swallows, iridescent fish with wings, layers of life above the water, under the trout."

Yeah.

It was written by a lady named Judith Nicholls, and I loved how she explained the pretty birds to the trout.

Right

Pretty trout.

Where does your husband like to fish?

Pecos, and all over.

I grew up in Sedona on the Oak Creek, fished every day. I haven't done it in years now. I used to ice fish up on Eagle Nest Lake with a bunch of retired National Park rangers, and I fished over in Pecos. Once when I was fishing with my five or six-year-old son up past Mora, I caught a fish and banged its head on a rock. My son was so disgusted with me killing the fish. I haven't fished since.

Cool.

What do you do here in town?
My husband pulls teeth.

He's a dentist?

He's an oral surgeon.

He's an oral surgeon?

Yeah. Who's your dentist?

Kirk Macgillivray.

Okay, you could tell him if you ever need an implant or a tooth pulled who you want to go see. I think we just saw one of Kirk's patients last week. Is he still on Luisa?

He moved over off St. Francis by the clock tower.

I don't think I knew that.

I was going to that dentistry before Kirk bought them out. He bought out Dr. Zierman.

Oh, yeah, I remember him.

Many years ago.

That's right.

It's a small town.

Yeah. I was playing tennis two days ago, and it just popped. My knee just popped out.

On the court? Did they adjust it or...?

It wasn't like my knee popped out of its socket, something just popped.

Have you seen anybody?

I have an appointment Thursday, because nobody could get me in sooner, of course.

My lady turned around and tripped in our garden, and fell on a flower pot.

Ow.

She fractured the tibia, the plateau of the tibia, in an L-shaped fracture. It's amazing the way they didn't do surgery. They didn't put in any screws. It's amazing the way that bones can stitch back together by themselves.

Really? The tibia and fibula, which one's which?

The tibia goes all the way to the knee cap.

Oh, yeah, okay, so it's the one on the outside. So, did she just wear like a brace?

She wore a brace for a while and stayed in bed. She couldn't put any weight on it whatsoever, and so I had to take her around in a wheelchair for nine weeks.

Nine weeks?
Yeah.

Wow, I've never broken a bone. Well, that's not true. I broke my nose once, and it was like very, very achy. The PT at El Gancho who looked at it thinks it's the ACL.

Oh, boy.

Which is on the outside, but I don't think it's torn necessarily where I might have to be in bed. I won't be walking on it because I need to keep it elevated.

I'm having fun with my left shoulder, boy I'll tell you, rotator cuffs.

Ouch! And usually it's right, unless you're left-handed.

I've already had shoulder surgery on my right shoulder ten years ago. Ok, here we are.
All right. Thank you.

You're welcome. Thank you.

∞

— MEDICAL ANTHROPOLOGIST —

You interview people in the car? That's a good idea.

Well, thank you. My focus is just Santa Fe, people who come to Santa Fe, or live here – it's an interesting group of people.

You know, we're all anthropologists.

That's what they all tell me.

I'm happy you're returning the favor. Santa Fe is my favorite city in the entire United States. I love it here.

Where are you from?

Originally, I'm from upstate New York. I've lived in the south for over a decade in Alabama and now Florida.

What kind of anthropology work do you do?

I'm a medical anthropologist.

What's that mean?

Well, I study diabetes, community gardens and race relations – in child health policy.

I recently read a book called The Case Against Sugar by Garry Taubes in which he anthropologically studies the introduction of western diet into cultures that have never eaten the western diet. What he finds is that western disease such as diabetes, cancer and alzheimer's follow western diet. He says that studies have been done on mice where they get them addicted to heroin, then they introduce them to a sugar water feeder and they all switch to the more addictive substance, sugar. More people die from refined carbohydrates, such as sugar and white flour, than any other substances known to man. The other thing I

learned from this book is that the first largest users of sugar is the processed food industry but the second largest user of sugar as an industry is the tabacco industry. They started putting sugar in Camel cigarettes before World War I and they captured the market because it was a smoother smoke. After the war, Lucky Strikes were introduced, also with sugar and now all American made cigarettes contain sugar. It's the sugar in tabacco causing lung cancer. Each cigarette has about a half teaspoon of sugar, meaning a pack has ten teaspoons every day going into your lungs. So, what do you do in this field?

Well, I'm among the faculty at the University of Florida. I evaluate the Florida health care program. So basically, evaluating insurances plan providers to make sure that poor kids are getting quality care in Florida. Yeah, sugar is a real problem in our society.

That's admirable. Are you employed by the state?

I'm employed by the university. The university has a contract. It's a good job.

Oh, boy. In what part of New York were you raised?

On the other side of Lake Ontario – near the St. Lawrence Seaway. Small town there. So very northern, closer to Canada. About an hour from Syracuse.

What did your parents do up there?

My mom is a nurse and my dad was a school administrator. I still go up there to visit.

Do they still live there?

They do, yeah.

You've traveled around quite a bit?

I have, yeah, mostly because of being at grad school and going to anthropology conferences. I've done some international travel too.

Do they have a lot of anthropology conferences? This is huge; I can't believe it.

Yeah. This one is big. There's one that's bigger, the American Anthropological Association.

Where is that usually held?

Not usually in small places like this. It's usually D.C., San Francisco, Atlanta, Chicago, Denver, so bigger cities – it's so big they need a big convention center.

Well, does this conference here have any vendors with booths, or is it just researchers talking about the projects?

Yeah, there are always vendors. People selling books and things. But at the bigger conferences, they have folks selling software, systems stuff and things like that. It's mostly presentations and workshops. I'm going to a workshop this afternoon. It's going to be on implementation science.

Implementation science?

Yeah, so kind of using scientific knowledge to -- it's basically like, applied anthropology. So, solving real world problems – not just what the academics are talking about. I mean anthropology, you can study anything related to humans, anything and everything. So anthropologists are interested in human experiences, the human condition, and we study everything – health, food...

I always thought anthropologists just explored ruins.

That is one sub field of anthropology. So, there's archaeology which studies past human experiences. There's cultural anthropology, so I'm a cultural anthropologist, and we study current living humans. There are anthropologists who study human variation and human evolution. They are biological anthropologists. And then there are – there's a small number of anthropologists who study language and communication. They are linguistic anthropologists. There are four subfields of anthropology.

My daughter, she teaches the blind. But she was a linguistics major at UCLA. I've had great talks with her about language roots, where all these languages came from.

That's cool. I was a linguistics minor in college, and that was kind of one of my pathways to becoming an anthropology major. But I took a class called the history of the English language, just fascinating to learn about. You have to learn about political history, takeovers and ...

You seem to have a fascinating mind. You're a bright light.

Thank you. I like to learn and talk to people.

I can tell you like to learn. You get turned on by it. My daughters are the same way, both of them. What are you going to rent a car for?

Oh, well, I wish it was something fun, like going to Bandelier, but unfortunately I have a workshop, and my partner is teaching a workshop today. So, we just have to head out of town around 5:30 to get back to Albuquerque. We are getting a place for tonight, because the flight is at 6 AM tomorrow. We don't feel like getting up at 2 AM. This is my fourth time in Santa Fe. I have gone to Bandelier before. Everything here just seems brighter. My vision is clear here.

That's right. Artists come here. It's the light.

Yeah, it's bright. Everything is bright. I always just really have good conversations here, connect to people, and I love it here.

Have you eaten at any good restaurants here?

Oh, yeah. Maria's, I went to Maria's yesterday. It's my favorite. Went to tapas at El Meson. Oh, I went to Gabriel's outside of town.

Isn't Gabriel's fantastic?

Oh, my gosh, it's the second time I've been there. Their guacamole is fantastic. Total indulgence. I'm a foodie, so...

You're a foodie? Hey, thank you and thank you for letting me record you.

No problem. Good luck with your book.

∞

— GUATEMALA —

Are you part of this convention going on back here?

Yeah, there are a lot of people that came to this. Just a pretty good bunch of humans trying to do their very best.

Where you guys from?

I'm from North Carolina.

Yeah, and I'm coming from Arizona, so not too far.

What part of Arizona?

Phoenix.

I grew up in Sedona.

Oh, really? Sounds really great.

I like Sedona. I've been there. I went through Phoenix, but stayed in Sedona.

Yeah, Phoenix is a place that you have to get used to.

My daughters are living in Avondale and Chandler.

Oh, yeah? I never thought, but Chandler was a surprise. I've been through Chandler. Phoenix, it's like huge. It has all these suburbs that are just like extensions of Phoenix, like where I live...

Now what is your field of applied anthropology?

Well, I'm interested in cultural anthropology. Yeah, we were here presenting from research we did over the summer in Guatemala. We did our presentation yesterday, so we can just hang out for the rest of the week.

My Rotary Club does a whole water project in Guatemala.

Really? Where?

Up in the mountains, in the very rural villages in the Zona Reina region.

That's interesting.

It's near Ubinquinol. I'm not sure of the exact villages, but we've had that project for quite a few years, getting running water to some of these small rural towns that don't have any running water.

Yeah, I know that even where we were they rarely had running water, depending on what time of the week we were there.

And sometimes depending on the day we got there.

And what do you do in North Carolina?

I go to North Carolina State University. I'm not from there. I'm just in Raleigh to go to school.

Are you studying anthropology?

Yeah, I'm studying anthropology in social work. I want to lobby at some point.

Straight anthropology is good for that.

Have you been to Sedona?

I haven't been there. I've been to Flagstaff. I think I drove through Sedona, but —and I would love to go. I've heard great things about it.

It's weird, but I've been to, like my family makes it a point to go to different McDonald's when we travel.

When my son was a little boy, we did the McDonald's Monopoly game. We went to all these newspapers to get different Monopoly pieces. We found them in the newspaper.

Did you go to the Sedona McDonald's?

Yeah.

Did you really?

Yeah. I went to the Sedona McDonalds. We like, we don't really like to eat at McDonald's, we just like to go to them. Sedona is the only McDonald's without the golden arches. They have colored turquoise arches.

When I grew up there they didn't have any fast food places at all. But the great thing about growing up in Sedona back then is that us kids, we were all creek kids, playing in the creek or hiking. Billy, Timmy and me, their brothers and the girls, Jannie Mae, Mary Lou, Billie Bea and Nancy, we are all still friends. I think we had eighteen at our last elementary school reunion from the early fifties. The big thing back then was the skating rink at Indian Gardens and the fruit in the orchards. We did a lot of hiking. One time, way up past Jordan Road, we were hiking one afternoon. We had brought a shovel in case we ran into any rattlesnakes. Well, sure enough, we rounded a bend, and there under a low hanging rock was a rattlesnake. We took the shovel and jammed it down trying to get its head, but we missed, and when we tried to pull back the shovel, the metal part came off the wooden handle. We just froze, and

eventually the snake disappeared. During those days, they had one McDonald's on Central in Phoenix that advertised over four million hamburgers sold. We got to go there once a year.

That's funny. There are different kinds. What brought you to driving Uber?

Well, I like to get out and meet people. And I'm writing a book about my riders. Do your meetings all start at ten?

Most of the time. Well, it depends. There are a bunch of different talks and meetings to attend, so they technically start at eight, and then they go until like six. So, it depends on what your interest is.

Do you have different talks and seminars going on at different times?

Yeah, essentially, they have a lot of them going on at the same time, so you have to decide the twenty you're most interested in.

Yeah, it's mostly all the researchers talking together, and talking about the work they've been doing.

Are these researchers themselves applied anthropologists, or are they trying to get applied anthropologists to use their research? Do you follow what I'm saying?

I think it's both. Yeah, so it's like the findings from their research have not been applied yet.

Yeah, I would say it's both, but it's predominately the first one where its researchers presenting their applied research they've done. Does that answer your question?

So, they are trying to get others to apply it?

Yeah. So, here is, these are like the preliminary findings basically. Because there are all kinds of academic researchers. It just kind of happens.

So, you think it just happens in a random way?

Applying it?

No, what you are saying about research.

I think it's quite structured. Someone gets an idea. They go forth to a company or university, get a grant for funding, go do the research, hope that it materializes well in that they find either what they were looking for or any type of pertinent information, go about presenting that research, and try to apply it to the field.

Yeah, there are lots of people doing research on disparity in medical care, so once that research is over, hopefully it can have some effect on medical companies and medical practitioners not having so many disparities in how they practice. Yeah, it still is anthropology. Applied anthropology research can be very complicated, which I suppose all research is.

I mean disparities in the medical system is something that is an anthropological question?

I mean, the cool thing about anthropology is that anything can be an anthropological question. I mean at the conference there are people doing research on medical disparities, medical treatment, on the experience of undergraduates in academia, on how people react to post traumatic stress disorders in conflict areas, stuff like that. Like anything really. It's just the kind of methodology that you use that matters.

Because anthropology is just the study of peoples, so you can take that to mean people and whatever course they choose.

Great! Thank you.

Yeah. Thank you.

∞

— DRONES —

Good morning.

Hi. Was it you that I had the conversation with about the drones?

Yeah. I'm sure it was. I'm into drones. There was a big drone convention here in Santa Fe a while ago, maybe 500 drone experts from around the planet gathered here, and I picked up a lot of them - and learned a lot about drones. You see that pink can, that's to support breast cancer awareness,

A pink garbage can shows your support for breast cancer?

Evidently. Now the reason I know that is I picked up a guy recently who was part of a company that distributed those all over Santa Fe these past three weeks.

But not Waste Management.

It's not Waste Management, some other company that distributes – they're sort of a large company that just goes into these different towns, and distributes them, Strategic Cart Service or something.

Well, I noticed they were doing a lot of rental trucks.

It took them three weeks.

And so, they have no equipment to speak of.

They fly in the labor.

Yeah, not a bad deal, not a bad deal. Of course, with GPS today you can take anybody from anywhere and put them into any town.

I know. Whenever I go down to Albuquerque to take someone to the airport - sometimes I get a ride down there - I'm amazed at how well this GPS thing works when I don't

know the town. I picked you up another time to take you to a car place.

Did you take me to a car place or home from a car place?

I think I've done both.

Yeah, because I've got this, well, Beth and I have this old car that, it's still pretty new to us, and it's requiring a certain amount of catch up maintenance. Unfortunately, the person that had it before me, it pretty much sat in the garage for 15 years, and didn't get used, and a lot of seals and...

What year is the car?

'56.

'56! Well, was it used up to 15 years ago?

It was used – it only has 90,000 miles on it, so in 60 years that's not much miles. But it takes a toll on the seals and the rubber parts just sitting there.

Just sitting?

Just sitting. Yeah, it's not good for them.

So, have you souped it up?

No, it's fairly stock -- the engine has been rebuilt, but just minor upgrades.

How's the paint job on it?

Beautiful. It's teal and white, or Santa Fe teal blue and white.

What year is it again?

'56.

Well, that's a good year, isn't it, '56 for those Chevys?

They were very popular. They still are – '55, '56 and '57.

'58 is when they went into those odd fins.

Yeah. '58, '59, they started the – '59 was a bat wing.

I know a lady here in town who recently died who kept all of her old cars throughout the years. She had five or six of them: a '59 pink Cadillac with the big fins, a '55 Chevy pickup, and, I think, a '65 TR3, or something like that. As it turns out, this lady horded everything, particularly papers. She had every paper she had ever acquired going all the way back into the forties stacked to the ceiling in every room in her house.

That '59 Cadillac is quite a car.

Well, it only had 78,000 miles on it.

Did somebody local wind up with it?

I don't know who bought it. I had someone who would have bought it. It was a guy from Norway, and he buys Cadillacs like this, amasses them in New York City, and ships them in a container to Norway.

He's from Norway?

He refurnishes them. He has one specialty; Cadillacs.

I met a guy with a pink Cadillac, and I thought from his accent he was German. He may have been Norwegian, and I just didn't realize it. Did you meet the gentlemen, a pretty good-sized fellow?

I never met him. I just talked with him on the phone.

But he has got an accent. I wonder if it's the same guy. There can't be that many of them around here.

I bet it is the same guy.

Well, there are not that many pink Cadillacs floating around. We're going to the Quality Inn right up here on Cerrillos.

Your '56 Chevy is there?

Yeah, it's on up a little – the white sign on the top corner of the building, by the fire hydrant, the car is right there.

Oh! My lord! Look at that. That is beautiful.

That's what we said.

Oh, boy! Very nice!

All right. Thank you.

∞

— TV PILOT —

What is this on Rodeo Park Road?

Oh, it's a production office for a T.V. pilot we're doing out here.

Is it a western?

I think it's a murder like crime drama. It takes place on an Indian reservation. That's about all I know. Someone told me that, but...

Are you from California?

Yeah.

I used to live in L.A., around Sunset and Harper.

Oh, okay.

What part of L.A. you live in?

I'm in Playa del Rey.

Playa del Rey. Where is that, down near the airport?

Yeah, by the airport, just north of the airport, by the beach.

What are you doing in the film business?

I'm a cameraman. I'm a first assistant cameraman, so I make sure everything is in focus.

How did you get into that?

I started about 18 years ago, and I was in the production part of things, like kind of coffee getting and that kind of thing, and just kind of – so many different jobs to choose from. So, I chose the camera department.

I see.

Just kind of been doing it.

When I was a little boy growing up in Sedona, Arizona, my father loved to take me to watch the movies being made.

Yeah.

And they had all these westerns being made in Sedona – fake fire, fake rain.

Yeah. Pretty cool.

Fires. Yeah, it's fascinating. We met all the great actors and actresses of the day. Joan Crawford.

You met her?

Yeah.

Wow! That's very cool.

Not in a formal way, but I saw her doing a scene and I watched her walk up the road. I mean, after the scene was done, I said, "Hello Ms. Crawford." This is from the movie <u>Johnny Guitar</u>.

You were close to a legend. That's pretty cool.

There were a bunch of old time actors like Jimmy Stewart, Richard Widmark, Glenn Ford, those types of people all made movies in Sedona. One year, Tommy Rettig of Lassie fame came to Sedona to do a movie. I think it was <u>The Last Wagon</u>, and he started dating Little Nancy, one of the local fourteen-year-old girls. It was quite the talk of the town.

Yeah. I've been to Sedona, but only a drive through.

In the early '50's we had a fake western street out by Coffeepot. We had fake buildings on both sides of the street, and there was just a front for the buildings. Movies like the original <u>3:10 to Yuma</u> were filmed out there with Glenn Ford.

Yeah.

Stagecoach comes roaring into town with a whole team of horses. That was around what was known as Grasshopper Flats, now known as West Sedona. We had the rodeo grounds right out there, our baseball diamond, and on the other side up on the mesa you had the ever-growing Sedona Airport. I remember going up to Easter Sunrise service up on the dirt runway in the early fifties. People rode their horses up to it. Later they built a big cross. You primarily work in TV as opposed to movies?

I do more movies and commercials, but this came up, and I felt like getting out of town for a few weeks.

You should try Ten Thousand Waves while you're here.

I've heard of Ten Thousand Waves, but last summer we went to Ojo Caliente.

Oh, boy, that's the Real McCoy.

And that place is real nice. Now is that closer to Taos?

Okay. It's about halfway in between.

It is, isn't it?

Yeah. It's on the back road, you know, not the High Road or the Low Road, but the back road. It's about halfway there. It's about 45, 50 minutes from Santa Fe.

What road number is that, do you know?

I think it's Highway 285. You go through Espanola, and you turn left at the first stop light. And you just sort of follow that road to Ojo. Northern New Mexico is known for its hot springs.

It is, isn't it?

Yeah. No one seems to really knows that.

What about San Antonio Hot Springs, ever heard of that?

Yeah, that's up there near Jemez Pueblo.

A friend of mine was telling me. I'm going to try to go up there this weekend. Let's see if I can find that place.

There's a real interesting one called Spence Hot Springs on the way down to Jemez. You sort of have to find it on a map, because it's not marked, but you hike back in there, and it's quite a spring. Google it. Lot of people do it naked.

Yeah. There it comes up. Thanks.

Thanks. Bye.

∞

— MY WHOLE LIFE —

Hi.

Hi, we found you.

Yes. This is my nephew Austin. I don't know if you remember meeting me the other day, but...

Yes, I do.

I was telling him to enroll in The MASTERS Program.

That's true.

So, what is your book about, describe it.

It's about Uber riders. Just, you know, the interesting people that get in my car that I pick up here in Santa Fe.

Cool. Are you just going to type out what they say?

Well, I'm going to use the recordings as a base, and then revise and edit.

It was snowing pretty hard a few minutes ago.

What grade are you in?

Almost in seventh.

Where do you go to school?

La Mariposa Montessori, it's next to Waldorf.

I know exactly where it is. My son went there. He went there 23 years ago or so.

Him and I are the same age, yeah. He's 30 right, this time?

Yeah, he's 30.

∞

Nice school.

La Mariposa has been going for quite a while. It's a great school.

How long has it been open for, do you know?

Well, he was there the first year. I believe – he went there in the fourth grade. So, he was – so it's been 23 years.

Yeah, they've been working, I don't know for how many years, with the Assistance Dogs of the West.

That was a good program. How long have you been going to La Mariposa?

Like my whole life.

Since you were in kindergarten.

Yeah, kindergarten. I got mixed up.

La Mariposa only used to go through sixth grade. Do they have seventh and eighth now, or just sixth?

No, just sixth.

Where are you going to go next year?

Desert Academy, that's where they go.

That's what my son did too.

This is fine right by there by the recycling box.

Okay. Thank you so much.

Thank you very much. It was nice to see you again.

Bye-bye. Hey, here's a $2.00 bill for you.

Yeah! Nice to meet you. Thank you.

∞

— SACRED FORESTS —

You're with the anthropology group?

Yes. I bet you've been getting a lot of business from them.

Yes. I'm doing a book on my Uber and Lyft riders.

You are?

I record conversations. Is that okay?

Of course. Are you an anthropologist?

Not really.

You know we're all anthropologists in the world.
That's right.

Oh, you're doing an ethnography of your riders, and you know to ask for consent.

Yeah, right.

Is there a theme you're looking for, for your...?

Is there a theme? No. It's more just like a collection of what occurs in Santa Fe.

What occurs in Santa Fe? What's your best anecdote so far? Any real crazy folks get into your car?

Well, I picked up one guy at about 5:30 in the morning from the Drury Hotel. He got in the car, and obviously he'd been drinking all night, and he sort of slurs it out, "Take me to Allsup's. I need a pack of cigarettes." Driving down there he says that he had gotten into a fight that night down in Albuquerque. I asked him if he was ok, and he said, "Yeah, I'm a cage fighter. But I'm a perfect gentleman on the streets." The people that come here and live here are for the most part pretty fascinating.

Yeah, I bet.

I've had one guy who started six Silicon Valley startups and sold them all. And his latest investments are in flying cars. He says they are just around the bend.

Wow and I've been thinking of self-driving cars.

I know flying cars are definitely way cooler, much more exciting.

What kind of applied anthropology do you guys do?

Well, I study community based conservation and sacred forests protected by indigenous groups in southwest China.

Right.

So, I'm sure you get all sorts of anthropologists, do you? What do you think of anthropologists?

Pretty good sample size.

I've liked everyone I've taken. They all seem to be fascinating people in their fields. Anthropology is such a wide field.

It is, and especially this conference. It draws a particular kind of anthropologist because it's for applied anthropology. So, people are here using anthropology for all sorts of problems.

It's real multidisciplinary too.

Right, it's really, you have ecologists and engineers and all sorts of different kinds of people who are interested.

We heard a talk yesterday. He was a social scientist.

He was a computational social scientist.

What does that mean?

So, that means that he uses the power of mathematical modeling to model what different like social systems and power structures would look like given different sets of rules. So, like if there was this kind of market incentive and this kind of rule, like how would different people act or different groups act.

Now tell me about what you're doing down there in China again.

So, I'm working in the world's northern most tropical rain forest, which is beautiful, but it's lost 70% of its trees in the past, and they have real water issues.

And where is it located?

On the border of Laos and Myanmar. The region has been experiencing rapid environmental and economic change. I'm working with an indigenous group there, and I'm trying to look at their sacred forests, which are fragments of a threatened kind of ecosystem. And I'm trying to understand, like, if, when and how, like under what conditions can conservation and community goals be aligned, so that if we do conservation, we could do it in a way that's socially responsible, because a lot of conservation has been done in ways that are ineffective, and actually act to disenfranchise people who depend on it.

Well, how did you come across this project?

Well, I wanted to work in tropical rain forests. I wanted to work with something about people in nature. And I was born and raised in North America, but I have Chinese roots, and so I wanted to go back.

Yeah, and do something in China.

Yeah, do something in China.

And have you actually worked in the field there yet?

Yeah. I spent over a year living there.

Oh, boy. Oh, here we are. So, thank you.

Ok, thank you very much.

∞

— SHRIMP FARMING —

What do you do in anthropology?

We are environmental anthropologists.

What does that mean exactly?

We study the relationship between humans and the environment in general. So, I work in Vietnam with shrimp farmers.

You work in Vietnam with shrimp farmers?

Yeah.

What exactly do you do there?

You know one of the things we do is hang out and write about people's lives. We interview lots of people.

Tell me about shrimp farming. Are most shrimp in Vietnam, are they farmed as opposed to caught in the wild?

Nowadays, yes, because the wild populations have really diminished, both because of overfishing, and because people have cut down all the mangrove forests that are along the coast. And that's where the baby shrimp grow, and now there's no place for the baby shrimp to grow. So, most people are farming shrimp now. And it's devastating for the environment.

Are most of the shrimp that we get here in America farmed?

The ones that are coming from Southeast Asia, definitely.

Definitely.

Yeah, like the imported ones, most definitely. But, you know, in a lot of the supermarkets, like Sprouts and Whole Foods, and wherever, you know, they'll sell fresh caught shrimp.

That's the wild shrimp.

That's the wild. I see.

Yeah, yeah, because we live in Florida, so we often have the option to buy, you know, wild caught Florida shrimp. Or not.

What's your book about? Or so far what direction is it like...?

Well, there's no direction. It's just a study of the people that get into the Uber and Lyft cars in Santa Fe, and the type of people that come to Santa Fe and live here.

That's pretty interesting.

I don't really have a direction with it yet.

What's one of the most interesting things that somebody said to you?

Well, there's a lot of them. I had like a guy who grows roses in Ecuador who sells them to wholesalers all over the world. I had a lady who is a sock designer for forty years. I had a guy from Silicon Valley who bought and sold six startups, and he said that his latest investments are in flying cars.

Wow.

Flying cars.

I got into an interesting conversation with a Rasta lady, talking about Bob Marley. All the rides are fascinating.

I bet, I bet.

It's a good way of approaching it.

I know. I picked up one guy who has a 32-year-old autistic son who's getting married.

Oh, wow, okay, good for him.

And that was pretty interesting, isn't it? A rundown of the autistic world.

Aha, aha. And was he getting married here in Santa Fe?

No, in California.

Okay. I imagine this is a place for destination weddings, right?

Destination weddings, well, we had a huge one the other day.

Did you?

Down here at La Fonda they stayed, but then they got married at the Loretto Chapel, and it was formal. Everyone was in tuxedos. Two former Miss Americas spoke at the wedding, I understand.

Wow, it's beautiful over there. That'd be a nice place for pictures in fact.

Nice chatting with you.

Nice chatting with you guys.

∞

— ALASKA —

Hello. What brings you guys here to town?

I'm just visiting. I'm here for an anthropology conference.

Lots of you.

Yeah, there's a lot of us. The town is crawling with them, sorry to say. I'm avoiding them myself.

This is the last day, isn't it?

Today is the last day but I'm sticking around to go for an extra day to take a drive around the town tomorrow, maybe do Ojo Caliente or 10,000 Waves. The one in town is fancier, right?

It's Japanese. He's done a great job with it.

Yeah, I hear it's nice.

For in town stuff, yes. And the services are great. They employ like 150 or 200 masseuses.

Oh, that's no joke.

No, it's no joke.

Yeah, that's huge, but I don't need a massage. I'm married to a massage therapist, so just hot tubs...

There you go. Ojo Caliente is completely different. They have a lot of different mineral springs and baths. Where are you from?

These days Philly.

What is it you apply to anthropology?
What do I work on?

Yeah.

So, I've worked on a bunch of things. I've worked on disasters like post 9/11 and Katrina. I've done work in Alaska with indigenous communities. I've done suicide interventions and stuff in northern Canada.

That all falls under anthropology?

Yeah. I became an anthropologist mostly because I thought I could figure out what to do when I wanted to, and pretend like it was a profession. So, it semi-worked out. Like any profession, it actually kind of gets to you. You think you're gaming it, but in the end it games you in the sense that it forces you into certain kinds of professionalized behaviors, which change how you do things. And once you're in, you have to do certain things to stay in, and figure out the scheme of things.

How did you find your different jobs? Through like Craigslist or industry journals, or...?

No. I now have a permanent position teaching at a college, so I'm not...

Oh, so you're not an applied anthropologist?

I do applied work, but I have a regular job. For a bunch of years, I went from job to job. And that was more, it was more word of mouth than anything. Like a colleague of mine had a big National Science Foundation project in the Arctic. So, I went up there with him and spent time in Labrador for a couple years. And then I landed a job, a temporary job for a few years, out of McGill on a project for a community, a nationwide project on community mental health.

What's McGill?

McGill University in Montreal. So, I spent time there, and got to travel a lot, and got to spend a lot of time pretty out of the way in Canadian Native communities.

My lady's son lived in Greenland for two years.

Oh, wow. Doing what, resource extraction stuff?

He's a marine biologist. They were studying crabs for environmental purposes in different populations.

I've never been to Greenland, but Labrador has a close, if not similar, ecosystem.

My lady went to Greenland to visit her son. Her grandkids speak Inuit. They learned it so quickly.

Oh, they do? Cool! Yeah, Santa Fe seems like a good place to live. Seems like though in midlife it may be a hard place to make a living, I can imagine.

A lot of people live here, and make their living in other places. They have businesses that support them.

Oh, like where they can like have web based businesses?

Yeah, all different types. A lot of people fly in and out to L.A, New York.

Like film industry people?

Film people, yes, a lot of different industries.

Yeah, because it's such a nice place to live.

Weather changes every 10 minutes.

Yeah, I like that. Philly is all right. It's not my favorite place to live though.

I like the music aspect of Philadelphia.

Philly has got good music and good radio.

It always had good music.

Yeah, I mean jazz and soul.

Rock 'n Roll came out of Philadelphia. You know Bobby Rydell, Frankie Avalon, Fabian and Chubby Checker, they all are from Philadelphia. Fabian and Chubby Checker actually went to the same high school together. I used to listen to them all on KOMA, from Oklahoma, 50,000 watts.

We'd get it in the evenings when the sun went down. I used to dream of girls and far-away places, listening to radio and all those records. Also, American Bandstand was from Philly. We didn't have a TV growing up, but whenever we traveled, my older brother Jeff always had his eyes peeled on American Bandstand. Sometimes we'd visit friends over in San Bernardino. They had a TV box about four feet tall by three feet wide that had a little six inch black and white screen.

A lot of it, yeah, it still has good music. You know I think probably these days what they're known for is hip hop. And there's kind of a younger indie rock scene right now. It's like younger kids that kind of engage in it. But probably there's some pop bands.

Okay. Thank you.

Thank you, man. Be good. Good luck on the project.

Thank you.

— BLACK ACTIVIST —

Where are you from?

Well, I live in Albany, New York. But I'm originally from Greenville, Mississippi.

Greenville, Mississippi. What do you do in Albany?

I'm in grad school at the State University of New York in Albany, where I study anthropology.

Lots of anthropology riders today.

Do they tell you anything about their work?

Yes, I've learned so much. It's unbelievable.

All different interesting things, I'll bet.

What is your particular field?

I'm a cultural anthropologist, but also do social linguistics. I do a lot of discourse analysis about the way that people talk about politics and different factors in their lives. I work mostly with activists.

What kind of activists?

Primarily black activists. I work with activists from Black Lives Matter. I work with activists from mass incarceration organizations. I work with different activists, and really just talking to them, really exploring their lives, but also the work that they do.

And are you doing this as part of your studies?

Yeah. It's the focus of my dissertation research. I'm trying to get out studying and working with them to determine how the methods of activism influence what the state policy is and state actions, and what it means for us the general public. Those are some of the larger questions.

And what do you intend to do with this? Do you intend to make your career out of this in the anthropology or...?

Yes, like anthropology has been dedicated to how we can really study the human condition; to better the human condition. I study activism as a way of understanding how to deal with problems in our society. I mean, for example, how do we react as a society to different forms of activism, and how listening and studying as an activist can help us to understand the ways in which we can do better, and how to implement policies, and...

What prompted you to get into this field? I mean is it something in your early childhood, your parents, you know, like have you always had an interest in this?

Well, I was a student activist in undergrad, and I did a lot of work in history. My undergraduate degree is focused on history and psychology. So, I was obsessed with the way that people think, and how sort of the way that human thought has influenced different policies and actions throughout history. And it was really interesting, and so I did an ethnographic project in undergrad as my senior thesis. And my advisor, when I was graduating, she was like, "So, I know you're thinking about grad school. I think you should think about anthropology." And then I looked at her and I'm like, "What the hell is that?" And then she gave me some more information, and then I did a lot of my own research.

I took a year off before I even thought about planning my grad school. Then I took a few months before I thought of applying. I had a year off during the year, so I did a lot of research, and I applied to different programs throughout the country, most of them in anthropology. You know, it's like I figured I'd try it out, because I found it interesting. So, I started it my first year of grad school, and I've been like kind of hooked ever since.

That's cool.

In terms of studying activism, I didn't intend to. I was intending to continue actually my undergraduate project as part of my graduate research, which was focused on sort of family structures and methods of survival in sort of the urban south.

What were you like in high school?

Actually, in high school I was more business and culinary arts focused. So, I'm like I was totally different. I thought I was going to..., I went into undergrad thinking that I was going to study business. And I did start off studying business. I did economics, but I did a couple of sociology classes and then business, but I wasn't really passionate about business. And so, I decided to make a change, and ever since I've been happy with like sort of....

Your field of focus.

Yeah. With social anthropology, you get to see so many different ways in which you can put research to work. Right now, I've also done research on health issues around women and child birth within black communities. So, my research varies, but like my focus right now is the black community. What types of projects have you heard about?

A lot of medical, a lot of environmental...from indigenous cultures in the northern part of China bordering with Laos, and all different types of projects. There's a couple thousand people here at this conference.

Yeah. Actually, this is one of the smaller conferences. Well, it's the second largest. The larger one is like we have it in the fall, and it's usually anywhere between 5,000 and 10,000 people. Yeah, it's like really large, so it's really easy to get overwhelmed when we go.

So, you've been Ubering around town?

Yeah, and walking to La Fonda. And like now I'm exploring the area. The conference is pretty much over, so I'm doing the museums and stuff – touristy stuff. What brought you to Santa Fe?

A woman.

Wow, that's actually a first. Out of all the Uber drivers, different people, none of them were from here. I saw one guy last night. He was the first one who ever told me he's from here. One guy came here on a ski trip, and he just never left, literally never left. He came, like he was in his late teens, maybe early 20s, and he just showed up here for a ski trip. He decided to extend it to a week, and then he said the week became a month, and he never went back home. Thanks for the ride.

Yeah. Okay. Thank you so much.

Thank you.

∞

— FRENCH POLYNESIA —

Where you from?

I'm from Philly for the conference.

What kind of applied anthropology do you work in?

So, I study climate change in French Polynesia. I do the Society Islands, Marquesas Islands and the Tuamoto Atolls.

Where do you live?

While I'm there I usually try to stay in Papeete, Tahiti, but I kind of just wander around. I hitchhike. Someone invites me to stay at their place or boat, I won't turn them down. Sort of a nomad right now in the South Pacific.

I visited Bora Bora for two weeks about twenty years ago.

Oh, wow, how did you like it?

Oh, I loved it. We sailed around all those Society Islands with four couples in a boat with a captain and a crew for my friend's 50th birthday. Saw all the natives rowing in their outrigger canoes between the islands and lagoons. One night we moored up, set anchor and listened as the natives played the drums, sang on the beach and burned their fires. We even sailed to one small island that was occupied by only two people.

Yeah, Bora, Bora is beautiful. Did you stay in one of those over the water bungalow things?

I did, yeah. Very nice. I can't remember the name of the hotel.

I haven't. I've seen those, and they're really cool. I love Bora Bora. I also really like Moorea.

I didn't really go there. I saw it from an airplane close to the ground.

It's a little smaller. It's a little bit off the beaten path, but they have some, they have two beautiful bays and a couple of really nice hotels.

Papeete is like a huge city. I mean, it's like people are going nuts there, flying around on their motorcycles, and cars weaving in and out.

Well, it feels small compared to Philly. I think it's about 140,000 people.

Is that all? I guess compared to the rest of Tahiti, the Society Islands, it's the biggest city there.

Yeah, it is the biggest city there. A lot of people don't like Papeete, I think because they come to French Polynesia, and they're expecting, you know, just a beautiful sense of nature and coral reefs, and then they get to Papeete, and it's jarring.

Do you work for a government agency?

No. I'm a PhD student. Have you had other riders who work for...?

I've had all kinds of riders. It's amazing. Is the conference over yet?

I think it ends today. I toured stuff today. So, I avoided it.

What's the most interesting thing you saw in Santa Fe?

I really like all of the churches. I think they're beautiful, the San Miguel. The Mission, that was my favorite. I went to what is it, it was the...

Did you go to the Cathedral, the Cathedral Basilica?
Yeah, that was pretty too.

Are you staying at an Airbnb while you're here?

Yes. I'm staying with a man named Christopher.

Oh, I know him. He's a very interesting fellow. Musician, writer, wood crafter and sculptor and among other things, he's a good friend of mine.

Well, all the reviews are saying he's very interesting, and, you know, that he's a great host, so...

Well, thank you. You'll enjoy Christopher.

— FAIRBANKS —

You visiting Santa Fe?

Yep.

Where you are from?

Fairbanks, Alaska. I tried walking down here but then they are all closed on Sunday. So, that didn't help me out, and I don't have a car.

Yeah. What do you do up in Fairbanks?

I'm an acupuncturist.

Do they grow a lot of stuff up there?

No, an acupuncturist

Oh, an acupuncturist. I thought you said agronomist.

Yeah, yeah. But we do grow a lot of stuff up there, because we have sunlight in the summer all day long. So, our vegetables are huge.

How big is Fairbanks?

I think it's about 200,000 in the borough. It's kind of spread out. How big is Santa Fe?

Santa Fe proper is about 80,000. In the county, I think, it's about double that.

It's beautiful. I love all the stucco. It's really pretty.

Yeah. The Land of Enchantment they call it.

Where do you guys get water from?

We have a reservoir system for the rain, and then we have a whole bunch of wells, what they call Buckman Wells, near the Rio Grande. Is there a lot of fishing up there?

Not in Fairbanks, but in Alaska there is, yeah. We are a little too far north. I mean, when you think of Alaska, you think of big salmon, right? Or halibut? But it's mostly like lake fishing, pike and trout and stuff like that. But most people that live in Fairbanks go to Valdez or Homer or Seward and go fishing every summer. There are lots of places to get salmon. We have caribou and moose and bear and lots of hunting. We got tons of snow this winter.

How much?

Oh, jeez, we probably got about eight feet in Fairbanks. We got a lot of snow this year.

Well, hello there! Do they get the streets ploughed?

They try. It's pretty rough though, you know, because they can't do it all at once. It takes time to get to all the roads. Most everyone I know have a four-wheel drive. Cars get pretty beat up, because it's super cold. That's hard on them too. At 40 below, your vehicles don't like to start. So we plug in our cars in the winter. We have little heaters on the oil pan and the battery. Yeah, otherwise your car will be dead and never start.

It's a different way of living. What's the coldest it gets here?

Well, last winter, first week of February, I don't think it got above 10 degrees. That's probably not cold in your terms.

Anything above zero is pretty warm to us. Ok. Thank you.

Thank you.

∞

WEEK THREE

— EPILEPSY —

We got to be down at the courthouse in twenty minutes. But first we got to go to this UPS Store across the street and then come back and pick her up.

Straight ahead? Ok, I see the UPS store.

It took me doggone seven months to send this computer. Seven months, man! You're talking about seven months, shit happens, man. But at least I know it's ready now. And my son will be like, "Dad, you finally sent it? Wow!" People, I don't even believe it. Shucks man, I get to go see my son now!

Okay, here is the UPS store. You want me to wait here for you, or shall I go back and pick her up?

Okay, if you could wait that would be great. Appreciate it. And it's John, right?

Yeah.

Okay, thank you, sir. I'll just only take a minute. Thanks, John.

Get it all done?

Yeah, sure did, man, long overdue. Appreciate it. Can you hold it a sec. Damn, look at her.   That's crazy, huh? She's got my wallet. I put my wallet in my pocket, I thought. I'm sure I did.

That could have been a problem.

Oh, yeah.

Listen, I've had people leave their wallets and their phones in my car.

Oh, I know, that's a pain.

I got one phone in my glove compartment right now that no one ever claimed. That's a Sony phone you have?

Mm-hmmm.

I've never seen a Sony phone.

Yeah, I could have got a better one, but it was spur of the moment.

Sony makes pretty good products.

Heck, yeah; heck, yeah. That's why I use it and my Sony headphones and stuff. Yeah, Sony is good. I mean, you know, I wouldn't trust it with my home theater per se. Oh, there she goes, crazy girl.

There she goes?

Uh-oh, she's coming. I guess I'm going to court and waiting. Hey babe, law court's on now.

No, I have the key.

All right. If you don't mind taking me over here, I'll go with you downtown and we'll – baby, you mind this gentleman. Oh, no, she's all right, she's all right, she's all right, she's all right. She's under a lot of stress right now. It's okay, baby. Baby, baby, it's ok.

Is she epileptic?

Yeah.

Should I take her to a hospital?

Let me go in the back seat and see if I can help. My baby.
That's all right, baby, all right now, okay. She's – you'll see,
she's going to be ok. Yeah, now I got to go and lock the door.

Are you sure you need to leave her and lock your door?

Yeah. Yeah, I'm going to go and lock them. She'll be out of it
for a few minutes.

Okay.

Thank you, man. Sorry it took so long. That's an interesting
way to start your trip, huh, John? Okay, the crazy part is like
when she wakes up, it's like she was asleep. You know what I
mean when you have seizures?

Does it conk her out?

Pretty much. It's just the better part of it is the end. Baby,
baby, although I guess the answer to your question would
be, yes, at that point, because it's like waking them up. Baby,
sweetheart, hello, baby. She's real worried about this court
thing. Baby, well, she's all right, John. All right. I'm just here
for you.

Okay.

Okay. She's all right.

You want to sit in the back with her or....?

Yeah, yeah, yeah.

Here he is. Here's your boyfriend.

It's ok. I'm going to go with you, all right?

What?

What?

What?

No, you went out sweetheart.

What?

Calm down, calm – let me hold you, okay? You're in the car. We're on the way to the court office. Don't stress yourself out. Relax, please, please, because that's why you're confused right now. You got too excited. What you thought? I left you? You seized out as soon as you got in the car.

I what?

You seized out. You had a seizure as soon as you got in the car. I figured it was because you thought I left you, and then I think you realized I didn't. So now I'm going to court with you. Hope this doesn't take too long.

I'm just concerned about her being okay, and getting you guys down to the court on time. I hope she's okay.

Yeah, she is, yeah. That's my baby. You didn't think I left you. You know I didn't leave you, okay? You know I didn't leave you. I know you've been concerned, but nothing's going to happen. We're going to walk in and walk out. It's all right.

Does she have seizures sometimes when she gets stressed?

When she gets stressed, yeah, wouldn't you say, babe? I get so frustrated with the fact that I hadn't done it, that I didn't call him. He's eighteen. I've been giving him a lot of advice and stuff like that. But because I love him so much, I told him I was not going to call him until I sent this thing off.

There you go.

So finally sending it off, sending him the tracking number, and then I can call my son as I wish.

Very good. Where does your son live?

Philadelphia. Yeah, that's where I'm from. But I haven't been back there in 10 years now.

How often does she have a seizure?

Only when she gets stressed out, man. As soon as you sat in the car, baby. Yeah, that's why I figured you thought we left you. I'm not going anywhere, but John was kind enough to stick around, because we knew – because I told him that you're still getting ready.

I was in the car? I was in the car? I kind of felt one coming on.

Thank God, yes, yes. Yes, you were.

Here we are. Thank you.

So, thank you, John, for your customer service and patience, my man.

Thank you.

Yep, have a good one.

∞

— FANTASY WRITER —

You're writing a book? That's an interesting project while you are driving. I'm a writer also.

Are you?

Yeah, fantasy writer.

Where are you from?

San Francisco area. I'm going back now.

What kind of work are you in?

I do freelance writing and stuff, just different odd jobs.

How do you get the jobs?

Usually through Craigslist. I shop around.

People advertise that they need someone and you just apply?

Yeah, a lot of the time I work in the Silicon Valley area, so it will be like tech writing jobs, which is alright. It's not that fun, but it's good. I'm working on a novel, so I try to get jobs where I can work around that.

You're doing a novel? That's a big project!

Yeah.

My lady published a book called Hold My Hand: A Mother's Journey.

Oh, really?

Macmillan in London published it. And, you know, the interesting thing is that these editors and publishers – like for her book she presented four sample chapters that she had written, and sort of like a paragraph on the rest of the chapters.

Interesting.

They like to get involved early on in the project if they can.

Yeah, I've heard that.

And they like it to where they can do – I mean editors are a major piece of the whole publishing equation. It's amazing the influence an editor has.

Yeah.

But they get so many projects before their desks. They don't like to read the whole book word by word up front.

They also do want you to have the full book written up, so it's like a balancing act. You've got to show them what they want, but have more in waiting.

Have you ever seen the movie <u>Genius</u>?

No. Is it about a writer?

It's about three writers: Thomas Wolfe, Ernest Hemingway and F. Scott Fitzgerald. Those three were all edited by the same person. All three of them had the same editor.

I didn't know that.

And the story is about him. His name is Maxwell Perkins. But it's also about his writers.

Interesting.

It's a very interesting movie.

So, are you planning to write a book about the Uber riders?

Yeah.

Are you going to do it for a certain amount of time, then write the book, or are you going to just do it for the longest time?

I've been thinking about that. Probably just like a certain slice of Santa Fe at a certain point in time.

Interesting. What interesting things have you found out about the Uber riders of Santa Fe?

It's a wide selection of people. Like this past week we've had an anthropology convention here in Santa Fe. 2,000 applied anthropology people from all over the world came here. And it's just interesting to me, the way that people get into anthropology.

My parents are anthropologists.

What field?

My dad is not really doing it anymore, but they both did cultural anthropology before, and now my mom teaches like the virtual world through online communities and stuff. They've been doing it for years. I have to ask my mom if she knows that conference.

Yeah, it was gigantic. I mean for Santa Fe it was gigantic.

Yes, I love Santa Fe. I want to come back. It's nice.

It must be difficult to be a freelance writer. I mean economically you've got to keep going all the time, don't you? But the people who you write for, if you do a good job, they will ask for you again, right?

Yeah. That's the idea. I'm kind of starting out, but, yeah, hopefully I'll build up a reputation and it will work out.

I met a guy one time who was the printer for manual books for like the iPhone in the beginning, you know, like he said his business almost evaporated completely when they stopped giving you a manual.

Yeah, my dad did a lot of that work, and the same thing happened to him. It's hard to get the technical jobs, and they don't always pay for that anymore, because people figure out how to do it and post their own stuff online.

I learned from my daughter and granddaughters. I mean these kids, they just go so fast, and they're not worried about what buttons they push.

And it goes in waves of how many businesses are opening and stuff. There was a burst like there was in the nineties, and then there was a little bit of a wall, and everyone lost jobs, and then it came back.

Had you ever been to Santa Fe before?

Yes, I've been visiting my friend here. I've been here a couple of times to visit her. It's fun and pretty cool. I went to this big moustache party on Friday, and it was fun.

A moustache party?

Yeah, it was a moustache party; everyone had moustaches.
I've never seen nor heard of that.

Yeah. Apparently, it's a yearly thing.

I was once going to put on a mustard party.

A mustard party?

Yeah, where everyone brings their favorite mustard. My wife at the time thought I was crazy though.

I don't know if I have a favorite mustard. You would have to be a ...

But then I went to this museum in Wisconsin, called the Mustard Museum, and this guy had every kind of mustard you could possibly imagine. He was a retired lawyer from New York. I asked him, "Hey, have you heard of anyone who has done a mustard party?" He said, "Well, everyone does mustard parties, don't they?" I said, "My wife thought I was crazy." He said, "Well, I have therapy for the condimently impaired." Yeah, he had a whole movie on mustard about how it's grown and processed. I met a fellow on an airplane that told me he gets leg cramps at night sometimes, and the minute he gets one, he eats a teaspoon of mustard, and it relieves the cramp immediately.

Are there like different types of mustard? What are the different types of mustard?

Well, there are like hundreds of them. I don't know how many, but he had like 2,500 different varieties.

Wow! So, do you know a lot about mustard too?

At one point in time I had about 100. Here in Santa Fe, down at Farmers Market, some of the best mustard is sold. It's green chile mustard.

Yeah, I know. I miss the green chile when I go back to California.

Then they got pecan mustard with pecan nuts and flavor. It's very good.

Mustard party?

Everything is green or red chile in Santa Fe. Kids who grow up here, when they leave, they really miss it a lot.

I miss it. Just being here a couple of times. I like the green chile a lot. We have a lot of spices and good food in California, but it's not quite the same as New Mexico green chile. My brother lives in El Paso.

What attracted him to El Paso?

My brother went there for a job; he's a professor of ecology, so he's at the university down there. So, I can get more green chile when I visit him.

There you go. He's close to Hatch?

Yeah, I did a big road trip in the winter where I drove all around this area. I have a friend in Phoenix, and I have this friend here, and then there's my brother, and then I went to Las Vegas. So I went to all the big cities around here.

So, that on the left is a Buddhist Stupa they call it.

Hey, there is actually a lot going on in Santa Fe.

There is. One of my projects is creating the insides of Buddhist prayer wheels.

I like the weather you guys have here too. It's kind of exciting. Like when we came out of that party, it was snowing. We weren't expecting it.

Santa Fe definitely has exciting weather patterns. I mean every ten minutes it changes. We just had some good snow. It was coming down pretty good. Which is your favorite restaurant in town? Did you go to any?

I went to a few that were good. I used to go to Bobcat Bite.

But they got kicked out of their place; they were there for years and years. They've been recognized for making the Number One Hamburger in America for years.

Yeah, it was so good. The cheeseburger with green chile on it was really good. It was my favorite meal.

Yes, Bobcat Bite was really good. Okay, well, here we are.

Yeah, thanks for the ride.

You're welcome. Thanks for letting me record you. Good luck and have a good flight.

∞

— MUSLIMS —

Headed home?

I'm headed home to Western Michigan.

Western Michigan.

Yeah. Hopefully it's not snowing there anymore, but it's so cold.

Did you come here for a conference?

I did, and then I stayed a few extra days and played hooky.

The anthropology conference?

Yes, that's right.

What kind of applied anthropology do you do?

I work in Detroit. I work on Muslims in America, and how they are contributing to building up the city.

Muslims in America?

Yes.

And what kind of organization do you work for?

University of Western Michigan.

Aha. I know there are a lot of problems with Muslims in America, but what do you study exactly?

I have a few different projects going on. The applied version of my project deals with how Muslims in certain institutions are developing. They are trying to help solve city problems like water scarcity, hunger and homelessness, and even civil liberty problems through organizing together, and they are doing charitable and volunteer work through their religious organizations. And I have another project too that has something to do with just how Muslim Americans are becoming incorporated into the city in other ways, how they are building mosques and organizations, and just dealing with getting their needs met, their specific needs met for certain accommodations, daily living and organizing.

My lady, back about 40 years ago, she emigrated from Wales, and her first stop here in America was in Detroit. She helped start the first Head Start program in the ghetto of Detroit.

Wow, that's amazing.

She had three little towheaded boys with her when she moved here.

And she still found time to do all that?

Well, she needed a job, and so that was – She had run into a guy who started the program, and she wrote him a letter saying she needed a job. And he said, "Come on."

Wow!

Detroit has really turned around.

Yeah.

People came from all over the world to this conference.

That's right, yes, they sure did.

Picked up a lady from Pakistan the other day.

Yeah.

I had a lady this morning who had an epileptic seizure in my car.

Oh, my goodness, that's so scary. Have you ever had that before?

No.

What did you do?

Well, I took her boyfriend to a UPS store, and then we were supposed to go back and pick her up. And she was a little bit frantic when we picked her up, because she had walked away from her door. She was trying to find him, and she got into the car, and immediately had a seizure.

Was she in the backseat?

Yeah, she was in the backseat.

How did you tell at first that this was going to be like...?

Well, the boyfriend was sitting here in the front seat, and he turned around and said, "Okay, don't worry about it, but she's having a seizure."

Right.

"Just drive back to the house. I've got to lock the door, and we've got to get down to the courthouse." And he just like really consoled her, and said, "It's going to be okay, baby." She was completely conked out from the seizure. Then after about ten minutes, she woke up and was completely disoriented.

Did you do something like put something in her mouth, so she wouldn't bite her tongue?

No. He said, "She'll be okay. She was frantic! She was afraid that she had lost me," or something like that.

She had what? Lost him? She had a seizure, because she was upset, like her emotions triggered it?

Yes, something like that, yeah.

Jeez. Oh god. That's scary!

Yeah. But about 10 minutes later she was pretty much coherent again.

Yeah.

Is there a big fear in the Muslim community about what's going on in America right now?

Oh, yeah, it's terrible. Muslims in America are living under horrible fears, but they are doing something about it. They are organizing, and they are reaching out. They are trying to make really good connections with organizations in order to protect their reputation and their status. The people in their community are incredibly engaged, and their community is incredibly well-educated, above the higher mean in terms of income, in terms of education. And so most of them have ways of reacting and trying to band together, and doing something about it. They are a very active community. For the newly arrived ones who are not fluent, some of them come not fluent in language and things, it's even worse for them. Most Muslims in America live in urban places obviously, in big centers, so they can be networked. But, then there's also those who live scattered around, and it's really bad for them.

We have a Muslim community up in Abiquiú about 80 miles north of here. It's where Georgia O'Keeffe lived. There's a Muslim community up there.

There's a mosque?

Yeah.

Wow, interesting. You know anything about their history, like where they are really from?

They built it out of adobe on 1000 acres back in 1981. I think they call it Dar al Islam. It was financed by a wealthy Saudi prince or something. I took my son there one time to play with one of his classmates. They drove him from Abiquiú to Santa Fe every day for him to attend Montessori. I don't know how active it is any more, but they used to have upwards of sixty people in their community.

Very interesting. Such a tiny little airport. I like it.

I know, people love it. Our parking is three dollars a day. Thank you so much.

Thank you.

Have a good flight.

∞

— TRAIN —

Hi there. Good morning.

Good morning. How are you today?

I'm good.

How was the train today?

Good. Good.

Do you ever eat there at Adiamo's? I wonder if they have gluten free pizza.

Oh, I do eat there, yeah. Don't know about the pizza though.

Is it very good?

Yeah, it's pretty awesome. Sometimes it's really busy during the day.

I try all the gluten free pizzas in town. Pizza Centro has a really good pizza.

Pizza Centro is better by far.

It is. Isn't it?

It's really good. So much better.

Well, their gluten free is phenomenal.

Awesome to try, it's great. It's nice to mix up.

We had a fish dish over at Il Piatto. Have you ever eaten there?

Yeah, I know Il Piatto.

Well, that place is really good.

They're good. They have a happy hour half price special on appetizers.

Oh, they do?

Yeah. It's pretty awesome. It's like from 4-6.

Yeah, I check out all the gluten free things sometimes. Have you ever heard this place called Love Yourself Café? It's 100% gluten free vegetarian. Also, they have a great wellness spa called Light Vessel, which is probably the most advanced spa in the area.

Yeah, my friend worked there for a while. Just so happens, we were both adopted. She was able to find her birth parents fairly easily. I was able to find my birth mother through the Canadian Family and Child Services. My birth mother and I had both registered with them and I got a call right after college that they had found my birth mother. Eventually I met her, and when I did I asked her who was my birth father. She told me his name, and I spent the next two or three years intensely trying to find my birth father. I probably made 3,000 calls. I wasn't able to find him, but I did find a half-brother, and a cousin, and learned that this person had died. I did my DNA test on Ancestry.com, as did my half-brother, and I learned that, through DNA, he could not possibly be my father. I went back to my birth mother and told her the person she said was my birth father could not possibly be my father. She said she had had a one-night stand with another guy but she couldn't even remember his name. But Ancestry did find a possible match with a person who could be my second cousin. Through this second cousin I found a name of one of his parent's siblings and asked my mom if she had ever heard of this name. She said, "Oh my god, I completely forgot about him. It was only one night." I Googled his name, found him, and the rest is history. I just met with him a week ago. He had no idea he had a child. But we sure look alike.

Wow! That's quite a story. I have a cousin that was adopt-

ed. But she never knew she was adopted. Her parents never told her. I knew she was adopted ever since I was a child, but my parents insisted I not tell her. I always felt this was terrible. After both of our parents died, her mother was the last to die, she called me and told me that right before her mother died, that her mother had some sort of a visitation from a spirit. When she told me that, I took it as a sign to tell her she was adopted. She never found her birth parents. Maybe this DNA thing through Ancestry could identify a DNA match, and maybe she could find exactly who her birth parents were.

Well, it sure worked for me.

Okay. Here we are. Thank you so much.

Thank you.

∞

— BOLIVIA —

I am from Bolivia. I think there's a sense of honor to be recorded.

Yeah.

In a culture that's so fleeting, and... I don't know.

Down in Bolivia, what kind of government is it? Is it just a democratic...?

It is. Sort of.

So, isn't that Morales or something like that?

Yes, I said sort of, because it's his third term now.

It's his third term?

Yeah, he's running for his fourth right now.

Do you have term limits?

Yes. But the constitution can be changed.

I see. The constitution can be changed, yeah, right. How old a guy is he?

I think he's in his 50s. I think it was a necessary experience for the country.

It was?

Definitely. We needed a change.

Do you have a strong military?

Not any longer, but we used to.

You used to?

Our history is plagued with military dictatorships. The last one was a long time ago. The progress wasn't working.

Can you tell by dialect where different people are from? Do people in Bolivia speak a certain type of Spanish, as compared to like the people from Argentina?

Yes, but that's not really the dialect. It's just the way they talk Spanish. The dialects are for indigenous people, and we do share some of their words, for example, we share little parts of Chile, parts of Argentina and Peru. But the way we speak Spanish, we can tell because the intonation is different. The slang is different.

I see. Well, the Bolivian people, are they from the Incas? The natives in Bolivia are they Incas or...?

Yes.

They're Incas?

Well, we have the Aymara people and the Inca people.

What's the difference between the two?

The Aymara are much older. Let's say that. I don't know if you've heard about them or not.

I never heard of them.

There are ruins. I mean very, very old ruins. We do have what we call a sun-up portal for the sun. On certain dates, you can see the sun raise through that portal.

Really?

Yeah, it's very interesting. And it's obviously very similar to other sun portals. The Incas were much more modern in a way. It was a big empire.

I see. They were more organized.

Much more, and newer. The big empire was born in Peru. Before we didn't have Orellana, Peru, we used to have Alto, Peru or the higher part of Peru. That was Bolivia and Sechin Bajo, Peru or lower Peru.

Bolivia is... isn't there a big lake?

Lake Titicaca, the highest lake in the world.

The highest lake in the world, but you have no ocean.

No, we don't.

So, you're land locked.

Some crazy people used to say the lake was an ocean before. As a matter of fact, it's salty.

Really? That's interesting.

There are many people that say they've seen UFO's coming

in to land. So, it is interesting. Did you forgot to take your medication?

Yeah.

I had a girl earlier who had an epileptic seizure in my car.

Wow, my god! That must be really rough.

What did you do? I mean was there a way...?

Well, she was with her boyfriend. And he was sitting in the front, and she was sitting in the back. He knew exactly what to do.

Oh, he did? Good!

He just really consoled her, and held her, and then she just calmed down. And after about 10 or 15 minutes she came back too.

It was over.

Yeah, he knew exactly what was going to happen, because he's been through it with her before.

I can imagine. I was just thinking when you mentioned that, I really wouldn't know what to do in case of with a seizure. I mean, my dog is like my offspring. He had seizures, but he's not a human, so it's different.

What were you going to do? Take the train down and then get a cab?

Yeah, I guess. I've never been down here.

I haven't either. This is in the middle of no place.

Oh, I know how we're going to get there. He's right, what we're going to do, take the train and then... I thought this was downtown. That's how much I don't know. She's doing a movie or something in a studio, the person that we're going to go see. So I don't know. That would be interesting. Aren't you glad that we took Uber? This is like ten miles south of Albuquerque.

Yeah, this is bizarre.

Because I had no idea. I thought that this was part of getting there. Q Studios?

There it is. I think this is the new Netflix studio.

Oh, my god. I was telling my mom we were going to be early. I was like, we can go to Starbucks, something. I thought it was downtown.

Good luck with finding a Starbucks out here. It's Q Studios, right?

Yeah. I'm actually glad that we missed the train.

Yeah, I think so.

Jesus, it's huge. She says she's in Building 3.

Building 3?

Yeah.

It seems to me the buildings are A, B, C, but we'll see. Here's the guard.

Okay Building A, sorry.

Building A. You're going to have to tell him what you're doing here.

Guard: Hi.

I'm here to see Sandra Tafoya

Guard: Why? What for? What are you doing here?

I'm getting my dress fitted. She said to come in Building A.

Guard: Okay, thank you.

He's like a comedian.

Thank you for taking the time to drive around and find the right building.

Thank you.

∞

— INDIAN SCHOOL —

Are you moving?

Yeah. I'm moving to a new place downtown.

It's amazing how long you live some place, the more stuff you accumulate.

Yeah. I'm realizing that. Yeah, I thought I had a lot, but it's all just like these little things.

What do you do here in town?

I run the IT department for the Santa Fe Indian School. So, where I'm moving is like across the street from where I work, which is great.

Yeah, it is.

Yeah, just right there, which works out. I don't have to drive to work in the morning.

Okay. How many students go to the Santa Fe Indian School?

Right now, we're tutoring 500 to 700 – I think 687.

And where do they all come from?

They come from the 19 Pueblos of New Mexico. Then we also take in students from the Navajo Nation and all the other tribes in New Mexico, because if they want to apply, they're accepted.

Well, with the 19 Pueblos from New Mexico, it's by choice if they want to go there, right?

Right, yeah.

I mean they can go to the regular school if they want, right?

Yeah. And that's the thing too, because a lot of like Southern Pueblos, they choose to go to like their local high school, or if they're like in Laguna, they stay at the high school over there. And then you have Pojoaque onboard...

If they're coming, you have dorms for them, right?

Yeah. We're a boarding school, and we also bus students daily.

Oh, you're bussing students?

Yeah, just from the couple of surrounding areas, not too far. The furthest we go south is San Felipe. We go to Santa Fe Domingo, and we go to Cochiti. Then up north we go as far as San Juan Pueblo, but the majority of our students are in dorms, so...Yeah. It's a small percentage that is actually bussed.

And that's strictly a high school?

Seventh through twelfth. Yeah, so we have two schools on campus. And then we also have our own district. We have all our administrative offices on campus. It's not somewhere else. Everything is just in-house on one campus, so we're a full-fledged district.

Well, you're not part of the Santa Fe Public School system, are you?

No, we're owned and operated by the 19 Pueblos. They manage all that, and then we have a board of trustees, and then we have a superintendent and two principals for the schools as well. And they all get together for the majority of the decisions.

Are you native?

Yes. I'm from Laguna and Santa Ana, but I was born and raised here.

Where did you go to high school?

Indian School. Yeah. My mom worked there for like 36 years. And so – yeah, so it's kind of a given that I had to go there, sadly. Yeah, because we lived in Santa Fe too, so yeah, so I lived in Santa Fe for quite a while since I went there, which is easy. Where did you come from originally?

Northern Arizona. About 27 miles south of Flagstaff. Sedona.

Oh, Sedona, okay. It's really nice down there.

When I went to school in Flagstaff, they used to bring all the Navajo and Hopi kids in for the semester, and they lived in these Quonset huts from World War II. So, I grew up with – I mean I went to high school with all these Navajo and Hopi kids. Every Fourth of July we had a huge Pow Wow and parade in Flagstaff with a gathering of all the tribes from across the U.S.

Yeah, that's cool.

It was you know – you become friends with them. We used to go up to the reservation, watch their dances, be welcomed into their homes and go on the roof tops. I don't think they allow it now. I remember being on the roof overlooking a Hopi village square, and watching the Butterfly Dance and the Corn Dance. One of the most special was watching the Snake Dance, and them coming

out of the kiva with a rattlesnake in their mouth, and then dancing with it. Before the dance there wasn't a cloud in the sky, and after the dance it poured down rain. Now, when I go down to the Plaza for Indian Market, I see some of the Hopis that are my age that I went to school with.

My parents used to have foreign travelers stay at our house all the time. One time during the early sixties three Russian travelers stayed with us, and I drove them up to the Hopi Reservation. We drove into Oraibi, and I showed them around. You know little dusty Oraibi is known to be the oldest continuously inhabited settlement in America. Well, this one Hopi came up to us, and asked if we could take him to Second Mesa. We said sure. While driving up, toward the end, he asked where we were all from, and they said from Russia. He turned to them, and said, "I fought you fuckers in Korea," as he was getting out of the car.

Right. Hey, thank you. Nice talking with you.

Thank you.

— LAURA —

Laura?

Yes, Laura.

Hi there. Thank you.

I'm doing a book on my Uber riders. Are you okay if I record our conversation going down to Meow Wolf?

Sure.

Okay. Have you been to Meow Wolf yet?

No, it's my first time.

Oh, really? Did you go to the Folk Art market here?

I did.

What do you think of that?

I liked it, but I was here more to see just the straight off Native American stuff, so then I went over to the Wheelwright.

What do you think of that?

Oh, I really liked it.

It's fantastic. Isn't it?

Yeah. I actually enjoy a smaller museum.

Well, she was the Real McCoy Native American art collector. It was built in 1937, originally to preserve Navajo religious practices and their creation story. It's been here a lot longer than the others. She was from Boston, but teamed up with a Navajo medicine man.

Yeah. I read about her.

Well, you're about ready to have a sensory overload at Meow Wolf. Where are you from?

I've lived in San Francisco for about 23 years. But I'm from Chicago.

What side of Chicago?

Southside. Near University of Chicago.

My granddaughter is there today at the University of Chicago.

Oh! It's one of the best in the world, I suppose. What is the topic of your book?

Just the diverse group of people that get into my car. I've done over 3,000 rides with people from all over the world.

And just spending five, ten minutes with people, I've recorded a lot of them.

Wow!

I had a heroin addict in my car yesterday, and she said, "No way. I don't want to be recorded." But we had a whole discussion about her spiritual quest, and her quest to stop heroin. She knew she had to. She had been clean for one week. The professions that people have and how they got there is of interest to me.

Yeah. I suppose the whole reason I wanted to come to Santa Fe in the first place was Georgia O'Keeffe. She has been a big influence on me my whole life.

Yeah. Are you an artist?

No. But my mom introduced me to art when I was very young at the Art Institute of Chicago. And then my first job out of college was working for a food photographer in Chicago. This was in the early 80's when southwestern food and Whole Foods was becoming a big thing. So, he used to spend a lot of time shooting here. And he would bring me back photographs of Santa Fe cuisines. Photographers would – I would hold down the floor when they were here, and I just couldn't wait to get here, but that was 30 years ago.

Is it all you expected?

It is. And ironically, I didn't even realize it. I stayed at the hotel where they used to stay, the Inn of the Anasazi. And I just went downtown walking. I saw this restaurant with a James Beard award, and it was fantastic. But there were a couple of locals who were talking about why was it so crowded. They were talking about too many tourists.

You might want to check out the Nedra Matteucci Gallery. It's phenomenal.

I'll check that out.

And the garden, she has a secret garden in the back. There is a little door that they don't even...

They don't advertise it?

No. But you go back in this garden, and it is just chock-full of unique sculptures.

I'll check it out.

It's right on the corner of Paseo and Acequia Madre.

So, it's funny. As I was paying my bill, I realized this restaurant had all these vintage looking calendars.

The restaurant in the museum?

No, this place downtown. It's called Pasqual's.

Pasqual's, yeah.

Pasqual's. So anyway, I realized that they used to give me back calendars from Pasqual's, like 30 years ago, and here I was. I just randomly – that was the first place that I went into today.

All right.

And I met a really, really beautiful older lady at the Sage Bakehouse.

Oh, really?

Sage Bakery. You'd probably know her if I just said her name. She is a famous opera singer Regina.

Regina Sarfaty?

I think so. And we just fell into a really natural conversation. We ended up talking for an hour and a half about everything.

One thing is for sure here in Santa Fe, you never know who in the world you're going to run into next.

We surely needed to have the conversation. We talked everything about love and motherhood, politics of course, tech industry, Silicon Valley. I mean we probably covered 15 topics.

All right.

It's really nice. You don't usually get to talk to too many people when you're traveling. I took this trip without my boyfriend, and when you travel with someone, you don't necessarily need people. So that's why I like to travel by myself once in a while, explore. Have you been to the opera?

I have, many times.

Yeah. I think next time when I come back, I will plan it around something that I'd like to see. But I imagine a lot of this wasn't here 30 years ago.

Yeah. The Santa Fe population itself has only increased from 60,000 to 80,000 in 30 years.

Oh, that's good.

It's primarily in the county where it's expanded more.

Well, that's good to know. Tonight is my last night here. What would you recommend?

I'd recommend definitely going to Meow Wolf, which you're doing right now.

Yeah.

But for dinner, since you are already down on this side of town, I'd recommend this place right over here called Jambo Cafe. It's a combination of African and Caribbean.

Oh, yeah. Well, I can just – a friend recommended I check out a bookstore called the Ark.

Very good. The Ark, I would say, is the number one – okay, it's where I go every Christmas to buy my gifts.

Perfect. Yeah. I heard they have a lot of books on spirituality and...

Well, I'll tell you, they sure do.

Yeah. I think a bookstore sounds nicer right now, plus a peaceful dinner tonight.

You could spend hours in the Ark.

Yeah.

It's – they have everything of a spiritual nature happening in there.

Good.

We have several great Buddhist centers, Mountain Cloud Zen Center and Upaya, and several Christian retreat centers.

I went to Ten Thousand Waves.

There you go.

It was the day that it was snowing. It was perfect. Late afternoon and I did the whole thing, hot tub, massage and dinner. It's kind of a perfect place to chill out.

Absolutely, it's ideal. Well, here we are.

Here we are.

You see, this place used to be a bowling alley. You can tell by the bowling pin right there. They gutted it, and built this 70 room Victorian House.

How long has this been here?

A couple of years ago. You've come on a perfect day. Sometimes there are lines way back...

Oh, really! Thank you so much. Have a good evening.

Okay.

Thank you.

∞

— DNA BIOLOGY —

What conference were you here for?

It was DNA; it was a biology conference. It was about DNA damage and repair.

DNA damage and repair?

Yeah, you know everything that's going on in cancer. It's usually linked to DNA damage and replication of cells. It's a pretty amazing field of research. I work for a company. We do products to detect these kinds of changes.

To detect DNA changes?

Yes.

And that can forewarn for cancer?

It helps actually to better understand what leads to cancer, and also of course then how to treat it. So, it was really amazing. It was in the convention center for like four days.

Really? How many different people came to it?

Well, there were around 500 participants, many from Europe and Asia. Most of the participates were from the U.S. from different research centers and cancer centers.

And did they have vendors?

No, not really.

Or people doing presentations?

Exactly. Presentations. Discussions. It was really good. We were sponsors actually.

You were sponsors?

Yeah, so that is why I came. I came from Paris, actually. It was a very long travel.

Really? My Lord!

To come to Santa Fe, it was worth it. It's a nice place. Unfortunately, I didn't have much time to visit, but kind of had the chance to walk around a bit and eat the food.

Yeah, right, so from your view are there cures for cancer? Or are there clues as to how to cure it?

There is a lot of great research going on everywhere in the world. There are great cancer centers as well. But it's still a struggle. There are amazing ideas everywhere. The problem is that we do not completely understand how cells become cancer with different kinds of tissue. Because like the cancer in the brain is not the same as cancer on the skin.

Right.

So, the most important thing is for us to understand how the whole thing works, so you can apply treatment.

What was one of the most interesting discussions you had here at this conference?

I mean a lot of the discussions were about how DNA is organized in the cells. How it is folded, and how it unfolds to do cell division. DNA replication - most of the errors happen there. That's why cells become cancerous. One of the most interesting talks I heard was a girl who was talking about treating cancer cells with salmonella infection, which was crazy. She kind of discovered that using salmonella on cancer cells can stop them from growing.

Can stop the cancer cells from growing?

Yes, it can kill them, actually. They showed how they injected these mice who were suffering from cancer with salmonella infection. Then they visualized how the infection spreads, and they ended up seeing that all the salmonella infection went to the tumor and shrank the tumor, which is pretty amazing.

Does it have residual effects?

I don't know. Because to use the idea of treating cancer cells with a virus, its already tested and it pretty much works. The biggest problem with cancer treatment is that it is not specific to the tumor. Like chemo therapy will kill a lot of cells other than cancer. That is why people get pretty sick when they are getting treated, because other cells around the body are dying. The idea of virus treatment is to direct the treatment into the cancer cells, and that way you can be very specific as to the type of cells you are killing. So, yeah, I found it fascinating.

Do you ever have incidences where they inject the cancer cells and like blow them up?

Well, yes, there are ways. Every cancer cell has its specific signature. Like the receptors that are around the cells, they are specific. So, you can target the cancer cells, and tell them to kill themselves. So yes, it is possible. You don't blow them up, but you tell them to die, which is great.

How do you tell them to die?

So, there are specific, what we call pathways, signaling and messaging within a cell. Every cell has all these receptors. They desire things like to communicate with the outside world. So, there are, for example, hormones or kinds of molecules that are circulating in your blood that can go on to a cell and tell them what to do. So, these molecules can attach to a receptor on the cell, and allow a whole pathway of messaging inside the cell, that they, for example, have to go in the nucleus where the DNA is and tell them to do whatever. So that's how you tell. There is a whole messaging between cells and from outside into the cell to tell them what to do. That's how cells are communicating with each other, and how your brain controls hormones, for example. How your brain controls a lot of things. It's by these messaging signals.

How long have you been with this company?

Two and one-half years. It's pretty amazing. It's really interesting. I love everything that has to do with genetics. The discoveries are mind blowing. Every day at every conference you have something new discovered.

When did you discover that you wanted to get into this field? In high school or grade school? Did you always know?

Yeah, I remember the exact moment I decided I wanted to become a biologist. That's really funny. I was in high school, and I was studying for a biology exam. I was studying the photosynthesis of plants, and how they use carbon dioxide to make oxygen. I kind of found it so fascinating, the whole physics in biochemistry, that I completely fell in love with it. I found that how the human body or any living thing works, it just takes your breath away. How it is possible to work so perfectly is amazing. Imagine in your cells there is an error every moment and you can still live like 100 years. Because your body is functioning in a perfect way. So even if we hurt our bodies with all the shit, it still manages to go on. I think that is why. That is the moment. But I don't, to be honest, like research, even though I did it for six years. I do love science, but I didn't like the academic and research part. Because I mean I'm a very social person. I like to meet new people. I like team work. I like to discover new things. I

don't like to stay on the same thing for a real long time. And
when you do fundamental research you really need to be on
your thing like every day and work alone, and, you know, kill
the poor animals, whatever, I didn't like the mechanical part
of the research, the whole bench work, pipettes and animal
studies. I didn't like that part. I love to discover things, write
publications, go to conferences, but I didn't like being stuck
with something for a really long time. That is why I decided
to go into industry, because it is closer to applied science.
I wanted to see what you can find, and if you can use it for
something. So that is why. And I feel pretty good in what I
am doing. And I think I am good at what I am doing. I have
a lot to learn. And I get to travel.

Do you travel all over the world?

I travel mostly in the States, because I am responsible for
sales a little bit here in the United States. So, I spend at least
a week a month here, mostly on the east coast. And then
conferences wherever they are. I'm lucky.

**Well, you are very, very bright, my lord, at such a young
age.**

I'm not that young. I look young, but I'm not that young. I'm
thirty-four.

**Yeah, right. My girls are in their fifties, and my son is in
his thirties.**

Oh, my gosh. You don't look like someone who has kids
that age. It's amazing. That's really cool. I think you are the
coolest person I have met all week, and I've met a lot of cool
people at the congress.

I found it fascinating, this idea of Uber. Like, I do a lot of
Uber in Paris as well, because we do not have a lot of taxis.
Well, we have a lot, but they are always occupied. I also
use Uber Pool, which is also really cool. I usually hate that
because I don't like to share. But sometimes it is so cool to
go home, like on a Saturday night after a dinner, whatever,
and you meet someone and maybe he is a bit drunk, but he's

funny. I love it; it's cheaper. In the U.S. it's more fun to ride Uber than Paris. People are more closed minded in Paris.

In Paris people are more closed minded?

Yeah, they are not as chatty. Like, that is why I really like to come to the U.S., because there is always a way to chat with people. People always have a nice word for you, or a smile for you. I love the French people. They are so crazy, but they don't have this thing. When you meet someone in the street they are not talking to one another. In places, for example like in Santa Fe, people know each other. We can talk, and we can just walk on the street, and you smile. I'm a very open person.

I can tell. Are you ok with me writing about our conversation?

I mean it depends if you are going to write like, "I met this completely crazy girl, and she was so boring," then maybe not.

Right. Well, I'm just writing about the conversations. I've only had two people say no. Yesterday I said, "Is it ok for me to record you?" She said, "No, I just got out of the psychiatrist, and I can't deal with it."

Oh my god. Yeah, she was crazy. This airport is so small. Thank you so much.

Ok, thank you.

∞

228 · EVERYONE'S GOT A STORY

EVERYONE'S GOT A STORY

228 · EVERYONE'S GOT A STORY

228 · EVERYONE'S GOT A STORY

— DNA CHANGES —

What brought you all here?

We had a scientific conference that was at the conference center.

Oh, the DNA thing.

Yep, that's us. Taking over Santa Fe for a week.

Yeah, I just had a gal in here that was from that conference. She'd come all the way from Paris.

Yep, there are people from Australia. The people we were standing with just now are flying back to Germany today, people flying all over - India, Israel.

What's your focus?

So, well, I get into how changes in DNA happen. How mutations happen when DNA replication or cell division goes awry.

Aha, for cancer purposes?

Yep, largely for cancer and also evolution. Cancer is sort of a microcosm of evolution. So, everything applicable to cancer is applicable to evolution.

Where are you all from now?

I'm from ... well, I live in Boston now, but I'm originally from New York

I'm from China. Off the coast, but roughly in the middle.

Are you in this science field too?

Yes. We are colleagues and work on similar things.

Is most of this work in the bio-DNA field cancer related?

It varies heavily. Usually for funding purposes having a cancer focus helps. But people are working on anything and everything. There are other genetic disorders people are looking at. Something that was spoken about a lot at this conference was Fanconi anemia which is a condition where you do have anemia, so you have red blood cell issues, but you also frequently end up with leukemia, or other genetic issues later on in life.

Oh, from it?

Yep. There is Spartan Disorder, a lot of different generic disorders.

How did you both get into this field? What drove you to it?

It's interesting and exciting. You are on the cutting edge of knowledge. You're the first person to know new things about how the world works. Are there often conferences in Santa Fe, big groups taking over the city?

Well, last week it was a group of 2000 anthropologists. And they were fascinating. I had a lot of rides with anthropologists that week. And, you know, their focus, it went from A to Z.

I was going to ask. So, they weren't all into Native American research.

No, like a lot was medical. A lot of it was evolutionary, evolution stuff. Environmental.

Actually, one of the models for evolution comes from an-thropology. I don't know if you've heard of gradual evolution versus punctuated evolution. There are two models of how evolution happens. One of them is gradual changes over time, and the other one is that there are gradual changes with other times of stability. So, you only change at certain periods of time, and the rest of the time you are stable. And this second model was actually produced because of antropology. How influences change. How long have you been in Santa Fe?

31 years.

Seems nice. Nice small-town feel.

It is. It's very pleasant here. Lot of little communities. My lady and I met at our dance group. We are both dancers. There are like 600-800 people in our dance group. Maybe 80 of us dance on a given Thursday night at the Railyard. It's been going on for 15-16 years.

Wow. That's a pretty good size group. What kind of dance is it?

Just free form. Sort of based on 5Rhythms by Gabrielle Roth. Our variety of it we call Embodydance. Does DNA change by itself?

How do you mean? Like mutations?

Yeah. Well, not mutations, but mutations tend to be an illness. Right?

Not necessarily. That's actually a very common misconception. I mean between you and me we have, ah, ... so the human genome is around 3 billion bases of DNA, and roughly every thousand of them is going to be different between two individuals. Not everyone is genetically the same, obviously.

Right.

And that's due to mutations, mutations that happened long ago for the most part. There are also new mutations. When you are born the mutation rate is quite low, so it's not very often that ... you may change a base or two, well, maybe more than that, but ...

Can your thinking or your intention change your DNA?

No. Your DNA is permanent. Or mostly permanent. There actually was a scientist who published something recently saying that when you learn, when your neurons reshape and reform, when you are learning stuff, you do have DNA breaks that can lead to mutations very briefly. So, there are niche cases where it is possible, but for the most part the answer is no. Your DNA is atypical to change with most conditions. I mean you can get changes if you are exposed to environmental hazards. That will cause change. Certain radiation is incumbent on an x-ray. Then there are things called epicenters, which, those are how...so you have all this DNA, but not all of it is actually functioning at once. Your DNA is a blueprint, and epigenetics helps you focus on one section of the blueprint at one time. Not focusing on the whole thing. And there is a possibility that some epigenetic modifications can also lead to DNA changes. It's like rewriting the blueprint. But, hey, it's not common. Essentially the answer is no to your question.

There are actually medical cases of genetic up-mutations curing disease, for example, curing genetic disease. The unfortunate part about that is that there was a mutation to produce the disease in the first place, so that initial mutation was a bad thing. But there were later mutations that have fixed them. So, yeah, not all mutation is bad.

I see.

Cancer is an example of bad mutations. Other cool things are, you see, humans have 46 chromosomes. But certain cells, such as your liver, especially after exposure to toxins, say, for example, if you drink alcohol, that will actually cause your liver cells to become what is called tetraploid. So, they will double their number of chromosomes. Instead of having two copies of every chromosome, you will have four copies of every chromosome.

Wow.

So, you'll end up with 92 chromosomes, which it is unclear whether that is a good or a bad thing. It is partially believed actually to be a good thing. When your liver is dealing with a lot of toxins, such as alcohol, it is believed that DNA change enables you to better handle the toxins. That still needs to be proven, but that is the thinking.

Have you ever studied the effects of refined carbohydrates like sugar and white flour on cancer?

No. I never have.

Are you associated with a university?

Yes, I'm at Harvard University. She is from the University of Washington in Seattle. Thanks.

Ok here we are. Have a good flight.

— TOMMY MACCIONE —

Hello. Okay, where do I take you?

Desert Chateau. Down Cerrillos. You know where the Western Scene is?

Yeah.

It's right there. And I might need a ride back home too.

How long are you going to be down there?

I'm just grabbing my phone. This is my girlfriend's phone.

You go to school around here?

Yeah.

Where do you go to school?

I went to Alameda, and then I went to Santa Fe High. Where are you from?

Arizona.

Arizona. I'm from Oklahoma.

Oh. So, I'm taking you down here, you're going to pick up your phone, and then we're going to go back to Hillside?

Mm-hmm.

Okay. I'll just park right here.

I'll be right back. Thank you......

This is the phone I went to go get too. This one has my memory and all my music, my photos, my contacts. I need to get a new one though. Still works though, like a champ. I have anger problems. I throw it at stuff.

You what?

I have anger problems, I throw it at stuff. That's why the glass is all broken.

Oh, I see. I call the triangle park the Tommy Maccione Park.
The what?

Tommy Maccione, he's the sculpture there.

Oh, yeah. That little guy?

I knew him. Back in 1991 I was running the Ross Pert for President campaign here in New Mexico. I was state chairman. One day I get a call from Tommy calling me to his hospital bed, and he gives me this ten-page manifesto that he had handwritten on the back of paper placemats

about how everyone was being bought off in Espanola County. I wish I still had it.

Yeah?

He used to paint, stand right up here. It used to be a little triangle right up here at Acequia Madre and Paseo on the corner, and he'd stand there and paint flowers.

Nice. I don't know what it is about Santa Fe, but I always end up coming back here. I'll leave, then I'll come back. I'll leave, then I'll come back. I grew up here. I went to school here, but I'm not from here, but I consider myself from here.

Right. Yeah. A lot of the kids who grew up and went to school here always come back. My son after he graduated from high school went on a six month around the world journey, taking trains and staying at hostels in Europe, exploring the Sahara Desert, riding a camel at the Pyramids, sitting under the Bodhi Tree in India, rock climbing in Thailand, and then a month in Bali. But he came back.

Yeah, well, I hate where I'm from. I hate the Bible Belt. I'm never going back.

Why?

I just don't like it. I'm from Oklahoma originally, and I just don't like it. I'm not against religion or nothing, you know, I just don't like the way they do it down there. It's all self-righteous.

Oh.

Two to three million-dollar churches and stuff like that. It's ridiculous! Hey, right over here will be fine. Thank you.

Okay, man. Thanks.

∞

— RAW FOODIST —

So, tell me about your book, what is it?

I just talk to people while driving around Santa Fe and it's like visitors and locals. It's a unique perspective of Santa Fe, unique perspective on a whole bunch of other things, like their jobs, how they got into what they do...

It's just what people are willing to share.

That's right.

That's wonderful, and it makes your job an art process.

Totally.

It is an art process.

That's kind of absolutely fascinating for you.

I'll probably be working on a radio or TV program of it too.

Cool! How are you going to do that?

I'm not going to use the real people, because I thought about just doing a video on my iPhone, but I think people would be less inclined to speak if they're on a video.

Totally.

Would definitely affect the situation.

And so, I'm going to get actors to do the script that is based on all these interviews. You live in L.A. too?

I live in L.A. She just moved here.

That sounds like a really smart idea. I really think that that has a lot of possibility.

We'll see.

Great idea. Are you a film maker or photographer?

Not really.

It's cool, seriously.

My daughter put the app on my phone when I went to San Francisco for a conference, and I rode around San Francisco as a rider. I was so impressed I decided to try it, try to be a driver down here in Santa Fe. I wanted to understand these new technologies like Uber and Airbnb and for my company to develop a media arts division for publishing, videos and apps. My company currently just works in nano science.

That's a wonderful idea.

Where you all from again?

Los Angeles.

I'm her mom. I'm visiting from... I live in New York.

Are you a vegetarian?

Nowadays I eat wild fish and organic chicken, organic turkey, but I haven't touched beef in forty years or so.

Me too. I rarely, rarely, rarely, I have to say I rarely eat meat. The whole thing is very upsetting, killing all the animals. I don't eat pork either. I don't know how I ever rationalized having a bite of hamburger.

When my son was six or seven we were driving past cows in Colorado, and when I explained to him that you had to kill a cow to make a hamburger he got completely disgusted. I was a raw foodist for 10 years. I only ate fruits and vegetables, nuts and seeds. It was a fascinating experiment with my body. But later he put a bumper sticker on my refrigerator that said, "Save a Cow – Eat a Vegetarian."

How did it make you feel?

Clear and clean. But my kids thought I was too gaunt looking. I was down to 165 pounds and my kids said, "Dad, you look too thin," and so I went into Ayurvedic cooking.

Ayurvedic?

Yeah, it's like an Indian way of cooking with turmeric, black mustard seed, and many other spices and herbs and different things that fire your digestive system. I made a lot of kitchari. Then my lady, she likes eating fish, so then after a couple of years I started eating fish.

Do you feel different now that you're eating animal protein?

Not really. Except when you're a raw foodist it's a completely different energy level.

Wait, what is it? Is it being on a higher energy level?

Yeah, you have more energy. The way you use the most energy in life is through your digestive track. And so, when you free up utilizing all that energy for digestion, you have more energy. There are different techniques, such as food combining, or just mono fooding, where you just eat one thing at a time, and that really increases one's energy.

Interesting.

What do you mean, at a meal you have one thing at a time?

Yeah, like you eat an apple in the morning, then maybe an hour later a papaya, an hour later avocado. That's another way to do it.

Just kind of graze throughout the day.

Yeah, and it's a completely different energy level. And lifestyle too.

It is. And then I got into... along with that I would have a green juice drink every day with spirulina and that was pretty good. I did that every day for years. You talk about life style change. The lady I was with at the time was always complaining about the price of food, and not having enough money for food. I showed her how to eat like a king for free. Every day at Whole Foods, and most other grocers, they rotate their fruits and vegetables on a daily basis. Usually they put the older foods into big green plastic bags, and people come by and pick the bags up for their animals. For three months I picked up those same bags full of fruits and vegetables, and juiced them or just ate them. A raw foodist magazine I read recommended raw foodists to taste their pee every day. It's supposed to taste just like water.

Wow! Oh, my goodness, look at those pink trees. Aren't they gorgeous? Just like, a week and a half ago or so they were in a super vibrant pale pink.

Then they disappeared because of the frost.

Right, the poor flowers. They'd just started coming out, no way.

I know. Apricot trees are not the... they're not the brightest things on the planet.

Yeah.

Let me show you a picture of what was in our backyard this past October.

Wow.! He's like a twelve-point deer.

He lives up in the hills, we think. The other day we saw three deer, two males and a doe. One of the males was kissing the doe, very sweet. The males lose their rack every year. Right now, the antlers are only about six inches long covered with velvet.

Right here? Right downtown?

Right here on Garcia Street.

Is this a reindeer or an elk?

No, it looks like an elk, but it's a big, big, huge deer. We know it's a deer, because it was eating the leaves. Elk eat grass.

That is an awesome thing. I love it.

Okay, here we are. Thank you. Hey, it's been a pleasure ladies.

Thank you.

— CONGRESSMAN'S WIFE —

Welcome. Where you from?

I'm from Washington D.C. Yeah, just visiting for the week-end, personal visit.

Just for vacation to see what Santa Fe is about?

Well, the Democratic Party has an event here.

Oh, with Ben Ray Lujan?

Yeah, so I am here for that.

I went to high school in Washington D.C.

Is that right!

In the Library of Congress.

They had a high school in the Library of Congress? What was it called?

Capitol Page School.

Oh.

I was a page in the U.S. Senate.

Were you? You know they discontinued it.

No, they still have it in the Senate, but they don't have it in the House, and they don't have it in the Supreme Court anymore.

Okay. Was it a useful experience for you?

Very. What do you do with the Democratic Party?

Nothing. My husband is a Member of Congress.

He's a Member of Congress?

Yeah, I'm here with my husband.

What state are you from?

Maryland. This is a wonderful thing, preserving the majesty of the landscape here. What's the population here?

80,000. How does your husband like being a Congressman?

He loves it. It's his calling in life. He's perfectly suited for it.

You work in government too?

No, I run a non-profit. The focus is on policy, so I pay a lot of attention to government.

My lady runs a non-profit here in Santa Fe that provides free home care for people who fall through the gaps and cracks of our medical system.

I'm sure she is quite busy. Our medical system has too many gaps unfortunately.

How many Congressmen came out for this event?

You know, I think that there are about 20 of them here.

Is the leadership here?

We have got leadership and staff that helps, so it's a pretty good turnout.

I think Nancy Pelosi came last time.

Hmm, she came this time too.

Do the Speaker and the majority and minority leaders, do they have Secret Service protection?

They have protection, but I don't think it's through the Secret Service. I think it's the Capital Police.

Capital Police?

Yeah. Secret Service is just for the President and executive branch.

I was back there in the first two years of the Kennedy administration, and the last few months of Eisenhower's. One time, President Kennedy was coming up the elevator in the Capitol, and the doors opened, and he was right there. We shook each other's hand. He says, "Who appointed you, Sonny?" I said, "Senator Goldwater." "He's a good man, a good man." That was my entire communication with President Kennedy.

Memorable.

Very memorable. You know when I was a page I'd go around getting everyone's autographs. I got 101 U.S. Senators to sign my Capitol Page yearbook. My friend Walt Michael, who was a Supreme Court Page, got the entire Supreme Court to sign my yearbook other than Felix Frankfurter, who was very ill at the time.

Oh, where did you get the extra Senator from?

One died.

Oh, that's terrible. So that means you got every single one.

I got every Senator, the Supreme Court, Vice-President Lyndon Johnson, the Speaker of the House and Bobby Kennedy, who was Attorney General. What we got to see was amazing. I was the youngest page during Kennedy's inauguration, and so I was assigned the job of opening the doors leading from the rotunda to the inauguration stand. So, I saw the inauguration from the rear. But then right after the inauguration for the new president's luncheon in the old Senate Chamber, I was assigned to take everyone's hat and coat. It was a very cold day, and that is where I first met Harry and Bess Truman. I met the seven original astronauts, Yuri Gagarin, the Shah of Iran, Harold Macmillan and many others.

Wow. Did you enter into a career in politics?

Not really. Although a lot of the pages did. I was New Mexico State Chairman for the 1992 Ross Perot for President campaign.

Sounds like you're still into politics.

Not really, but I do track everything.

Ok, here we are. Last night they went to the Museum of Native American Art. I wonder what we will do tonight. Thank you.

Thank you. Ok.

∞

WEEK FOUR

— BEHAVIORAL HEALTH —

I'll bet you get to meet a lot of nice people driving Uber. People from everywhere, too.

I meet a lot of nice people. I sure do.

I think that would be the fun part of the job, to meet all kinds of people from different places.

Oh, yeah. One of the things I ask a lot of people is how they got into the job that they have.

How I got my job, that's a good question? I work for the state in the Behavioral Health Division of CYFD. Getting my job with the state actually was just kind of luck. I had been applying for different jobs with CYFD. I didn't really know what this job was, and I thought, well, I meet the qualifications - I'll apply. And, I am glad I did, because this is a really good job. It's a lot of fun.

Do you have to have a particular education?

Yes, you have to have a master's degree in social services, a degree of some kind.

I see. Where did you go to school?

I have my bachelor's in psychology from UNM. And then I have my master's in addiction counseling from Hazelton Graduate School of Addiction Studies in Minnesota. It was fun out in Minnesota. Very cold, but it was fun.

How long were you at Hazelton?

It was a one-year program. It was a condensed two-year program into one year.

Where did you go to high school in Albuquerque?

I went to St. Pius High School.

Is that like St. Mike's up here?

Yes, it's a Catholic school.

My granddaughter is graduating from Xavier Prep in Phoenix. It is the Catholic girls' school in Phoenix. Just yesterday she interviewed at Northwestern in Chicago. I'm not sure what she wants to do though. I guess that's why you go to college, right? Figure out what you want to do?

Yep. Well, hopefully, you already have an idea, because college is so expensive.

She is talking about some kind of medical research, you know, or medical anthropology, or medicine itself or something.

I did not know there was such a thing as medical anthropology.

Well, I learned all about it from this convention that they recently had here. They had 2,000 anthropologists from all over the world come here.

Wow!

I learned there are four different fields of anthropology: archeology, which studies the past; cultural anthropologists study the current; biological study human evolution; and linguistic anthropologists. Some are much bigger than others. And medical evolution and ecology, are all different branches of anthropology. Some even study the way people eat.

I'll bet that was interesting.

I used to be a raw foodist. I only ate raw food. And one of the things I learned about addiction was, among raw foodists, they say that more people are addicted to bread than anything else on the planet, and that bread kills more people than any other thing by gluing up your system. So, I quit eating bread during that period of time, and lost a whole lot of weight. Now I only eat gluten-free bread.

Did you notice a difference in how you felt?

Yeah. When you don't eat wheat, it has a major league impact on the body, because it eliminates a whole class of foods, which typically include a lot of sugar. Plus, in the production of commercial wheat and corn they spray Roundup on them during the last week of growing, so your body is getting all these toxic chemicals. My major thing now is no sugar and no refined carbohydrates. There's a book called The Case Against Sugar by Gary Taubes. He traces introduction of the western diet into cultures that have never eaten the western diet, and western disease follows the western diet. Some of these cultures had no diabetes, cancer, HPV, Epstein-Barr or even alzheimer's until the western diet came along.

Wow, that's really fascinating. It looks like it's going to be a beautiful day.

It does, doesn't it? Thank you.

Thank you very much. I appreciate the ride. Good luck with your book.

I appreciate the conversation. Thank you.

— CHICAGO IT —

Good morning, how are you today?

I'm good, beautiful morning turned out. Can't complain.

How long you lived in Santa Fe?

I don't. I actually live in Chicago, but my mother lives here. She's lived here for – on and off for 30 years. So, I've seen quite a bit of the change.

Yeah. Cubs won last night.

Yeah, it was exciting to see them last season.

It was, wasn't it? I've been a Cubs fan for 71 years, or close to it.

Wow. Yeah, it's nice to see what appears to be a good team, not just the players, but ...

Yeah, everybody. I used to live at Belmont and Sheridan.

Oh, okay, I'm not too far from there. I'm at Belmont and Ravenswood, little bit further west.

My granddaughter just interviewed yesterday at Northwestern.

For medicine or for their college?

For their college.

Yeah, you can't get much better than that.

Is Northwestern private?

It is. What brought you to Santa Fe?

A woman.

Yeah, that's what brought me to Chicago. I grew up in Florida.

What do you do in Chicago?

I'm a technology consultant.

For like computers or...?

Yeah, my current client actually is Navistar. Maybe you've heard of the International brand?

Right.

They have a joint venture with GM. They are building a new truck, and I'm helping them with the technology involved, because all those components now in the trucks all talk to each other and then they wirelessly talk to somebody else. It's absolutely crazy how your cars nowadays and trucks are basically, you know, computers on four wheels. It's not just an engine anymore.

Some companies are talking about those driverless trucks.

Yeah. I think those will be commonplace within the next 10 years, maybe five years and not so sure about how long driverless cars will be around but I don't think they will take off as fast as some would like. The money is with driverless trucks, and if corporations and insurance have anything to do about it, that's where their focus will be.

I had a rider who told me that his big investments these days are in flying cars. Says the infrastructure is already there, it's just going to be above the roads. They are going to have to follow the roads.

Yeah, you know, he could be right. As you known growing up, and I'm 50 myself, and all I heard about growing up was flying cars. So, hasn't happened yet. We'll see. That would be very interesting.

He started six Silicon Valley startups, and sold them all.

He's in his mid 30's. He says flying cars are just big drones.

That's true. Again, I think the first big drones we will see will be flying across the oceans. It costs a lot of money to, the big tankers, but also the freight ships, most of the money for those is with the personnel, and the captains, and everybody who has to run the ship, and because of that there is a premium on speed, so that they can make as many trips as possible. They were talking about flying drone freight vehicles or airships that will be driverless, obviously. Nobody on board. May take a little longer, but because of the cost savings and everything, and the number that they can produce, driverless freight across the oceans will become bigger and bigger and cheaper and cheaper. That will definitely be here within the next five or ten years, and again it's going to be all driven, I think, by the cost savings. So, that will be the first big, I believe, the first big change in shipment. We are living in an interesting time. There are so many things on the cost side. It's going to be interesting what actually takes off.

Yeah.

Whether it's a medical breakthrough, or a computer breakthrough, or energy breakthrough, we are very close to major discoveries, and, I think, I hope, that if we do have one of those, we will use it right, not exploit it. But who knows, who knows.

I had a fellow from Los Alamos Labs speak to my students. I started a school. They are in high school, and he said that the next Bill Gates and Steve Jobs of the world are coming from the energy sector.

Yeah, I believe that.

And everyone is going to have their own personal energy pack that provides energy for their home, their car, everything. It's just like computers. We used to have big IBM 360s occupy football fields. You can store more on a cell phone now than you could do on that. He says the same thing will

happen with energy. What would they use to power something that could go across the ocean, petrol?

It would be primarily – it could be a combination of different power sources, depending on the way they build it. Solar could be used, because it would be unobstructed, right? So, you power parts of the ship with solar. Batteries would be used for certain parts of the ship, especially for takeoffs and landings. Maneuverability would be propeller driven. So, it would be, my understanding is it would be a combination of all. But I think for the mass majority it will be solar. It would be essentially a blimp type of vehicle with a large payload below, and, you know, the entire outer structure would be solar panels. So, you said you started a school here?

Yeah, a high school at the community college called The MASTERS Program. MASTERS stands for Math, Art, Science, Technology, Engineering, Reading and Service.

Sounds perfect to me.

It's a dual credit program with the community college. All of our students graduate with some college credits. Some graduate with an Associate's Degree at the same time they graduate from high school. We hired a principal, Anne Salzmann, who used to be principal at Verde Valley School in Sedona, where I'm from. We actually had many of the same elementary school teachers.

How long has that been going on?

We are in our 7th year. We are in the top ranked schools in New Mexico. Anne has done an excellent job.

Wow, and you do Uber just for fun, or to meet people, or just to keep busy?

All of the above. I am doing a book on my Uber experiences, sort of a study of the kind of people that come to Santa Fe and live here. People are fascinating. Everyone's got a story. I like to have various projects that I work on.

The mail box is up here on the left.

Okay, here we are.

Thank you very much. Good luck with your book.

∞

— MUSEUMS —

All set?

Yeah. Is the Folk Art Museum close?

Just up the road.

Okay. Nice, so it's just up the hill right there.

All right.

They have a good menu too.

It's very good. Smell of passion fruit is good too.

Yeah.
Where are you all from?

All the family is from Massachusetts but now we live in Boston, Washington, D.C. and Florida.

Wow.

And we met here.

For the first time.

Are you all sisters?

Yeah.

There's actually four museums on this hill.

Oh, this is Museum Hill, right?

Yes, this is Museum Hill. There's the Spanish Colonial Art Museum, Museum of Indian Arts and Culture, Folk Art and then the Wheelwright. I will show you all of them. I used to be on the Museum of New Mexico Foundation board, so I learned quite a bit about them.

Wow.

The Wheelwright is very classic Southwest. It was first opened in 1937 by Mary Cabot Wheelwright and assisted by her friend and Navajo medicine man and artist Hastiin Klah as a repository for the beauty and dignity of the Navajo religion.

Wow.

I know, we just went to Folk Art and then we went to Native American Cultural Art Museum.

The Folk Art that you just came from was founded in 1953 by Chicago heiress Florence Dibell Bartlett. They now have one of the world's largest folk art markets in the world the second week in July. People come from all over the world. So, that over there is the Folk Art.

It's really a beautiful weekend.

It is gorgeous.

And this is the Museum of Indian Arts and Culture that opened in 1987. MIAC is actually a combination of two museums. One opened in 1909 by anthropologist Edgar Lee Hewett, and the other, the Laboratory of Antropology, was founded in 1927 by John D. Rockefeller. They combined in 1947, which created the most inclusive and systematically acquired collection of New Mexico artifacts in the world.

Wow!

Wheelwright is right over there. Museum of Spanish Colonial Arts is over there.

Everything is really close and convenient. Thank you so much.

Thank you.

∞

— UBER INSURANCE —

How are you doing today?

I am doing good.

We are going to the Santa Fe International Airport.

International? I like that. I like that.

Another gorgeous day. Every day we have been here, it has been really nice.

Where are you all from?

Miami.

Miami.

But I don't know if we are from there.

That is where you currently live?

Yeah. We are plotting and scheming how we can end up here. It's so nice.

Just here on vacation?

Yeah. Our daughter made plans of her own for spring break, and so we decided to do our own escape.

Your daughter goes to college?

No, she is in high school. She got invited by her friend and her family to join them.

Oh. Have you ever been to Santa Fe before?

Yeah. We were once here about 22 years ago.

Oh, boy.

So, we thought we would catch up and see what's happening here.

Did you notice much difference?

Well, we both think there's a lot more to do or maybe we are just noticing these things. And then the food seems really good, including all your grocery stores. I don't know if they were all here then.

Did you go to Whole Foods?

Yeah.

It was not there 22 years ago.

And the Co-op, I don't know how old that is?

The Co-op has been here all along. I think from the seventies.

Yeah.

But it used to be on Alameda closer to downtown. It's on Alameda right now, but further down at Solana Center. It moved about 10 years ago.

We actually went to the one in Los Alamos yesterday.

Is the Co-op there the same one as down here – La Montanita?

Yeah, I think so. It's in the new area sort of outside of town.

Just south of town.

What did you do in Los Alamos?

We went up to-

Valles Caldera.

Isn't that something else?

Wow, it's beautiful.

Yeah, it's so beautiful, and it's only an hour away. It's quite amazing. You didn't happen to drive past the caldera, did you?

Just slightly.

Well, we went down into it, because it was...

Did you go to Jemez Springs?

We went to the visitor center.

Oh, the visitor center, yeah, right.

The road is only open as far as the visitor center right now in May.

If you keep going down, not the road to the caldera visitor center, but on that paved road...

Yeah.

You go down to Jemez Springs, and along the way there is all this hot bubbling water, bubbling up...

Oh, really?

Oh, my gosh!

Bubbling up from the road.

That's cool. Are there...

That magma is still hot. It comes from the Jemez Volcanic Field.

Oh, sure, it surprised me. Well, just like in Yellowstone.

That's right. I believe this is one of the country's largest young calderas. It's 13 miles across, and still considered to be an active volcano.

It's quite dramatic when you come over the ridge, and you look down into it.

It is, isn't it?

So, we just drove on that road probably where you're talking about, and got out and walked along the east Jemez River which is really like a spring almost.

Did you happen to see any deer or elk?

We did see deer. We saw some white-tailed deer, but no elk unfortunately.

Somebody was saying that it's mating season.

For the elk?

In the mountains.

Oh, I don't know.

I think not, because now is the time when they should have calves.

In the spring.

Yeah. I think they were talking about when it was mating season, they were running and doing all their drama.

What do you all do down in Miami?

I work in the insurance business. How about you? Is this part time, keeping you busy kind of thing, or how do you like driving Uber?

Oh, you know it's a creative project. I'm doing a book.

Oh, really?

On my Uber riders, and just the interesting people that come to Santa Fe.

I think you definitely have some characters and color here.

I write notes on riders, and I record a number of the conversations.

Yeah. I find it fascinating. I think it's just like being next to somebody in an airplane. I get so many stories from Uber drivers. You're doing a front seat to back seat, but I'm usually back here and I ask the drivers stuff. People just tell you any amount of intimate details about their lives and interesting stuff. So, have you written a book before?

I have, but I didn't publish it. I've gone through the process. My lady is an author.

Say it again?

My lady is an author. The lady I live with. She has written a book published by Macmillan in London.

What is her book about?

Well, it's called <u>Hold My Hand, a Mother's Journey,</u> and it has to do with an ordeal she went through with her 20 plus year-old-son down in Australia. He was mugged and was in a coma for four months. He came out completely quadriplegic, and he didn't fit into the Australian medical and immigration systems. They kicked him out after a couple of years, and she went to England. It's complicated. She had to get volunteers to care for him, and it carried

over into an organization that she founded here in Santa Fe called Coming Home Connection that provides free home care for people who fall through the gaps and cracks of our medical system. Now she's doing a free hospice house in Santa Fe.

It's great that she's doing that. How has her son done all this time?

He died four years after. Her book is a four-year ordeal of what she went through in the late eighties.

And he was in his 20's when this happened, you said?

Yeah.

Oh, I don't know how you get over that.

You don't get over it. You learn to live with it. She wrote a book about – maybe doing a movie about it.

Yeah.

She's in the middle of a script for it now. She has a script writer, but it was published in Polish, Dutch, Chinese and Italian, plus 22 pages in <u>Reader's Digest</u> all over the world.

I didn't think <u>Reader's Digest</u> ever did a story longer than a couple of pages.

This was 22 pages in <u>Reader's Digest</u>. It was amazing.

And the two of you met later in life?

About 15 years ago. We're both dancers. We have a dance group here in Santa Fe called Embodydance. It's sort of free form dance. You dance with a partner or by yourself or with someone else. Every song changes.

But it's not like ballroom dancing?

No. No, no, no. no. It's free form. It's just movement, anyway

you want to move.

So just like people dance, right?

Yeah. The great dancers in Santa Fe all dance there. It's a very intimate group of people that have been dancing together for a long time. We have like 800 people in our group.

800 people?

In our group, yeah. Not everyone dances the same night. Usually 80-100 dancing on a given Thursday night. It has been going on for quite a while.

Where do you do it?

At the Railyard Performance Center, right near downtown across from Farmer's Market.

That's cool. What great stories have you heard in your Uber experience that so far are going to be shortlisted for the book?

I picked up a guy in his mid-30's. He has bought and sold six Silicon Valley startups. He started six and sold them, obviously very wealthy.

Yeah.

He says most of his current investments are in flying cars. And all the different components.

Is that right?

"This is just around the bend," he said.

So, he was involved in what companies in Silicon Valley? Do you remember?

I don't know. I didn't ask him.

Well, a lot of people are betting on this flying car thing, I think big companies are too. Oprah is doing it.

They are doing self-driving cars.

And I read that in Dubai they have already launched something, or they are about to.

Well, you see, Dubai, the United Arab Emirates, countries like that, they don't have the regulations that we have here in America, so they are willing to try new...

Well, the thing is they just change the regulation, because they own, they own the whole place anyway.

That's right.

Our son is studying over there. He's in Abu Dhabi.

What is he studying?

NYU has a university campus over there. He's in that program. It's a liberal arts course.

My granddaughter is just deciding on which college she's going to go to.

I think we're getting close to the airport. We are 11 minutes away from it my app says.

Yeah. You know that mountain, the Jemez mountains, they were almost double their size when that volcano exploded.

Well, they said it was 500 times the volume that was ejected at Mount St. Helens.

Really?

Yeah, there was a sign outside of the road. Mount St. Helens was a pretty formidable event.

Yes, it was. I wonder how they figured that. The disbursement of ash or...

I don't know. Maybe just calculating volumes.

What kind of insurance do you do?

I do all kinds of – well, actually, I'll tell you, I never tell people this. I actually work for Uber now.

You do?

I do, and I buy all of Uber's insurances in certain areas of the world.

My Lord!

I used to – I have been all my life working in the insurance business for the last 20 years with a big Swiss company. And then last year I moved over to be on the client side.

I was wondering about that with Uber insurance. They want us to have a special policy with State Farm here. They recommend this additional insurance. I was wondering how often they have a claim. How often do Uber riders file claims?

There are plenty of claims.

There are plenty of claims?

Yeah. Well, there are a lot of Uber drivers, many, many all over the world. Uber is in 80 countries now.

I know, it's amazing, isn't it?

It is really something else. So, Uber buys a lot of insurance.

Well, it is pretty fascinating.

It's changing so many things; it's really interesting. And then to get to sit down with insurance companies in all these different countries. I try to get them to do this stuff. A lot has never been done before, and there is not a lot of information. It's quite a challenge. You must make up new stuff as you go along. It's interesting.

So, is yours like an agency or insurance company or brokerage?

No, I work for – I am an Uber employee.

Oh, you're an Uber employee?

Yeah, a pretty small group of people just does insurance. Very sophisticated people. We have a lot of the same kinds of capabilities as a fairly big insurance company, in terms of actuaries and data science.

I had a passenger after about a month of driving who I took to Albuquerque, he and his girlfriend. His girlfriend was up here doing a documentary, a PBS documentary on the film industry in Santa Fe. And I'm driving them down to Albuquerque; I'm fascinated with films. About halfway there I asked the guy, "What do you do?" He was 26, 27 years old, maybe early thirties. He says, "I'm an Uber executive."

An Uber executive?

Yes. Oh, my god! The guy is so young. His phone is just ringing off the hook.

So, I'm 53, and there are a lot of twenty something, early thirty something people in this company. It's quite amazing. And really a very, very high average of intellect in this place, from all the best schools and interesting experiences coming out of the people who have founded a business and sold it. We run into a few people from Goldman Sachs, all kinds of different folks. I find it to be quite interesting – people, very, very young, super informal, bring your dog to work. Although in San Francisco you don't see dogs, in the Miami offices you see dogs.

How many offices do they have around the country?

Oh, gosh! I don't know for sure, but I think probably seven or eight.

This guy was out of the Phoenix office.

Okay. Uber executive, I like those kids. I should make sure that I start saying I'm an insurance executive. It's got a ring to it.

Right. Sounds like it has some clout to it. Here's my card.

Well, that's a famous name. Bishop is a famous name around here.
Well, it's the Bishop though, Bishop Lamy, who is the famous one.

Okay, I got you. So, you're not claiming all that?
No. Ok, here we are. Adios.

Bye.

∞

— ST. JOHN'S STUDENTS FROM CHINA —

It's really hot today.

It is, where are you from?
I'm from China. I study at St. John's right now.
What part of China?

It's a place called Changsha, capital of Hunan province, like in the center.

In the center. What year are you at St John's?

I'm a freshman.

What are you studying in freshman year?

Basically, we read great books, like classic books, with lab, seminar, math and Greek language.

What are some of the classic books that you read?

We read <u>The Iliad</u> and <u>The Odyssey</u> by Homer and a bunch of like Greek authors, ancient Greek authors like Aristotle, Plato and Sophocles among others. Do you live in Santa Fe?

Yes, 31 years.

That's a long time. Where were you before moving here?

Los Angeles for 10 years, but I'm from Arizona.

Okay.

Sedona, Arizona.

Sedona, I've been there actually.

Have you?

Yes, it's really beautiful, all those cliffs, and I've done a road trip in Arizona from Phoenix all the way to the Grand Canyon and back. We passed Sedona and stayed there for like an hour or two.

Yes.

It's really beautiful.

Yes, how did you find out about St. John's?

My friend studies here, and he recommended it.

You have a friend from where you're from?

Yes, but he's not here anymore. He kind of described the curriculum to me and life in Santa Fe. He said it was really beautiful, and close to nature, like there's a mountain behind our dorm. I can climb it any time I want.

Mt. Atalaya?

I've never been on the Atalaya trail. I'd like to sometime in the future, if I have the chance.

What's the main difference you find between Santa Fe and China, United States and China?

If it's talking about like Santa Fe, it's really dry here. I'm not used to the weather. I'm from a very humid region in China so this dryness, I'm not liking it. I don't feel good about it. I think one of the main differences between U.S. and China is that if you want to go anywhere in the U.S. you have to drive a car, but in China you don't have to own a car to go anywhere. Mostly it's walking distance. But when you travel long distance, you can take public transportation, which is very convenient.

I see, so you have a much better public transportation system in China?

Yes, I think so, like we have the high-speed train. That's become really popular recently.

What do your parents do in China?

My father is a business man; he sells industrial ointments, lubricants for machines. And my mom, she's a lab technician and she works at a hospital.

Oh, why do you want to make a book?

Just the study of humanity. I've had 3,000 different riders. People are fascinating.

Like different characteristics in humans?

The different things that people get into. Why and how they get into them. Do they have a scholarship program at St. John's for students from China?

I think so, yes. They have the Trustee's Scholarship. It covers like a third of tuition, and there's also the St. John's Fund, which is $5000 per year, so it covers some cost.

How much is the basic tuition?

I think it's like around $60,000.

I see. What do you think of all the concepts of God that you study at St John's?

The concepts of God?

Yes, that's what you study the second year right?

Like reading the Bible, we have Greek gods right now, which is so different from the Christian kind of God. The Greek gods possess more humanity. They're definitely not perfect, you know. They drink wine and have sex just like humans do, which is very, very different from the Christian God. The Christian God, which is perfect, is like the paradigm of morality.

Most of the people from your area are Buddhists, Zen Buddhists or nothing or Christian?

Most people are not religious.

Not religious?

Yes, but there are a few Christians and I think a few Buddhists.

Are they spiritual?

What do you mean by spiritual? Oh, here we are. Bye.

Thank you.

— ST. JOHN'S STUDENTS TO LAMY —

You're going to the train?

Yeah, Amtrak.

You're going to Lamy?

Lamy, yes that's it. At the station.

Oh, so you want to go down to Guadalupe and get the shuttle?

Yes, but I don't know where the destination is. I just follow the map and the Amtrak guide.

I'm not sure. So, there's a shuttle to Lamy?

Yes. Forty minutes.

Okay.

Because there is an Amtrak station there.

I know. I didn't know there was a shuttle.

Yes. Interesting.

Where are you headed?

Oh, Chicago.

Is that where you're from?

Oh, I'm from China. I'm a student at St. John's.

Yes, I know.

Amtrak is very expensive sometimes, very expensive.

Amtrak?

Yes. I like to be cheaper than a flight, and you can enjoy the view during the journey.

What time does the shuttle leave?

II:30.

Is school over now? Is St. John's out for the year?

Oh, no, no, no, no, no. School is not done. It's just that I have a special appointment in Chicago. And then, I have to fly to China from Chicago to Hong Kong. So, I have to get this taken care of. The semester is ending May 18.

May 18?

Yeah. Not too many Asians at St. John's. And if you see Asians in Santa Fe, 90% says he's a student at St. John's.

Yeah. Do you like Santa Fe?

Yeah, I like it.

Anything like it in China?

In China, we call a small city, maybe one million of the population. So, it's very different. My hometown is medium sized in China. It's three million.

And that's medium?

Yeah. And you know, Shanghai? Shanghai is 24 million. Beijing is 10 million.

Shanghai is 24 million?

Yes, and New York is 8 million - three times of New York. And Hong Kong is 8 million.

I've been to Hong Kong. I've been to Guangzhou.

Oh. You have been to Guangzhou? My hometown is in

Guangzhou. Guangzhou is 16 million. So, why did you go there?

A trade show.

Oh, a trade show? I think this year Canton Fair is just two weeks. Guangzhou is an involved trading city in China.

Yes. What do the Chinese people think of Trump?

It depends on the classes. Different classes. Different sorts of classes. Yeah, but most of the... Not the richest, but the scholars or elites or something, they see Trump as ... How can I describe it? They don't hate him.

They don't hate him?

Yeah, they don't hate him. Sometimes they see him as a movie star playing a dramatic role.

What do they think of North Korea?

North Korea? Oh, that's an interesting question. They think of Korea as being like China 30 years ago, 40 years ago, in the day of Mao Tse-tung. And now, they see North Korea, I think, the same as Americans. They see North Korea as a very weird country.

Very weird?

Yeah, a very weird country.

Do most people see the United States as very weird?

I don't know. I think so.

Do they?

Yeah.

What about you? Do you think it's weird?

Oh, I think it is weird in the 21st century. But, in fact, it is China 30 years ago, 40 years ago. But we had the reforming so... Deng Xiaoping.

Yeah.

But many young men enjoy to go to North Korea to have trip as a rancher or something. It is not very peaceful in North Korea now. Maybe Trump will, I don't know, attack. Attack North Korea.

Okay, I think that you get your shuttle right over here. Thank you.

Okay, thank you.

∞

— LILACS —

I just came back from Italy with my friend. We used to spend half the year in Florence.

Oh, you did?

Yeah. We just moved here two years ago. We love it, just love it! It's beautiful here. What can we say? Exciting!!!

You don't have to say anything.

Beautiful day and spring is here. It's just a long way, and this is my first experience this week using Uber.

Is it really?

My dear friend said she uses Uber all the time. My car is in the garage so I'm using Uber now, plus I use them a lot when we go out at night.

I do too.

You do too? I bet you do.

If I go out, and if I'm going to have a drink, or if I have a parking issue, I'll use Uber. I don't like to deal with parking.

I don't either. Now that I've been using it the last couple of days during the day, I'm going to do it more. It's fabulous.

I'm going to check into it for my house.

Have you been to the Nedra Matteucci Gallery?

I think it's the best gallery in town.

My friend paints portraits, so she wants me to check out some of the best galleries in town.

You know, they have a secret garden?

I love that garden.

We take our great granddaughter there. We have a great granddaughter, and she loves to play with all the sculptures and the... It's her secret garden.

I've been to parties in that garden.

Me too.

Wonderful I think.

Aren't they fantastic?

Now how long have you lived in Santa Fe?

31 years.

Oh, I've been 38.

You've been here 38 years? I've seen you around, I think, but I don't remember. But before here I was 10 years in L.A.

Okay, Los Angeles. Working?

Yeah, I had a business in L.A.

We have a grandson who's an actor. What kind of business did you have?

It was called Day Runner. The Day Runner Organizer, that you write your addresses, agenda, notes and everything in.

Oh, that's right, the Day Runner thing, yeah.

I sold my interest in Day Runner in 1986, and moved over here to Santa Fe.

Good for you. Well, this is nicer than L.A.

Yeah, this is.

The traffic in L.A., by god, I never want to drive a car there. Well, where I am in Silicon Valley it's worse. Sometimes it takes three hours to get to the office.

What do you like best about Florence?

Artwork, the Renaissance, the museums, the buildings.

Because you go over there for long stretches of time, right?

Yeah, three months at a time, which is the limit. The visits are ones that don't require a visa.

Is that the limit?

Right. But I am working on a visa. If you teach English, it helps to get a visa quicker, I think. You got to wait at least a year. The people are all so wonderful in Florence. They are very friendly, very friendly. And they look you in the eye when they're speaking, and when you're speaking they look right at you instead of like ignoring you. And the food, oh, wow!

The food?

Yeah, the food is fantastic.

I notice that the blue sage is in bloom now. And also, the lilacs. I noticed them along here. They are a little bit lower. Well, there is more sun here. It's better down here than up there where you are, yeah.

You are going to see a real one blooming down here right at the corner of Acequia Madre and Garcia.

Yeah, well, they just started to come up. If you put some of the blue sage in your hand, roll it around and smell it, it's fantastic.

Yeah.

I lost a few ones. I mean, I didn't lose the bush, but I lost the buds, and so I only have branches. I think I live too high up.

Look over here to the right.

Oh my gosh.

Isn't that gorgeous?

Yes, tulips. Oh, how beautiful! See that? It's close by Canyon Road, but I feel like we should come back this way after we do Fenn and Gerald Peters galleries.

See these, oh, how beautiful! Wasn't that nice?

Thank you! Absolutely gorgeous!

Now check these lilacs out. Let me tell you, it smells fantastic.

Oh, I'm glad you came and got us. There's more lilacs over here. Wonderful! This must be the largest lilac bush in Santa Fe. Oh, yeah, this is fabulous. You see this is where the garden is of the gallery. Do you want us to jump out here?

No, I'll pull up here.

Thank you, John. It was nice meeting you.

Thank you so much.

Thank you.

∞

— COLLEGE ACTIVIST —

Hello.

Good morning. Santa Fe Community College?

Yes, please.

I'm doing a book on my Lyft and Uber riders.

Yeah?

And I record conversations, if people let me. Are you okay with that?

Oh, you're writing a book?

Yeah.

Oh. Ok.

Do you go to the community college?

My son goes to the community college, and I plan to take some classes this summer. Looking for a second half to my career.

Boy, lots of things to do out there. That's one of the things you really realize driving Lyft and Uber, the number of different occupations that people have. It's just amazing.

Yeah, right.

"How did you get into that," I always ask people.

Everyone's got a story, right?

Everyone's got a story.

Interesting. Inspiring me to be a driver. That would be fun, listening to people's stories. Take you out of yourself, right?

It does. I started a program out here at the college called The MASTERS Program.

Oh, did you – that high school?

Yeah.

That's cool! I've been home schooling my kids, but we were thinking of doing that for my daughter. She's fourteen. She's totally capable of the coursework. But she's not old enough. You have to be an accredited home school, I think.

Yeah, it can be an accredited home school too.

But I'm not an accredited home school. I'm just a mom, and I hang out at home with my kids and teach them stuff.

Well, there's ways you know, if she can pass the test.

Placement test?

The college has an Accuplacer test.

She can probably do that.

Then you see, it doesn't matter what you do. You can just go directly into the college courses. But the advantage of doing it through THE MASTERS Program, is that the school pays for all the books.

Right. But also, there is a high school program, where they teach some....

If the students don't qualify for the college courses, then we have to teach the high school courses.

Oh, I see. I see. Well, that's good to know. Wow, how lucky to have you as my Uber driver. I'll look into that. I'm looking into law school actually. And I'm going to take some paralegal classes, just to kind of get my feet wet. And my daughter, she would love to take them with me. She's going to take them with me even though she won't get credit for them. But if she could actually, somehow, it would work for the summer, but we can look into that when she gets older. That's great. There's a lot of interesting stuff to learn and do in this life.

Let me tell you, the more you learn, the more you know you don't know.

That's right. The bigger the radius...the whole Universe.

I have learned so much from different people driving. I've had 3000 plus rides. I mean the different conventions that are held here in Santa Fe, like the other day there was a big bio-DNA convention, 500 bio-DNA people. There were 2000 anthropologists here in town several weeks ago. Boy, that's an interesting group of people.

The anthropologists? What's so interesting about them?

Anthropology covers everything. Most people think anthropology is digging Indian ruins. And stuff like that. Well, anthropologists, probably their biggest field is medicine.

Oh, that is interesting.

And their next biggest field is environmental – ecology. They study indigenous cultures in rain forests, shrimp farming in Vietnam, civil war survivors...They study everything from A to Z. I never knew that about anthropologists.

I didn't either.

There are four branches of anthropology that cover these different fields: Past, present, biologic and linguistic.

Yeah?

To hear these people speak about what turned them on to anthropology is amazing. It's like a branch of life that they completely love and have got turned on to.

That is very cool. So, do you have a traditional educational experience?

I didn't go to college. I mean I did a few college courses for six months, but I didn't really go to college.

Have you been in Santa Fe a long time?

Thirty-one.

Since 1931? No, I'm just kidding.

Yeah, right. I'm getting up there, but I'm not quite that old. How about you? How long you all been here in Santa Fe?

We moved here in the late 1990's, so twenty some odd years.

I always wanted to be, I was trained to be a lawyer. My father wanted me to be a lawyer. But I've been mentored by some great lawyers. I actually did a case *pro se* one time, by myself without a lawyer. It was so much fun. My one chance to be a lawyer.

Yeah, if you know where to start. I have an interest in prison reform. I think we have sort of a problem in our society with this experiment with mass incarceration.

Boy, you're telling me.

One of the things I've done through Upaya Zen Center is have correspondence with a few prisoners. I think they responded to an ad that Upaya placed in Shambala Sun or some New Age magazine like that. They are so grateful to have someone to talk to. Just a companion to hear them. It's so important to people.

I used to go out to the Old Main facility out here before they closed it.

The prison out here?

Yeah. I did it for quite a while. I talked to prisoners about what they can do right when they get out, as far as how to make a living.

Right.

How to get quick cash. What kind of jobs pay instantly. We have the highest incarceration rate per capita in the world.

In the U.S.

We have, in the United States, the highest rate in the world.

Yeah, it's a big problem. Some of them ask me for legal help. And I really wish I could do something. Someone sent me all his papers. I mean of course he's always going to say he's innocent, well, not always, but it looks like he's completely powerless within the system. And he agreed to do something he didn't want to agree to. I'm just like, oooh...

I say do what your heart tells you to do. If your heart tells you to do that, go at it with all your might.

Well, that's what I am doing, Mr. John. There are quite a few people that are really upset with me right now. Because I am powerful. I am determined, but they want to knock me down. No. This is what my heart is telling me to do. I stand up to bullies, and bullies don't like it.

You should meet my lady.

Yeah? I'd love to.

We live right around the street from you. She cares for a lot of people here in town. But, boy, she is a social justice ...

Warrior.

Social Justice Warrior. Yes.

I love her. I love her.

You two should really meet. Her thing is not necessarily prisoners. But its people that fall through the gaps of our medical system.

Yeah.

Particularly toward the end of life.

And people who are powerless.

People who are powerless.

Yeah, people who can't seem to make it in certain realms. Well, good for her.

I know a lot about the prison system. More than probably anybody you're ever going to meet.

Really, how do you know so much? From the inside?

That's right.

You do? That's ok. We all have a past. What did you do?

It was a marijuana offense.

Oh my gosh. Back in the days when that was criminal.

Yeah. But initially I was in a maximum security federal penitentiary called McNeill Island in Puget Sound. No one ever escaped from it. They have since closed it. This was many years ago, more than forty. Initially I was a pile driver building docks in Puget Sound, but later they discovered I knew accounting, so they moved me to the accounting office. Later they transferred me to a minimum secure facility at Safford, Arizona, where I got

to know this guy, John Ehrlichman, from Watergate and the Nixon administration. We played tennis and Scrabble practically every day. He worked in the boiler room. I was also the camp accountant at Safford.

Yeah, that's a familiar name.

He's one of the reasons I moved to Santa Fe. I bought his house up off Cerro Gordo, this huge double adobe duplex that overlooked the city off Montoya Circle. I was in prison with John Ehrlichman, and we became very good friends. There are so many stories in prison. It's unbelievable.

Unbelievable.

Ehrlichman told me the only reason he was in prison is that John Dean lied before the grand jury. Also, Ehrlichman said that he was approached by another prisoner at Safford that told him that he used to fence cars for Maureen Dean before she married John Dean. And that Maureen later moved to Washington, D.C. where she worked for a call girl operation. He said that Larry O'Brian had a list of call girls in his desk in his Watergate office that included Maureen Dean's name, and that it was John Dean who sent in the Plumbers to raid Larry O'Brian's office to get that list of call girls. And that's how Watergate happened, according to what John Ehrlichman told me.

Wow, that's fascinating.

But I did get a pardon from Governor Bruce King. Even though it was a federal offense, governors can pardon in their given state, and then each state is reciprocal to the other states. So, it's just as good as a federal pardon, except you can't own a gun.

Wow. Well, you got a lot of stories to put into a book. Have you already written something?

Not yet. I'm thinking of self-publishing.

Good for you. Do you know David Bedrick?

I don't think so.

Publishing. He's an advocate for marginalized voices.

Oh, here in town?

Yeah. He's one of my favorite people in the whole world.

Marginalized voices. Wow, that's a good one.

Yeah. And it encompasses the homeless, the sick, the impris-
oned, the bullied, all of these.

**Let me tell you what I've been working on at Old Main out
here. Yeah, you know the old prison out here on Highway
14 that they closed ten years ago? I've been trying to turn
that into a homeless center where instead of locking
people up, people will have their own key to their cell.**

Yeah, yeah. Beautiful.

**I'm calling it the Freedom Foundry. I don't know if it will
ever happen, but I've written a letter to Governor Martinez
and one of her cabinet secretaries about the project. I
think that would be a good place to have a homeless
center. Its completely empty. All these facilities around,
you know, that are completely vacant, state facilities, and
stuff like that, we can turn them into centers. We could
create a work force out there. Put all the homeless people
to work.**

Yeah, community centers. Gathering places where we
support each other.

I'll give you my card.

Yeah, I'm so inspired. I don't have a card.

Follow your passion.

Yeah, that's it. That's the trick to life. Thank you so much for the ride.

Bye.

WEEK FIVE

— MONTEREY —

Let me get that for you.

Okay. Aeroporto por favore.

Santa Fe or Albuquerque?

We are going to the Santa Fe Airport. I flew in to Santa Fe, which is wonderful.

It is, isn't it?

Oh, gosh, yes. What a day! It's a little colder. Well, it's paradise here. Everybody is right. It is paradise.

It is pretty nice today.

Today we went to that darling little gourmet chocolate shop called Gourmet Today. It's in that little courtyard next to Pink Adobe. The food is fantastic. It's all fresh.

I'll have to try it.

She made it that morning. Do you have family here with you?

I have my lady.

Good for you.

She has two great grandkids that are here.

Good, wonderful.

And her son is here. My two girls live in Phoenix. My son just moved from here to Sonoma County.

Okay. Near Petaluma, yeah. Close to San Francisco. Petaluma is the chicken capital of the world. It's noted as the chicken capital. They raise beautiful, rocky free range organic chicken.

Oh, yeah? I didn't know that.

Okay, it started right there. And eggs, wonderful eggs, and chickens. Yeah. It's a beautiful area. Have you been up there?

I don't think so. I used to own a house in Nevada City, California. What do you do up in the Monterey Bay area?

Well, I'm actually living in Moss Landing. It's a little community, a tiny fishing community. That's where the condo is located in a development by the...

Is it on the ocean?

It's right on the ocean. I watch the whales go by, and it's actually close to Carmel and Monterey.

Oh, really?

You've been to Carmel, I'm sure?

Oh, yeah, I have a house situation in Pacific Grove. So, we are going to be up there for several months.

Yeah, okay. Good for you. And I'm glad to hear that you got a lady, because my husband died two years ago. And I've just met a gentleman friend, and I'm still in a state of shock.

Oh my Lord.

You know how it is when you meet somebody after someone dies? I'm just absolutely shocked. He's so nice and so sweet that I still can't believe it, because I thought, 'Okay for the rest of my life here I am alone.' But no, I don't think so. I've got a card somewhere, and I was going to say you guys can call me when you go to PG.

That will be great.

I go to PG a lot for dinner.

Do they have nice restaurants up there?

They do. Yeah, we have some good food in PG, good shops.

How far is PG from Carmel and Monterey?

10 minutes.

That's it?

Yeah. 10 minutes. I'm going to write my name on this to-do list.

Okay. Do you have kids?

No. I was married very young, and then went back to school and worked and all that. And I got married to my sweet husband when I was 40, and he was 54. He just died two years ago. He has four kids, married and grandkids. But since he passed away my friendly stepchildren have just kind of written me off. That's okay. That's life. When I have time, I go to France. I go to Italy. I have a good time, and I paint water color portraits. I have a group of women that I paint with.

How did you meet this guy?

We shared a dinner table in Florence.

You shared a dinner table?

The restaurant was crowded.

There was a community table or something?

No, there was one little table in the backroom. The restaurant was packed, and I said, "Uno por favore." Uno, that's one in Italian. I said, "One more?"

Yeah.

So, then he said in Italian to the waiter, he said, "Maybe she can share a table with me?" Since it's hard to sit one person, when there are eight people clamoring for a table. It was so full. And he said, "Share?" So, I'd been studying Italian for years.

Is he American?

No, he's Italian.

He's Italian?

What do you think? He's a bicycle rider. He's almost a professional bicyclist. So, anyway, we just kind of hooked up at the table, and he wanted to see me again. I said, "I don't think so." So then he ran off, and I ran off. But I took a picture of him, because I said, "I do portraits and I need a model. Let me take a picture." About three weeks later I thought, 'Now where the hell is that guy? I'm lonely. I got to find somebody.' My girlfriends all said, "Go to Italy, you are going to find somebody. It's ridiculous! Your husband has been dead for two years. You got to find somebody." I said, "No." So, I thought, 'I'll just go to the restaurant, and see if they know this guy.' Sure enough, he's one of their best clients.

Oh, my Lord.

I said, "He told me he lived on the same street that I've rented on." "Yeah, he lives over there." Everything he told me turned out to be true. So, I said, "Okay, when he comes back, here's my card." And it had my name and phone number on it written in Italian. I said, "Have him call me. I want him to see a portrait that I did, and I want to make sure I've got his name correct, because I always put names down." So, anyway, the restaurant guy said, "Well, I got info he's gone for a month. He's in India." I said, "Oh, then I'll never see him again, fine. But if he comes in just tell him that I made it." Two nights later my doorbell rang. He had just come back from India. I said, "I don't believe this." So that's the way we hooked up.

That's interesting.

Yeah, interesting, isn't it? You can't plan anything, because it never works out. If I had gone out looking for somebody to go out with, it would not have worked. It was great. It's great. So, I'm going back in September.

Relationships at our age are a little different than in our 20s and 30s.

Absolutely. Tell me about it. Yeah. And remember when your heart used to go boom?

Yeah, right.

And you think, 'Okay, can I go and talk to this person again? Will this person call me?' I don't care. I don't care what this guy does. He doesn't even support me. I'm not looking for children. I'm not looking for...It's completely different! It's fun. Isn't it fun when you are not having an agenda?

Right.

It's just loosey-goosey and friendly. It's just wonderful! And as Pooh, the teddy bear used to say, "Life is too short to live alone." And she's older than you, that's good. And I bet she looks fabulous.

She does. She took me to Wales just a couple of years ago, to the Pembrokeshire Coast way out in South West Wales. Boy, it's an amazing area.

Wow!

She grew up in a little town called Dale that has experienced a huge population increase. It went from 90 to 190. It's a very small world. She went to school in Cardiff.

Yeah, tiny. Good for her. Did you meet her here in Santa Fe?

We are both dancers. We have a dance group here in Santa Fe called Embodydance. She's an excellent dancer. It's just free form type of dancing. You move anyway you want. It's just movement.

Oh, I love it, yeah.

You move anyway you want.

I used to go to all the discos in San Francisco back in the 70s. I loved it. I went to all the gay discos with my gay friends. We would dance all night long. Good for you. So, how long have you known your lady?

I think going on 16 years.

Good for you.

We do a lot of community things around town.

Sure, sure.

She has a nonprofit that cares for people, provides free homecare. She provides homecare for the very wealthy and very poor. The very wealthy, they contract directly with the family and the nurse, but she uses the same nurses for her volunteer care for people that don't have any money, that fall through the gaps and cracks of our medical system. And it's substantial, as far as the medical issues in our society.

Yeah, yeah.

She cares for quite a few people here in town.

Good for her, that's wonderful! We are all in the same boat. It doesn't matter how much or how little money we have.

It doesn't really.

It doesn't. We are all on the same boat. And I have met the nicest people in my travelling solo. I don't need my girlfriends to hang on to me, and say, "Let's go shopping for handbags." I want to go out and talk to the gypsies, a lot of old people, and I've had a ball going to Italy by myself, sitting in wonderful restaurants, and getting to know the people.

I know a lady here in town who's a little older than I am, and she's travelled the entire world by herself.

Yeah.

I mean she's climbed Mt. Kilimanjaro by herself, or with a group sometimes, but she travels all over the world by herself and spends weeks, sometimes months, like in Angkor Wat, Cambodia.

That's what I'm going to do. Great, good for her. I went to Cuba for Christmas, not this past Christmas, but Christmas a year ago, a year and a half ago.

It must have been interesting.

I loved it. This was my first big trip after my husband had died, and I thought, 'No, do it.' I drove to the airport by myself, parked long-term parking. I said, "Screw it, if somebody takes my car, I don't care." And it was wonderful. You can actually do everything that you want without somebody tagging along like a piece of Velcro, if you stop and look at every tree or stone or whatever. It's great. We don't have to be hooked up with other people. We don't have to be legally married to function today. We don't have to do that. And my dear friend, she's very active in socializing around, meeting friends, and she took me, and this was a very special yesterday afternoon, to Mary Huling's house, Mary, Clark Huling's widow, and she's lovely. So, I got to see some wonderful paintings at the house. Now what is your lady's first name?

Glenys.

Okay. So, you guys call me sometime. I'm leaving at the end of August to go. I was going to do three months here, or three months in the States, and three months there. So, I'm going to see how that works out. I had all this planned in my brain before I met this very nice gentleman, and my husband knew right away. He said, "No, we've been to Italy about 25 times."

Oh, boy.

I loved it; I love it. I've been in the classes over there, and he said, "You know, when I die..." We would talk about the future, and I said, "You are not dying. No, no, no, you are going to live to be 100." He said, "No, when I die, within a year you are going to be in Italy. You are going to be living in Italy." I said, "Probably." So, all my friends know that I want to go back to Italy, and maybe rent for a year. So, I've been working on a visa.

Oh, yeah, right.

Oh, god, with EU it's so difficult now. You have to show six months of bank statements, two years of your tax reports, medical plan, what you have, all your investments.

You got to show everything.

You got to show everything. I didn't have everything organized, went out there thinking, okay, I'm going to Italy next week. I left January the 1st , and I thought I could be gone for six months. I have a visa. She's like, "No, no, no. First of all, you have to apply for permission."

"Okay, I'll just stay three months this time." Took my cat with me.

Took your cat with you?

Sure. That's my baby. He had all of his documents. He was fine. They just looked at me thinking, "Okay."

See these signs right here, these yellow signs? They are for movie shoots. To direct the crew.

Okay. There was something being filmed two days ago downtown.

What were the initials?

Oh, god, what was it? It's one word on television, the name of it.

LM is Longmire. There's a whole bunch of them around here.

They had the food crews out there on the sidewalk right in front of the palace. Okay, and they were filming.

Yeah, they were doing Burro Alley there.

Yeah, that's where they were.

I don't know what they were shooting.

Well, it's one word, just kind of like Alamo, or I don't know.

Is it Scalp?

Could be. It's one word, and I thought maybe that's part of a new television program, or it's for a television movie or something. I don't know. But it was one word. Because we thought about going in there, but it was all reserved at the Palace for the crew.

I'll get in touch with you when we arrive there.

Oh, yeah, please do, it's just lovely. Wonderful beach to walk on, wonderful grocery store right downtown, independent. You've got everything right there. And if you play golf, there's a wonderful little golf course there.

I do, but I haven't because of my shoulder. I have an issue.

My husband had an issue. He had a specialist in San Francisco. He had a torn ligament. It was awful. He rolled a golf cart; it just ruined his shoulder.

Oh my god.

So, they did a reverse technique in San Francisco, and it was wonderful. So, if I see you again...

What does that mean, a reverse technique?

Well, you know, how it would go this way - they would flip it around.

Oh, yeah, right.

And so, the kids would say, "Well, dad, when you turn your shoulder this way, you are going to be going that way." I said, "No, no, no, no, no." But they do all these wonderful and special stuff up there. It was his left, no, it was the right shoulder. Yeah, it was the right shoulder. But there are some wonderful surgeons out there working on shoulders. We call it the poor man's Cypress, you know Cypress in...

Yeah, right.

Well, poor man's Cypress golf course is right there in PG. You can walk to it, and it's right there on the ocean. Wonderful! How busy is it during the Indian Market thing that they have here?

In August the whole town is pretty busy.

Yeah,

For locals, I don't go downtown during that period of time.

That's the way we are in Carmel when AT&T is playing.

Oh, yeah, right.

Yeah, that's what we have. I have friends who collect Indian art, and they come every year. They say, "Maybe you should come with us."

Well, it's interesting once or twice.

Yeah.

I've done it. I've been here 31 years. I've seen a lot of it. I go down every once in a while.

Yeah.

Sometimes I like to go at 6:00 in the morning, so that I don't have to deal with the heat or the crowds.

I wouldn't like that too; the crowd makes drivers crazy. Everybody wants to go to Carmel. Bye.

Thank you so much. Have a good flight.

— HELP WITH PARENTS —

Are you John?

Yeah. What brings you here, just vacation?

No, I've moved here. My dad is 86 and his wife is quite ill, and he's in an assisted care place. He needs family here. It's too easy to have things looked through. We had a caretaker who was kind of caring for both of them, and we found out this last weekend that she has been verbally abusing my father. I grew up in west Texas.

Oh my god. That is terrible.

I am a little stressed about it.

I pick up quite a few older people from Quail Run.

I live there; I live with those old people. He lives at Montecito, and then she is at Sierra Vista. When I showed the picture of the caretaker, because the caretaker knew where I lived, to security, and said, "Do not let this woman on the premises." They were like, "We need to talk to you about the elder care abuse and filing a claim." They thought my dad was living on site, and they were like, "You need to go talk to Montecito about filing the claim," I was like, "Aha, I am on my way." There were lots of really old people. We started staying there I guess like 19 years ago when my son was itty bitty. We would come out here for the summer, because Austin was hot and unpleasant to stay in the summer. So, for about 14 years we would always come here and rent an apartment. When I came in October I thought 'things aren't going well for my dad.' He called and said, "We need a place. Rent us a place. It's better that way." So what hours do you drive?

I drive during the day sometimes, part time.

Not bad. And do you keep both apps on, and just switch back and forth?

Yeah.

Santa Fe seems very friendly for ride sharing. Is it?

Yeah, it's very friendly. I have had over 3,000 rides, and I've never had a problem.

That's great. I think that's wonderful. Like I said, we live in downtown Austin, and my husband kind of drove for several years, and it made all the difference.

Yeah, I know. It does.

So, do you find you get more tourists or locals?

I was analyzing that this morning. I think about 60-40. 60% tourists and 40% locals.

And then they spike I guess over the summer?

Yeah.

I think it's wonderful. So, here's one of my funniest Lyft going to work stories. I got into the car, and there was an older gentleman. I said, "How did you get into this?" He goes, "Well, I retired." I thought that makes sense. He goes, "My wife and I discovered we were at home the same time." And I said, "Oh?" He said he wanted to buy a car and she said no. He said, "Now, in order to drive Lyft, I got to buy a car. We are not always home at the same time, and everybody is much happier."

That is funny.

Can't you just see it? He was a funny man. Now there's Lyft in Albuquerque as well?

Yeah.

That's nice. Are there other ride shares or sharing services that have tried coming in too or is it just the two of you?

I think there is another one here in town called 'BOLT' that only does Teslas.

That's pretty cute. In Austin we have Ride Texas, Fasten, Get Me, which their navigation system never could find me. And there is another one where you can schedule rides. I can't remember what it's called.

You can schedule rides on Uber; I don't think you can schedule on Lyft.

Can you hold two walkers in your trunk?

Yeah.

Would you consider doing it on Saturday night?

I don't work on Saturday night.

Well, can I get your information?

I will give you my card.

Good. So that if I need things done for my dad...

Yeah.

That will be great, because he needs a high up car to get in. My husband and I ended up buying an SUV because it holds his walker, and he can get in it. I made it through two kids with no SUV, and then I started looking at people who were driving SUVs. They are all my age. They are not kids. So that would be a big help.

Here's my card.

Thank you, John. Excellent. Okay, one bag in, and I need to schedule. So mainly 8:00 to 4:00. It's a big help.

If you need any help with your parents though, let me know, and I will hook you up with my lady.

Okay
Thank you.

— ARCHITECT —

I was just settling in when I got a call that I was needed at a client's house.

So, you're going to a client's right now?

Yeah. I'm an architect.
It's at the very top of Cerro Gordo?

It's a good-ways up, I guess. It's pretty close to the trail head up there.

Should I go up Canyon Road or Cerro Gordo?

Good question. You know, I never drive up there.

I see. I think Canyon Road will be a little bit quicker.

It might be. I think usually that's the way we have gone, because we go by the Gentle Nudge School, which is there.

Yeah, right, right, right. My son went to Gentle Nudge.

Oh, really?

Twenty-seven years ago.

Oh! I always feel like, you know, it should be, the Gentle Nudge Elementary, and then, like, the Firm Hand Middle School.

Oh, yeah, I see!

And then, the Hard Shove High School. And then, the University of Hard Knocks! Any idea what was happening on Siringo this morning? It looked like they had the whole thing sort of...

Blocked off.

Yeah.

Accident?

You know, I don't know. So, I was coming...

I didn't see it.

I was on, what was it, Yucca, and normally to get to the office, I turn right on Siringo. And that was all blocked off. And then, I saw on Llano, the bottom of Llano was blocked off at Siringo. And I couldn't see anything else, but it seems like almost that whole section of it was blocked off around the school. I wasn't sure if there was anything going on there.

Could have been.

I know. Nowadays, you know...

I didn't hear about it though. Nowadays, you never know what's going to happen.

Yeah.

I took you to work the other day.

I remember. I was telling somebody the other day about, I think you told me about the guy who walks around Santa Fe. You know, the wounded Vietnam era veteran.

Oh, yeah. David. He hurt his leg and left arm in a tank explosion in the '60's, and ever since then he has had to wrap it every day, and walk ten miles to keep his circulation up.

Yeah. I was telling somebody else about it. After that my wife and I passed him at some point, and just as you said, he was looking down to the left, and we actually saw him bend down and pick something up, and put it in his little bag.

Yeah. Everyone's got a story.

Yeah.

You never know what it is either. He is one of the more interesting guys around town. Very well liked within his church. And he dog sits sometimes.

I can't quite seem to wake up today.

Wow! I like to take naps. At my age I like to take one every day.

Yeah. I just try to keep awake with coffee, but I think a nap is a much better idea than coffee.

I took a course on coffee and milk about 40 years ago. It said if you drink more than three cups of coffee a day, your best investment is a dialysis machine.

Oh, really?

For your kidneys. And they said about milk, that it is the cause of osteoporosis in our society. In Third World countries, Africa, they don't have osteoporosis.

No?

What happens is, is that, what this seminar taught was that cow's milk is good for big bones quick and small brains - what cows have. It's good for cows. But with humans, we don't know how to digest that milk in the same way a cow does, but when you put a protein into your body, part of the digestive process for protein is it sucks your natural

298 · EVERYONE'S GOT A STORY

calcium out of your body. So, when you are eating more protein, particularly supplementing it with milk in addition to meats and stuff like that, it's that you are not only sucking your natural calcium out, but the calcium that you are putting in with your cow's milk is non-digestible. So, that's why in Third World countries, they don't have a lot of osteoporosis.

Are goat's milk and...

No. Different.

Is it better?

They said our bodies can digest it better.

I wonder about cheese made from cow's milk, if there is anything with the process there.

Yeah, I know.

You know, growing up, I didn't actually drink much milk, because I've always hated it.

You've always hated milk?

Yeah. And I am...

Lactose intolerant?

Somewhat lactose intolerant. I don't know if it's possible to be so. You know, I've come to think lately it's not even necessarily the lactose in the milk, because I switched from... You know, just in cereal and stuff, from, you know, just regular milk to organic milk, and it sits so much better with me. So, it might just be...

The organic milk sat better with you?

Yeah. So, it might be the hormones or drugs or whatever in milk that was bothering me rather than the lactose. But I grew up not drinking much milk, but eating a lot of cheese.

A lot of cheese?

Yeah. I've never broken a bone.

When I was a little boy in Oak Creek, I'd walk over to our neighbor's house, Clyde Etter, to get our milk. We'd go down to the barn and milk Elsie the cow, and sometimes squirt milk in the cat's face from the udder. We'd put the milk in these glass gallon jars, and watch as the cream would rise to the top. I hated the cream, but my mother loved it. Where did you grow up? Wisconsin?

No, Maryland.

Maryland? I see.

No real connection between location and the cheese, just, you know, I just liked it. Yeah, Maryland doesn't have a lot of dairy farms.

Yeah, but I think they make cheese almost in every state. The vegans have a cheese they make from tapioca root. I think it's called Daiya Cheese.

Oh, really.

They make cheeses here in New Mexico, that's for sure, in all different ways. My youngest daughter was lactose intolerant growing up, and as an adult has had major digestive problems. I remember her sitting in her high chair and me feeding her a jarred baby food called Blueberry Buckle. Evidently it had milk or something in it, because shortly after I gave it to her it came shooting out of her mouth in a steady stream for about six feet.

Boy. Maryland is more of a fishing and crabbing state, though I don't eat crab.

I don't either.

I don't eat shellfish.

I don't either. I don't do shellfish at all. My mother in her seventies became allergic to shrimp and other shellfish. One time she had an allergic reaction where her body ballooned up within minutes of eating the shrimp, and she couldn't breathe. It's called anaphylaxis.

Yeah. I don't eat shellfish, but a lot of my family who live in Maryland, they sure do, you know, the crab capital. And my girlfriend's family... My girlfriend? My wife! That was a slip! My wife's family lives in Maine.

Wow!

And, you know, that's the lobster capital.

Right.

And then, we go see some of her extended family on Cape Cod, which is, you know, scallops and that. And so, everywhere we go, I can't really eat the thing that comes from there.

Now, why is it you don't eat mollusks?

That's a good question. It's partly being Kosher, but it's partly I just never liked it. So, I don't eat pork either. I haven't eaten pork since I was 13.

Do you eat beef?

I do eat beef. I think I should give up beef, but...

I haven't had beef in 40+ years.

It is so delicious! I'd like to give it up. My wife is a vegetarian. Well, she's a pescatarian. She eats fish. But, yeah, I don't know. You know, the thing is, I don't really eat meat at home. I only eat it when we go out.

She doesn't like to cook?

Well, she doesn't like to cook, and, you know, she's told me, "You know, if you want to cook meat, you can cook meat," but

I don't want to cook a meal for myself.

Just don't do it here in the house!!!

Yeah, that's true. But, you know, she doesn't even mind it. Like, when we go visit her family, if they are grilling meat, she likes the smell of grilling meat. But, you know, I'm just not going to have it in my home.

Yeah.

Cook a whole, like, steak or something just for myself to eat, and then she'd have to make a meal for herself. You know, if she's out of town, I'll make beef but mostly... So, I eat probably less meat than most people, because I only really eat it when we go out. But, you know, it's hard to give anything up entirely, especially brisket.

Brisket?

Yeah.

I was a raw foodist for 10 years.

Really?

Nuts, seeds, vegetables and fruits.

Why did you stop?

My kids thought I looked too gaunt. And my lady didn't like it. You know, with raw food, you graze all day. You don't really sit down and have a meal. She missed that. So, now I eat fish, a little bit of organic chicken and turkey. The problem is, when you go out to restaurants and stuff, you never really know what you're getting, whether it's farm raised fish or just regular chicken. I just like to eat more of the organic, wild side of things. We always split an entree.

Yeah. At least, you know, restaurants are becoming a little more conscious of it.

They are. Some of them are, yeah.

So, you know, you can at least... You know, even at, like, Harry's, they now say on their menu, "We use organic eggs." And I don't remember if their chicken is or not.

Yeah, I know. A lot of people are allergic to eggs.

Counter Culture is probably pretty good for organic eggs. I like it there. I don't go there very often either, because it's sort of out of the way, but I've always had a good meal whenever I've gone. I want to try, there is a new Persian place.

Yeah, up there on Canyon Road. I think it's called Milad's. I haven't tried that yet.

Me neither. My boss did. He said it was good. I haven't tried that. Do you know if... Oh, what's it called? I'm blanking on the name. But somebody drove into them.

Jambo's.

Jambo's. Do you know if they are open again?

They are. I went the first day.

Oh, really?

I had lunch there a while ago. I like the owner. He's created a foundation that supports a whole medical clinic on this island off the coast of Kenya where he's from. He supports it from the proceeds of this restaurant. That is one of the reasons the city supports him so well, I think.

That's really great. Well, it's good to know they're open. My father-in-law is in town, so maybe I will suggest we go there for lunch or something. Yeah, I wanted to support them while they were closed, but I was never really motivated to sit in the parking lot.

I did it once. We got it to go from their truck. It was good.

Were they just serving from the truck, and still using their kitchen, do you know?

No, they were using the truck kitchen. Well, they may have been prepping back there. I don't really know.

Yeah. My wife and I, we did the reservoir loop trail the other day.

How was it?

It was good, except we got to the end, and then it said no trespassing, like the last half mile of it.

Is that right?

And we couldn't figure out how we were supposed to get out. And so, we clambered down the hill at a couple of places, and there was a big fence in the way. So, eventually we just did the rest of... You know, we went in reverse. Hey, thank you.

Ok. Thank you.

∞

— FISH —

Welcome. What brings you to Santa Fe?

Just vacation. See the sights. It's a lot different than Monterey.

Oh, I'm probably going to be up there pretty soon. What do you do in California?

Well, I'm a research scientist at an NGO. I do a lot of paperwork now, but I used to work in the field with aquaculture. I've done research on many different types of species and systems all over the world.

For fish that are grown? Aquaculture, is that a term for farming fish?

Yes, that's a term for fish farming.

You study that all over the world?

Yeah. Our main goal is to access the sustainability of all fish that come into the U.S. seafood market. And the U.S. imports like nearly 90% of its seafood supply.

America does? From where?

From everywhere.

And what percent of that is farmed as opposed to wild?

I don't know exactly, but currently its somewhere around 50%, but the farm portion is growing, particularly because consumption is growing. There are fish farms in the U.S. as well. In the south, there are fish farming operations for like shrimp, catfish, and tilapia. You get some salmon farming up north on the edges, and then you also have people doing recirculating aquaculture on land.

So, are most of these aquaculture operations, are they actually farms in the ocean that are netted?

Some are, yes.

Is that the typical way to farm fish, or are there other common ways of farming fish?

Well, there are a lot of ways. It depends on the fish you're farming, and the environment you're farming in.

One of the reasons I'm asking this is that I read this article about the ten kinds of foods to avoid, and one of them is always farm raised salmon. Now, we eat a lot of salmon. And I'm like, 'Oh, my god, I shouldn't get farm raised salmon.' And then I started researching it, and one of the

reasons that I read is that there is a lot of fish poop that sinks to the bottom. And it's not cleaned out or properly hydrated. What is the truth here, and what is your view of that?

Well, first of all I know the exact article. I absolutely hate it. I've seen it in many different iterations. It's one of the things that gets me really angry. It's this article that says a lot of random things that is designed to make you really worried and scared about your food, but it doesn't really back it up. As far as the question of feces in fish farms, that is one of the things that we evaluate when we are researching the sustainability of a farm. Because, yes, fish do poop. But, there are like nets in the ocean or lakes, the impact to the bottom of the water body is about the same. What really is important is that there is enough current to moves things, and in most countries where there is salmon farming the basic government regulations are pretty stringent. So, the idea that you have a net full of fish and the poop falls to the bottom, and doesn't do anything, is a bit far-fetched.

Well, in my mind's eye, when I was a little boy, I grew up by a creek and they had hatcheries. Or fisheries. A hatchery is a fish farm, right? Well, they had several hatcheries right there in the canyon to stock the creek. Now, are those farm raised fish?

Absolutely! The techniques employed at hatcheries are the exact same as used in a commercial fish farm. In fact, sometimes, the feed they use is exactly the same. So, yes, if you are catching a wild salmon in most places there is a good chance it was raised in a hatchery to begin with, then stocked, and it may just have been released into the wild for two days to two weeks.

One of the things is I go into Whole Foods, and I go to their fish department...

Yeah, I know. I'm very well acquainted with the Whole Foods fish department. I actually used to work with them in their sustainability sourcing. I used to do audits for them, and manage the audits they did at their fish farm facilities.

Well, that is my question. I go up there and look at their fish, and it says, I just tell you what goes on in my mind. I mean I eat a lot of fish. My lady is from Wales, she just loves fish.

I think it's a British Isles kind of thing.

Well, I was a raw foodist for ten years. I didn't eat any kind of fish or any animals. Now I go up there, and it says Wild Caught Alaskan Salmon. Then it says Farmed Raised Atlantic Salmon. Now, somewhere in the chronicles of my mind someone told me that there are no more wild Atlantic salmon. So, I don't know if there is any truth to that, but someone has told me that you can only buy farm raised Atlantic salmon. Then, these reports about farm raised salmon being the second leading cause of cancer.

I've never seen that before. What kind of cancer?

Oh yeah. Well, I don't know what kind of cancer.

I'd definitely like to take a look at that research.

Anyway, it's on the list of top ten.

Who puts out this list?

I don't know.

You've got to know your sources John.

I'll find out.

Yeah, I'm really interested in taking a look at that list.

But in my mind's eye, farm raised could be better. I mean particularly when you factor in Fukushima, you know. How risky is that for the wild caught Alaskan salmon from the Pacific Ocean? What am I supposed to be doing about salmon?

That was a big deal for a while. I know, it is tough to navigate when you don't have a background. Let alone when you do. It's something we talk about every day. I mean not the wild versus farmed. Because in our minds they are equivalent. But just the safety of both. You can have great farming operations and poor farming operations. You can have great wild fishery operations and terrible ones.

Now the other day, I learned that farmed raise salmon need carotene to get their color.

Yes, well, this is an essential antioxidant that occurs naturally in their diet. The carotenoid is called astaxanthin, and there are plenty of natural sources, like a yeast called *Pfaffia*, that you can use to produce it for fish feed without risking overfishing for wild sources. Wild caught salmon also get this carotenoid directly from their diet, since it naturally occurs in things like krill. If the feed companies didn't include this carotenoid, it could harm the fish's health, especially its reproductive health. The fact that it impacts the color of the flesh is a secondary effect that is rarely used anymore to market the fish. Also, different salmonids tend to have different flesh colors, so a Sockeye would always be very red, while a trout might be barely pink.

Now how did you get into fish?

I've always been into biology in general. My dad is a chemist. My mom's a nurse. I was always exploring the natural world in my backyard. I used to raise bees, and then dissect them under a microscope. My mom thought I was crazy. I never got bit by a bee until I was eighteen.

Let me tell you my bee story. When I was about ten, we studied bees in Cub Scouts. My friend Tim knew of a bee hive down in the ravine in a tree by his house. We got cheesecloth, covered ourselves, and started a little fire to make some burning sticks to stick into the hive. We thought we could find some honey. Well, the bees were going all crazy. We didn't find any honey, so we left. The

next day the Forest Service showed up at school, pulled us out of class and took us to their office. Our parents were there waiting for us. Boy, did we ever get a lecture. Seems like our bee endeavors started three or four trees on fire, and could have started a really big fire.

Wow!

Now in regard to my diet, you don't think there is a concern with me eating Atlantic farm raised salmon, do you?

No. And, I think there is a way to do it responsibility. The farmed fish at Whole Foods have to pass higher fish flesh quality standards as far as toxins go than the wild does, even though the wild is monitored by the U.S. government. You have to pass a higher threshold to sell your farmed fish to Whole Foods than you do if you sell wild caught fish. For instance, the government tests for 35 PCB's while Whole Foods tests for 209 of them.

Wow, that was fast. Here we are. Enjoy Santa Fe.

Thanks. Bye.

∞

— BLIND PERSON —

Welcome. Do you need help there?

No, I got it.

My daughter teaches people who are blind.

Oh, really?

Yeah, she's-- down in the Phoenix area. She's been teaching for a long time.

Oh, wow.

Like 25, 26 years.

So, teaching them in what way?

Well, she has...

The adaptability skills or...?

She has...

Like school teaching?

She has a class of preschoolers, through I think, sixth grade.

Oh, wow!

And then in the evening and on Saturdays she teaches adult orientation and mobility with a different program. She teaches cane management, listening at intersections, people with guide dogs...the whole nine yards.

Yes.

How did you get blind?

It's...

Progressive...

It's degenerative, yeah.

Degenerative?

Yeah, it's gotten worse over the years. But, I've been faithful to the local cab company until they closed last week.

I know.

Oh, no, no, my god no, the cab company closed.

It's pretty easy. Uber is pretty easy.

Yes, it's the smartphone. That's the trick.

Yeah, well, that's why they have this GoGo.

Yeah, my friend read that in the newspaper, researched it for me, I said, "Hey that's for me."

That's for me. We have – I have three or four riders that use GoGo Grandparents.

Are they fairly happy with it? I just have a flip phone.

They love it.

So why would I buy an iPhone, and pay $100 a month for service I only use once a week.

Well.

I know I could walk to DeVargas Mall, but today in this distracted driving world it makes me very nervous to have to cross at crosswalks.

I bet it does. The last time my daughter was here I had a big discussion about what she does with adults, and she taught me all about street crossings. That it's quite a chore to cross streets.

Yes.

What percent are you blind?

Oh, I can't even see the eye chart.

Aha.

I can see lights and darks.

Lights and darks?

Yeah. You definitely have to put your big girl panties on to go out walking with a cane in a place you don't know, because you don't know what's coming next. I've got my cane stuck in things. I've stepped off a curb to cross the streets, and they have one of those big drains, and I almost lost my cane, because I didn't realize it wasn't on solid ground. And that to me, that's the scariest part, when I can't touch ground.

Yeah.

I'm flagging down cars.

Boy, are you telling me?

But once you get used to it, being around...

Yeah, you've really got to listen at those intersections, don't you?

Yes, especially now with the hybrids, because they can sneak up on you.

Oh, they don't make any noise.

And if there's other cars around, you hear the other cars, but you can't hear the quiet one.

That's a real problem, isn't it?

Yeah.

You're goin' right out over here? Santa Fe Bar & Grille?

Yes.

Can I help you at all?

Oh, no, I've got this thank you.

Are you sure you've got it?

Yes, this is my favorite stop.

Okay.

Thank you, John.

Thank you so much.

∞

— ZACHARIAH —

Zachariah? You're Zachariah?

That's me. John?

You're still here at St. John's?

I am.

How long?

A couple of weeks out.

Then what are you going to do?

Right now, when I've been back to Houston, I've been working at a grocery store. They really liked me. They wanted to move me up to management, but I'm not certain I want to do that. I'm going to keep a few of my options open. I went to apply to a few of the museums in Houston to see if I could get a job in one of them. I just want to do a 9:00 to 5:00 schedule, get a decent paycheck and be around creativity.

You went to all four years at St. John's?

Actually, it took me five years. I ended up kind of messing up my second semester of my senior year back in 2013, and I took some time off trying to figure out what I wanted to do.

So, you came back to complete it?

Yeah.

Congratulations.

Thank you.

I guess sometimes you get the good things in life just by sticking to it.

Yeah. That's pretty much what I realized. I was spending a lot of time doing nothing and limping along, and I realized that was not what I wanted, that I had to make something happen and coming back here was confronting that.

A lot of traffic today.

Yeah. I've never known exactly what causes traffic in Santa Fe in the afternoon. Weird times, weird days. You lived here a while?

31 years. How old are you?

I'm 26. The town has changed a lot just in the four years I've been gone. I wonder how much it has changed over 31 years.

What's the number one thing that they teach at St. John's?

Do you know anything about it? It's kind of a weird curriculum.

The classics?

Right. Starts all the way back. I guess you can call the beginning the Iliad and the Odyssey, leads all the way up through this year. We just read 'The Dred Scott Decision Speech' by Abraham Lincoln. I think the number one thing that they teach here is really how to – I don't want to sound cliché - but really how to think for yourself, form your own opinions, because, you know, all these people, they disagree with each other throughout history, and you will have to come and rate how to weigh their arguments against each other and exactly what's valuable in an argument. You learn a lot about the structure of argument. They also teach you - this is going to sound clique - but really how to read a book, like how to really read a book and get the most out of it, and then how to hold a conversation, a very serious conversation about that book in a respectful manner, and also really kind of investigate it as a group. Ultimately, you kind of re-learn how to learn. No one ever teaches you that in school growing up, they just kind of feed you facts that you're supposed to know. This is true, because the teacher said so, and doing it this way you really kind of get to the basis of everything. You know when we learn math or science, we don't read out of a textbook. You go read a paper by whatever guy discovered that principle or that theory, and so we go straight to the primary source for information. We get to judge its validity on our own. It's very valuable. I think there's not a whole lot of...

It's very what?

It's very valuable. You feel like... There are not a whole lot of people these days who really go all the way down, and examine like their premises for thinking. They start at a point, and then they go from there. And it works for a lot of them; it works. Then you try to figure out the whole thing all over again. If I could go back, I would probably go to another school. This education cost a lot of money. Ultimately it's a BA in liberal arts, which in practicality terms, it doesn't go very far. There's a couple of RV's parked like right next to each other, and...

Okay, right over there. Thanks.

Bye.

∞

— PARKING GARAGE —

So we're going anywhere near the...

Plaza?

State capitol building.

And there's a parking garage next to it that we're going to.

Okay, the new parking lot, the new parking garage?

It seems pretty new, I don't know. First time we've been here.

Okay, we'll go down there and look around.

It's right across the street from the capitol building.

Right.

We got our car locked in there last night.

You got your car locked in there last night? How?

We missed the sign. It said locked at 9:00, and we showed up at 9:30, and we couldn't get to it.

Oh, boy. So, did you take a Lyft back?

We did. We took a Lyft back last night.

I hope they don't charge you for parking.

We'll see what happens. Yes.

We were wondering about that. There was a sign that said public parking, and there was no gate or sign on the entrance.

That said 9:00 o'clock?

Yes.

The only sign we had seen is as we came out the door. There wasn't a sign when we came out. But as we showed back up on the outside of the door there was a sign, but we didn't see it until we walked back to it. I hope we don't find a big ticket or a boot.

Have you ever had your car booted?

I never have, no.

I haven't either, that has to be quite a shock.

Yes.

Where are you all from?

Utah. Cedar City, Utah is where we're coming from.

Cedar City.

Southern Utah, kind of by St. George, if you know where that is.

How far are you from Zion and Bryce?

About an hour from Zion, and probably an hour and a half from Bryce.

What do people do in Cedar City?

A lot.

There's a university there.

Which university is there?

Southern Utah University is there.

I see.

And that's about it.

It's a small town.

It's located in a good place, if you like the outdoors. You can always get to somewhere cool.

How far are you from St. George?

It's about 40 minutes, 45 minutes.

How big is St. George?

I think there's about 150,000 people in the county. It's a pretty good size city. Its growing just incredibly fast.

From what?

I don't know. I think it's just that people like the weather and like to retire there. It's like one of the five fastest growing cities in the U.S., I think. I really don't know what else people do there. There is a lot of golfing, really good golfing.

When I was a boy, the big concern - I grew up in northern Arizona - the big concern over the St. George area was that the nuclear blasts were being done in Nevada.

Yes.

And they were sort of like downwind.

Yes, there's a generation of people who grew up at that time that have had a lot of health problems because of that.

Have they?

Yes. I think there was some sort of government payment for people who got cancer as a result.

They died, but they got some money from the government?

Yes, a little consolation, I guess.

What do you all do there?

We actually moved there a few weeks ago from Salt Lake City. I went to high school there.

He's going to do a little schooling there.

Yes, I'm going back to finish college.

Okay, folks.

Thank you very much for the ride.

∞

— STEM CELL CONFERENCE —

Beautiful day, isn't it?

It is. Where are you from?

Austin Texas.

What brings you to Santa Fe?

We are doing a stem-cell conference actually.

Is there a stem-cell conference here in town?

It's really small. There are like eight of us.

I have a shoulder issue, and I went to this guy who is not an MD – he's a DOM, Doctor of Oriental Medicine. He did an ultrasound on my shoulder, and said that I had a small tear on my rotator cuff, and that he could inject stem cells, and there were pretty good odds that it would grow back. My own stem cells.

Right, where was he going to harvest them?

I'm not sure.

So, you didn't do it?

I didn't do it. The regular doctor at Presbyterian sort of scared me from it. He said if it's really not done in a sterile environment you can get bacteria in there, and it can be disastrous.

Which is why I was surprised. I'm surprised you were going to use your own stem cells in a setting like that. I suspect they were going to use cord blood stem cells, which would be pre-packaged and fairly safe. But otherwise they are going to have to harvest from fat or bone marrow. Those are both surgical procedures. It's a fairly big deal, so I don't know how it can be your own stem cells. But I do think they are very helpful in orthopedics, and they have proven themselves in that area. You should feel safe if you do want it, and you think going down the path, someone who is a little bit more... I guess I would go back and kind of find out what it is they are really going to use. They can't really use your own stem cells, unless they are going to do it surgically, and that requires a surgical operating room.

No, it's not that. I thought he withdrew something with a needle.

Well, you can withdraw blood, and then filter blood and get plasma, which are protein, which has a little bit of stem cells. That's not the indication for a joint. For a joint you want pure stem cells, because it's a volume deal. You don't want to build a lot of volume into a joint, right? That doesn't feel good. Something sounds – either a miscommunication or something.

Or I just didn't understand. What's your specialty?

Environmental medicine.

What does that mean exactly?

Well, traditionally, it means I take care of occupations. So, for example, Chevron was one of my clients, and so I would really try to prevent disease in workers, and understand what would be the right inventory they need to comply from a regulatory standpoint. We need to do monitoring, and then placement, and if there was a disease process we can conduct experiments. But I retired from Chevron. I became interested more in the everyday person. That was more interesting to me. Now I have a genetics company, and I don't really see a lot of patients, but still it's interesting. So here I am.

Yeah, we had a big Bio-DNA conference here a couple of weeks ago. It was fascinating, all these DNA people in town.

Yeah. It must have been fun driving everyone around. It's pretty here.

Yeah.

Are you from this area?

31 years.

What made you move?

A woman.

Always a woman. Was it a good choice? Was it a good decision?

Yeah, we got divorced later on, but it was a good choice. We got a beautiful 31 year old boy. We are still great friends.

That's good. What happened?

I would say we grew apart, went different directions at the time.

What direction did she go in, and what direction did you go in?

That's a good question. I think we both went into solitude for a while. She's an artist and she really got into her art making and dream making and all that stuff, and I was into business and exploring different relationships.

Oh, I see, so you were more interested in looking at open relationships?

No, it has nothing to do with an open relationship. I just wanted to explore more, and just be involved with more people at the time. But she got married when she was 38; she'd been single all that time.

Did you marry young?

I married my first wife when I was 18. And then I was involved in that relationship for 14 – 15 years. I met my second wife, who was from Santa Fe, in New York.

What were you doing in New York?

Her booth was next to mine at a trade show in the gift and stationery business.

Well, that makes sense, so you went from one long term relationship to another long-term relationship.

And now I've been with my current lady for 15 years too.

Is that a better fit for you?

It seems to be a better fit, yeah.

That's all that matters. It's all about the fit, isn't it?

My lady is involved as friends with many different men and many different women all over the world and its fun for me to see her interfacing with all these different people. I am sort of a little bit of a home body. It is very interesting the way she operates her life. Very much different than me.

Are you her primary relationship, and vise versa?

Oh, yeah. We are definitely each other's primary relationship. She is not sexual with any of these people. I'm a complicated person to be with. I've always been with a woman, but I've always felt the most natural state is not to have a preset agenda of who to love, to be open to all relationships, women and men. I've certainly been attracted to a few men. But my lady and me, we are monogamous.

And would she stay there and watch you if you needed some kind of care?

Yeah. She's a natural born caregiver. She has an organization here in town that provides free homecare for people who fall through the gaps and cracks of our medical system. She has trained over 500 people to be caregivers.

She must be a dynamic lady.

Yes, indeed.

That's a very cool story.

It's fun to lead a full life.

Do you get to travel much?

I don't really like to travel. I have a business in Oregon that I go to every so often, and we vacation in La Jolla, California, so we go over there.

So, for you, fullness is defined by seeing a lot of different countries or people or...?

No. Fullness just is.

Yes, what I mean is, it's really interesting when you talk about people having to find a full life, it is so individual.

I know it is so individual.

You'll talk to different people, and they'll say I'm like happy fulltime. You try to find out why, and they may say they have someone who does things for them, or they just really want to explore the world, and they don't feel like they're really living until they do that.

For me, it's just about living in contentment. It's not about doing any one things. Okay. Nice sharing with you. Thank you so much.

Thank you.

∞

— LIBRARIAN —

How did you like Meow Wolf?

Oh, yeah, it was great.

Oh, yes. How long were you there?

We were there for two hours.

Two hours.

And how did you like it, young lady?

<u>I loved it.</u>

How old are you.

<u>Six.</u>

What brings you out to Santa Fe?

Just vacation. We drove through Albuquerque once, and said we should come back for a vacation one day. So here we are. I'm missing the mountains. No mountains in Missouri.

No mountains in Missouri? Wow! We got some good ones around here. What do you do for a living?

Well, I'm a librarian.

Librarian?

Yeah. So, you know...

How did you get into being a librarian?

Well, I used to be a special effects artist.

Special effects artist?

Yes, my undergrad was in – I did theatre technical design.

I used to work for Sony Pictures out in Culver City. So, I did that for a while, and then I moved out of L.A. But unless you work at night on the theatre circuit, that's the only way you're going to make a living as a technical designer, so you don't ever see anybody during the day. You can't do anything, because you work at night.

Okay, right.

Right, so I was working for a television program in New York. I left L.A. and went to New York. I was working for a TV show back in New York, but it got canceled. And then I was a substitute teacher, and I went back to school to get my Masters in Education. I was a high school teacher for 14 years.

Oh, wow!

And then I kind of got tired of that – they kept changing things, they kept changing laws, they kept changing rules and all this – I decided, I was just like well, you know what, education is kind of going to the dogs. I think I need to get out. So, I went back to school to get my Masters in Library Science, and here I am.

Now, what do you mean education is going to the dogs?

Okay. So just one – there are a couple of things that are bad. When I went to school they could still actually do something to children that misbehave in school.

All right.

Most ill-behaved children, because of bad parenting, they don't spend any time with their kid. They give them a video game console or set them in front of the TV, and let him do whatever they want to do. I know people have to work, but other parents have worked before and still spent time with their children, with the kids. So, they expect the school to raise the children. But because you can't put your hands on them, you can't expel them or discipline them, and they know it, they act crazy and they disrupt education all day along. And then, so there is no teaching going on, because you're babysitting 30 kids at a time instead. Because two kids can disrupt the entire classroom, and keep you from teaching. I just got tired of being held accountable for things I couldn't control. You won't – I can't control the kid's behavior, but you want them to have passed the test scores.

That's right.

And they come to me two grades behind. I just got sick of it, so I went out.

Well, the test scores determine how much money the schools get.

Right, and whether or not I kept my job. So that's the real thing.

They want you to test as opposed to teaching.

Right. I can't teach grammar anymore. I'm able to teach it, but I can't teach grammar. What kind of stuff is that? It was just crazy. And so I was like this is – it seems like it was a plot to make people stupid over a period of years. Like they kept making legislation, it seems like it was – it almost seems like deliberate sabotage to me. That's why I got out. At least in the library I'm with people that want to read and want information. Yeah, okay. And now I'm done.

I'd like to include this conversation in my book.

Sure.

Because it's important what you're saying there.

Yeah. You don't go into teaching for the money. You don't take out $50,000 or so of loans for a $35,000 a year job, which you turned out not to be a fit, and it turns out to be a $150,000 by the time you paid it off over twenty years. And then you have stuff like the kid doesn't do the work, and because the principal doesn't want that kid's parents to complain, we have to come in and change grades.

Well, tell me about library science stuff these days as far as... has the whole library thing changed itself?

Well, mostly the card catalog now is digital. Most libraries still use either Dewey Decimal or the Library of Congress system. A lot of old – a lot of newer libraries have gone straight into the Library of Congress system as opposed to Dewey Decimal. The library loan system has expanded, so now it's multinational. So now you can go in the index and find any book anywhere in the world, and have it sent to you, which is great, except for very special books. Some books they won't let leave the library. You have to actually go to that library. But mostly it's still actually the same, even though things have become computerized.

How about computers? Aren't there like computer stations in libraries now?

Yeah. We have computer stations to help you find stuff digitally. But for people that are going to school, you can't just go online and get your resource. It has to be a vetted resource, which means you got to go to the library, because like the library has subscriptions to like the American Journal of Psychology and all these other scientific periodicals, which to get a subscription these days costs $40,000, $50,000, $60,000.

Oh, I see.

Well, so the library can afford to get that subscription, and to allow you to get – it doesn't qualify, like if you buy the magazines that cost $40,000. But if you want the digital archive of everyone you've ever published at the beginning of their time, if you were able to download and print, then you got to pay that fee, right? So, people that are doing papers and stuff, they need to have sources that you can use in the bibliography. They still have to go to a library. And of course, little kids still like to go. Their parents care about their reading. There is still the summer reading program, still a lot of stuff going on.

It's changed a lot, but even now you can go – you don't have to get the physical book. You can go to the library, and get your library card. You can go online now to the library's website, and download the book to your Kindle or whatever. It will expire in two weeks or whatever and then it automatically erases off of your thing or you can renew it, if you want to renew it. That still counts as a patron, even when you do that, it counts as a visit. So that's how they get their money. They get their money based on population, and how many people use the library.

So as long as you keep finding new ways that count, every person that logs in – that's why when you go to a library that you have a little code to log on to. That's one of the reasons they do that. There are other reasons where they have to trace what people do, not what people do, but if something – somebody does something bad, they got to say, well, this person was there at this time. That's Federal, because otherwise you could be like a terrorist or something, going to a public library, and using it to destroy something, and walk away. So you can't do that. But it also counts – it also is a way to tell each person, and that person counts as a visit to keep their money up. So, it's got a little bit more complicated, but it's basically the same. I don't think it's changed that much, just gadgets and gadgets, and more gadgets.

Have the number of users increased in libraries?

You know, it's funny. Actually, for a couple of years it was going down. But now that all the libraries have started...Because there is still a remarkable number of people that don't have the internet, and that don't do video streaming. There are no more video stores around anymore. You got Redbox, and you might find one or two places that actually rent DVDs or...

There are no CDs anymore, or DVDs.

Right, but you can go to the library and get them.

Oh, yeah.

If you have a library card, you give them $4.50 or whatever they charge, and you can get it that way. There is always going to be a need for that. There is right now. If you go to most libraries, you'll find cassette tapes. Yeah. You'll still find VHS cassette tapes. And you're not going to find that anywhere else. A lot of things, like if you were talking about a jazz CD that was made in 1940 or something, it's not going to exist on a digital download. You have to get the original, or a copy of the original, and the library is the only place you can get it. So, and it's not obsolete yet. They've tried, but it's always going to be useful at least in some respect.

Okay, hey thank you so much. Now for my younger riders I always give them a $2.00 bill. So here you are.

<u>Oh, thank you.</u>

Thank you. You all have a good day.

— CROSS THE BRIDGE —

All righty, beautiful day. Headed for a massage.

It is very nice. Where are you from?

Michigan.

What part?

Right outside Detroit area. We have nothing like this there.

Nothing like this.

No. Are you from here originally?

31 years.

Oh, wow, originally from?

Sedona, Arizona.

Okay. Sedona is a similar vibe with here?

Similar kind of people live in both places.

Yeah, laid back, vortexes everywhere. hiking, more arts like here. I actually was just in Sedona.

Well, you were?

Yeah. My trip was Arizona and New Mexico. So, I did Sedona and now I'm here. I've never been here before, and I just absolutely love it.

What do you do in Michigan?

I'm an elementary school special education teacher.

Do you have both brilliant students and developmentally challenged?

Great question. I do. So, I'm a learning specialist, and my role works with kids that are exceptionally bright, but are disruptive like in one specific area. So, it comes out that they have a learning disability. And then I have other kids that are at average intelligence, and some kids that definitely are below the whole range. And then I've worked with students with severe cognitive developmental disabilities.

My daughter teaches students who are blind.

Oh, wow. Is she here?

Phoenix area.

Okay. It's got to be a challenging rewarding job.

She's been doing it for 25 plus years.

Oh, wow. Next year will be my 11th, and you can really get burned out. You get burned out. Does she like being in the Phoenix area?

Yeah.

So, you like Santa Fe more than Sedona?

Oh, completely different for me. Yeah, the great thing about growing up in Sedona back in the early '50s is that all of us kids are still friends. We did a lot of things together. Sometimes we'd go to the movies, which in the early days consisted of a screen they pulled up from a metal tube, maybe ten or twelve folding chairs on a dirt way under the stars. We'd do dances, plays, skating and we played a lot of sports.

That's really nice. Did you raise your kids there, or did you raise them in Phoenix?

I raised my kids in Tucson.

Okay. Great. In Sedona, you grew up in in a small community. New Mexico is pretty cool. We're going to check out Taos tomorrow.

Very nice. You should go to Ojo Caliente.

The hot springs resort? How far is that from Taos?

Well, it's on the way to Taos.

Oh, you pass it?

Well, there's three or four ways to get to Taos.

Tell me the way where I won't be on crazy, scary roads. I don't like crazy, scary stuff.

Yeah. But they're all pretty crazy.

Tell me the truth.

I'm telling you.

Should I take the high, is the high road the scariness or the low road?

Well, I'd take the back road, because I'd go through Ojo Caliente, and then you go on up to Tres Piedras and you cross the bridge.

Oh, I'm not going to cross that bridge! I've looked at pictures of it. I can't look at it. I'll close my eyes.

Okay. So, then I'd just take the low road up and the high road down. One up and one down, just because then you can see all the scenery of northern New Mexico.

Awesome. And I don't have to cross the bridge if I do that?

Right.

Okay. My cousin wants to cross the bridge, and I told him he can drive out and do it.

A lot of people have committed suicide off that bridge.

I'm sure. It's close to 600 feet in the air.

Yes, it's high. They put a big huge fence across it now.

People can't jump?
Right.

We'll check out 10,000 Waves tomorrow on the way home.

It's really nice. How did you hear about this massage place? Did the hotel refer you?

There were a few different places that I looked up. Have you heard of this one? The reviews were amazing just like a hidden gem.

Here we are. Hope you enjoy your massage.

Perfect. Thank you so, so much.

∞

— PAINTER —

Yeah, let's just put those bags back here.

Okay. Thank you. Do you live on Garcia Street?

Yeah.

Oh, yes. One of our neighbors said she really liked you.

Yeah, I live on Garcia...

She likes all the handsome men though.

I see. I see.

Is this a new RAV4?

This is a 2014 RAV4.

Wow! We have a 2010 RAV4; this is sure a lot better than ours.

I was going to get a 2016, but they didn't have a CD player in it. It's all Bluetooth.

Oh, gosh.

And my lady has so many CDs. Where are you folks headed today?

Minneapolis, Minnesota.

You go through Phoenix?

Right. It's sure nice we got the rain.

Yeah. How long have you folks lived here in Santa Fe?

Since 91'. How about you?

Since 86'.

It's really changed over that period, hasn't it? But still it's terrific.

Did you relocate here from Minneapolis?

Los Angeles.

Oh, Los Angeles, me too.

Oh, really?

I've been here 31 years. I was in L.A. for 10 years before that.

Oh, really?

What part of L.A. did you live in?
The west side. Where did you live?

West Hollywood. My daughter went to UCLA.

Yes, I did too. I grew up in Silver Lake.
I was born in Los Angeles.

Oh, you were?

Yeah, 1946. But I moved to Sedona when I was six.

Nice. You saw that grow up. They used to do a lot of films there.

That's what attracted my father. He was a movie buff, and he went to Pasadena Playhouse School to be an actor. Anyway, he got into another profession, and he decided to

move to Sedona. He used to take me out every weekend to watch the movies being made. I mean, I met people like John Crawford, Glenn Ford, Richard Widmark, all these old timers.

Yeah, it's sort of a hometown business there. Get a horse and a big hat and off you go.

I helped start a company in L.A. called Day Runner, that makes the Day Runner Organizer that you keep your notes and addresses in.

Oh, yes.

I sold out of that in 1986, and moved here to Santa Fe.

Oh, how terrific. Well, it must be fun to be an Uber driver.

I love it.

Because you work at your schedule, I guess.

You work at your schedule. I do it for a bunch of different reasons, but I'm doing a book and maybe a movie on my Uber riders.

Oh, great.

I make recordings and notes. I've done over 3,000 rides so far in a year, and it's fascinating the people that I meet.

Yeah, I would think so, particularly in Santa Fe.

Okay 3,000 rides, wow. I looked up this app. Do you know anything about it? GoGo Grandparent?

Yes, I pick up a lot of people who use that. Particularly people who are older. Like my lady. She can't figure out how to use a Smartphone, believe it or not.

Right, I believe it. It's very complicated.

She still uses the landline. So, people who use GoGo Grandparent can use the landline.

Oh, great.

You see, so it's for people that have a flip phone or a landline.

Not an iPhone?

No. You can use GoGo Grandparent on an iPhone, but there's no sense in it, because you can download the Uber app, and just push the button.

Is it through Uber? Is it connected to Uber?

It's a separate entity that has a relationship with Uber.

That's what I saw, but they didn't explain the point.

Yeah, I don't know exactly.

Clever idea.

It is, all kinds of clever ideas out there.

Anything that could be figured out that alleviates people of a certain generation having to get up to speed with the 21st century.

Yeah.

Because unless you have grandkids around...

My grandkids teach me a lot about these phones. They say - they call me Papa - "I'll put these apps on." My daughter put the Uber app on my phone when I went to San Francisco. I'd never really even thought about Uber. I went to San Francisco, and rode around as a rider, and I was so impressed with it, I said, "I've got to find out about this."

There's a point it makes sense that as you get older to a certain age, you don't need a car.

That's true. I chauffeur my lady around a lot. She has a nonprofit here in town that provides free homecare for people that fall through the gaps and cracks of our medical system.

Nice.

She cares for a lot of people whom have a lot of money too, but those people pay her nurses directly. But for people that don't have money, she uses those same nurses to care for them.

Oh, how nice.

So, I chauffeur her around to her appointed rounds.

That's great. What a nice thing to do.

I don't drive Uber at night. I never drive at night. It's too confusing for me with the lights. I don't go out at night very much, and if I do, I use Uber.

Yes, that's a good idea.

We don't go to dinner at El Dorado, Las Campanas or any place like that at night.

Right, you can get lost out there. What profession were you guys in?

I was in the banking business in Los Angeles and New York. And we retired in 91' and came to Santa Fe.

He paints. He retired to paint full-time.

Yes. I painted pictures.

What kind?

Landscape painting. I showed at the Nedra Matteucci Gallery for 20 years.

Really? That's impressive. I was one of the founders of the Santa Fe Rotary Foundation for the Arts here that provides funding for arts in education. We have an artist of the year every year, and we raise money. We've raised over half a million to give to art education programs.

Wonderful.

I've gotten to know a whole lot of the different artists like Agnes Martin. Do you know Agnes? She was amazing. I went to her studio in Taos. It was towards the end of her life, maybe two or three years before she died. She had me look at 10 of her big 5'x 5' paintings that she had just completed, and she says...

Wow! That's physically very hard to do.

Well, they were all pastel shades of lines and grids and stuff like that, and she says, "Do you know what I paint?" I say, "Well, tell me Agnes." She says, "I only paint one thing. I paint the pure love of a baby's mind. That's the only thing I'm interested in painting."

My goodness. Isn't that wonderful?

Isn't that amazing?

How much would it cost to go to Albuquerque?

It's about $90 from here. We do a lot of Albuquerque trips. Take people to the airport. Take people to meetings.

Oh, you do? Do you ever go to Albuquerque, and then wait for half an hour and drive back? We go to the dermatologist, and it's usually half an hour and you're done.

Yeah. We do that often, yeah. We take people to the doctors down there, wait for them, drive them back. Have you guys stopped driving, or do you still drive?

We still drive. Both of us. But we are thinking about the future.

My father, who was 84, got in three accidents in his last year of his life. Two of them in his driveway. Driving is a problem for people getting older, or it can be.

Oh my goodness. You never know. Now how do I pay you?

It's on your card. That's it folks. Thank you so much.

— WO CARES —

Well, it's just a book I'm doing on the type of people that ride Uber in Santa Fe.

A book? Oh, like are you a scholar or something?

Am I a scholar? No, I'm just a writer.

Oh, yeah, so interesting. Yeah, seeking for inspiration.

Where are you guys from?

Both from China.

A lot of Chinese come here to St John's?

I wouldn't say a lot. There's around 40 people in the community.

What part of China are you from?

I'm up from the east.

I'm from southwest China.

It's very different in southwest China.

I used to know a guy in L.A. who was from China. He was Muslim. Are there many Muslims in China?

In certain regions.

Certain regions?

Yeah, there are some, but I don't think many.

I think just students in the States are. I mean, Chinese students are not Muslims as far as I know. I don't know any single one that is.

Are they Buddhists?

Well, I mean, if they're religious, then more likely they're Christians.

Christian?

Yeah, if they're religious.

If they're religious.

Yeah. There are also Buddhists there. I mean like everywhere in the States.

Okay. I don't know any Buddhist Chinese on this campus.

I mean most Buddhist Chinese come from Hong Kong and northern regions.

I've been to Guangzhou.

That's very nice. Guangzhou is a great city.

I spent some time in between Hong Kong and Guangzhou in this industrial area.

Okay. What did you do there? Just curious.

Well, I was working with a factory there that made recycled paper products for me in the stationery industry. They had

600 employees and a big dormitory where they all stayed. They had a guard outside that operated a big gate, and he stood at attention and saluted each car that came in.

Aha, yeah, that's very organized, very industrial. Mostly that's how the Chinese university is like as well. There's huge dorms for students.

Is Wal-Mart in China?

Yeah, along with many other supermarkets.

Yeah, and also like just global supermarkets that are based in China as well, like Tesco.

They're in China, Tesco? What kind of cars are primarily in China?

Well, various sources.

I mean are there any U.S. or Japanese cars, or is it primarily just Chinese cars?

Well, it's very diverse. You have a lot of cars that just come from everywhere. American cars, you have like General Motors, Chrysler and Ford. Also like Korea's Hyundai and some Chinese ones.

You also have Toyota. And of course, Mercedes Benz, the most famous.

How do you pronounce Xi?

Xi. Kind of like between "c" and "she" in English.

Aha. Xi.

So, the Chinese presidents' names sound crazy. Our last one was named Wo.

Wo.

This one is Xi.

She.

Yeah. Who is 'She'? And Wo, when Obama was running for his campaign, now they have ObamaCare. In China we made the joke, ObamaCares, WoCares.

'Who' cares. I see. Are there still a lot of state owned businesses in China, or are they all private now?

Not totally privatized. There are still many state owned businesses in especially certain areas like banking or communication, and also like insurance.

Do you have unrestricted access to the internet in China?

Not quite. I mean many people have access to the internet, but no access to Twitter or Facebook or YouTube.

Oh, you don't have access to Facebook?

I mean, we have our own alternatives.

So, like Google, for instance, it's not the most effective search engine perhaps in China, if it's allowed, I mean. Before 2008 I think Google was allowed, and people still prefer like, the Chinese version, like Baidu for instance. It's kind of interesting to see different cultures and their adaptation. People nowadays are agitating Google to return to China.

How do most Chinese view North Korea?

I mean mysterious, like a lot of people travel to North Korea. And it's some people were joking, and saying it's just, I mean, in the nature of what China was like in the 1950s.

Yeah. So, like this one thing about North Korea is no one understands what's going on. Just no one understands. It's just like a different world.

Your premier's daughter graduated from Harvard.

Yeah. And other officials' kids like to graduate from good U.S. schools. Okay, thank you.

Okay you go in, and the Vision Center is right over there. Thank you.

∞

WEEK SIX

— ASIA —

Asia?

Yeah, I'm Asia. Hi. Oh my god, I'm so sorry. My grandma is not used to Uber. All I really...

It's your first time...

It's not my first-time grandma.

Let me know when you arrive.

Fort Marcy?

Fort Marcy.

Okay.

Okay thank you so much.

They are not used to...

No. I mean like, I'm 21 years old, so...

You're what?

I'm 21 years old, so it's kind of hard living with her.

Oh, well.

I know. It's difficult with me, and she's very concerned, but it's like...

She's concerned that you might be picked up by someone, you know, who's going to do something terrible to you.

Right, I know, I usually don't trust Uber drivers because of it. But I need it, because I don't have a car and they won't let me drive. That's another thing I need too. Hey, aren't you guys hiring to be an Uber driver?

Yes, they take on Uber drivers all the time. You can just apply online to be a driver. They have like 200 drivers here in Santa Fe.

No way. That's crazy. Yeah, because I'm already 21, and I saw online that you can apply.

Yeah, it's fun. Do you work at Fort Marcy?

No, I'm just going to the gym.

How long you lived in Santa Fe? You raised here?

Yeah, yeah. I've lived here for quite a while, so it's pretty nice. And then moved to Belen, and then I came back here. So, it's like a full circle. So, if you're applying to be an Uber driver, do you have to use your own car, or do they use whatever car they have?

You've got to have your own car.

That makes sense.

But sometimes in some cities Uber will lease you a car.

Really?

A lot of grandmas have nothing else to do but worry about their grandkids.

She's been holding me back since I was like 18, so it's been quite a while.

Oh, boy.

You know, it's just kind of hard to live with her. Yeah, it really is.

The other day I picked up someone who's blind.

Oh, my.

And she uses a cane, and we're talking about canes and crossing sidewalks and crossing intersections and stuff like that. She said well, yeah, you got to listen real carefully towards the direction of the cars, and you got to feel with your cane where the curb is. She said the problem is these hybrid and electric cars don't make any noise. So, you can't hear if a car is coming.

Exactly, that's crazy. When I see blind people, like, wow, they have so much determination, and so much knowledge, even though they're blind. They know where they're going. It's pretty crazy how they do it. You have to do everything on your own.

Yeah. Okay, well, you have a good work out. Good luck with your grandma.

Thank you so much.

Okay, adios.

Thank you.

— GREEN CHILI GORGEOUS SKIES —

Hello. How are you doing?

Good. Where are you from?

California.

California. I was 10 years in L.A. before I moved here.

Yeah. I was born in San Diego, and spent most of my time in the Bay Area.

San Diego is nice. I like the Bay Area, too.

I liked the Bay Area. It was so crowded though. There's a lot of things I miss, but I couldn't do the traffic, or just the numbers of people, or the high rises, or the building versus land percentage. I just ... I couldn't do that anymore.

Yeah, I like the laid-back lifestyle of Santa Fe compared to California. Do you work down here?

No, I have an appointment. I do still miss the road construction in the Bay Area, because it made much more sense to me. You know, there weren't places where you felt like you were driving into traffic!

Right. They have perpetual road construction here.

They do. It's mind-boggling to me. There was always construction in the Bay Area, but they did it in... You know, they threw all the resources at one section, and then they were done with it, you know, for 5 or 10 years. Not, oh, we'll do a little bit this year and a little bit next year, and, oh, let's get that group out of business.

Down here at the Interstate and Cerrillos, they've created... the worst nightmare. It's dangerous!

It's super dangerous, because you're driving on the wrong side of the road.

Yeah, not only that, but when you get off the freeway going south, I've witnessed, and I've almost gotten into an accident myself coming, and then going north on Cerrillos, getting off the freeway.

I haven't tried it.

It's a disaster!

My vet is out on Highway 14, so the first time I drove out there, I was like, oh my god, what the hell did they do? It's like, just follow the car in front of me, that was all I could do.

I know. It doesn't make any sense. I mean, they must have some $5 million, $10 million into that crazy exchange.

Yeah. That's probably right, and I need to let go of it, because it doesn't do any good to hold on to frustrations. But Santa Fe and New Mexico in general don't seem to ever learn from other states. You know? Like the drunk driving. Like other states have figured out how to do things and not, you know, spend $1,000, send someone out. "Oh, we can do it this way. We don't have to ...,"you know? So, when I get really frustrated, I have to pretend I'm living in Mexico, pretend it's Mexico.

Oh, there you go! That's a good one.

You know, manana time. You don't expect it to make sense down there. You don't expect the government to be official. I don't know. I mean, you expect the government to be corrupt, so it doesn't have to come as a surprise every day when you read about it. It's an interesting place.

Yeah. Do you ever eat over there at Jambo Cafe? It's very good.

Yes, it's very good, when it is not being run into by cars!

I ate there the first day they re-opened.

Oh, wow!

I ate lunch there. I had never had lunch there, but we ate lunch there just to support them. Then, I had dinner there the other day. I said, "Are you guys back to normal?" "Well, not quite. People still think we're closed."

You know, I follow them on Facebook, and I didn't see a big re-opening thing.

Right.

I know they had their truck parked there for a while.

I know. I went there one day. I tried it just to give them a little business.

That's the other thing here. Parking lots. They could have learned about parking lots from other places.

See, if I go downtown at night, I just take Uber. I don't like to deal with the parking downtown, if I have an event or something like that.

Yeah. I don't like to deal with the parking in most places. The one place that's just as bad in California as here, at least in the Bay Area, is the Trader Joe's parking lot. It's the worst one in Santa Fe. And it's awful in California, too.

Yeah, it's pretty bad here.

I always park up as far away from Trader Joe's as I can get, and still push the cart. But there's green chile here, and there's gorgeous skies.

There's green chile and gorgeous skies.

And sometimes good weather.

I'll tell you, the kids that were raised here, when they leave... They all leave for a little bit, but they all come back. They all miss their green chile, let me tell you. You really can't get it in the same way you get it here in New Mexico.

No. It took me two years to get used to eating New Mexican food instead of Mexican food. I got addicted to green chile. And then, it was like, oh, man!

I put chile on a lot of stuff. I even put green chile mustard on corn on the cob. I'm also into salsa. I love good salsas!

Me too.

A friend of mine, two years ago, he bought some acreage in Chimayo, and he's growing chile.

Wow!

Chimayo and chile. Last year was his first crop. He's, like, testing the soil for different nitrates and stuff. I don't know... He sends soil samples off to be tested.

He's being very scientific about it.

It is very scientific.

It's hard to believe we're going to have a full-on winter storm tomorrow.

Are we supposed to?

Yeah. A hard freeze and everything. So you'll be busier. Has it been busier since the taxi, since Capitol Cab, stopped?

Yeah, a little bit, I suppose. Some people freaking out. They are used to the cab service.

Yep.

I picked up a lady who's blind the other day. It was her first time to use Uber. She had been using a cab for a long time. She doesn't know how to operate a smart phone. There is this thing called GoGo Grandparent. It is for people that don't have a smart phone. And you just call on your land line.

Oh!

Or if you have a flip phone, you can call on your flip phone. They are hooked up with Uber somehow or another. I don't know how. But there's quite a few older people that use this GoGo Grandparent.

Oh, that's good, because that was my first thought. So many people don't have smart phones, the elderly especially. Well, now they have a way around that. Oh, good.

My lady, she only can seem to operate the landline. She doesn't like smart phones at all.

And you go straight. Yeah. It's this first driveway on your left. Thank you so much.

Thank you.

— SOUTH AFRICA —

Hello, hello.
Hi, how are you doing?

I'm doing good. Trader Joe's?

Yeah. That will be great.

When is school out here?
The official date is the 21st.

The 21st. Where are you from?

From South Africa. Three more weeks and we are all done.

How did you hear about St. John's?

I went to boarding school in the Netherlands.

In the Netherlands, really?
Yeah. I went to an international boarding school, and I organized a conference on philosophy, and one of the speakers who came ended up being the President of St. John's.

Oh, my Lord!

Just from the other campus, from the Annapolis campus.

Yeah. Is the President the same for both colleges?

Not anymore. We have two presidents.

You have two presidents?

And he spoke and then he took me out for dinner, because I was in charge of the women's conference. He was like, "Hey, you should come to St. John's. And then, I listened to him! Now, I'm here. Just not on the Annapolis campus. It's a cool school.

What year are you here?

I'm a freshman, so in the beginning.

What part of South Africa are you from?

I'm from Johannesburg.

Johannesburg is in the middle, right?

Yeah. It's close to the middle.

Yeah, I thought so. You have a very distinctive accent.

Really?

Yeah, it's different than Australian or English.

Oh, yeah, yeah. No, I don't have a British accent.

How long ago did Mandela die?

He died in 2013.

Did you ever meet him?

Yeah.

How did you happen to meet him?

Well, I met him a few times actually. I was really lucky. The first time I met him was in Italy. My father was working... We were living in the UK, and we had gone to Italy for a holiday, and Mandela and his wife, Graca, had flown to Italy for some, like, government conference or whatever. And my dad knew the people who were working with Mandela, and they were like, "Hey, you guys want a private tour of the Colosseum with Mandela?" And my dad was, like, "Of course we do."

Of course! So, you took a tour of the Colosseum with Mandela?

Yeah. And then he lived four streets down from me in South Africa.

In where?

In South Africa in Johannesburg. His house was four streets away from mine.

Oh, boy! What does your dad do?

My dad is an economist, but he worked for the government for a point, and then he worked for a government-owned company for a while. And now, he just works for the private sector.

Was he as charismatic in person as he seems to be?

Yeah.

Like on TV and everything?

Oh my god, he's fantastic. He's really, really... Obviously, he was old, like, but he was really charismatic and he and his wife, Graca, were just like the nicest people I think that I've ever met. And I think I'm very lucky, because, like, not that many people have gotten an opportunity to meet him.

Right. Well, apartheid was pretty much over when you were growing up though, wasn't it?

Yeah, I was born after apartheid ended. But I think the ramifi-
cations of apartheid are still...

Still there?

Are still there. There are still many issues that we are dealing
with.

My son-in-law is from a very rural portion of northern Namibia. His father was a member of the SWAPO opposition,
who were trying to gain independence from South Africa.
He worked in a mine in the south, but because he favored
SWAPO, the South Africans branded his chest and he was
never allowed to work in the mines again.

Yeah, there were a lot of terrible things going on back then.

When my son-in-law was sixteen, he joined the SWAPO
rebels in Zambia. But after a couple of years he and many
others of his age realized that a lot of the humanitarian
aid from the UN and other organizations was being
diverted by SWAPO leaders and not being delivered to the
people it was meant for. Major disagreements broke out
within SWAPO and some SWAPO youth leaders were
arrested and held for about 18 months in a special camp
under extremely brutal conditions. They eventually fell
under a UN mandate and when he was 23 he applied to be
a student at UCLA, got accepted, and was allowed to come
to the U.S. under a special U.N. travel passport. For around
twenty years he had no real passport. He eventually became a U.S. citizen. He got his PhD in mineral economics
and is a professor at a local community college now.

Wow. Quite a story. Thank you so much.

Thank you.

— YOGA TRAINING —

Welcome. Where are you from?

Houston.

What brings you to Santa Fe?

Yoga training.

Where do they have the yoga training?

Well, it's going to be aqua yoga. So I'm hopeful it's warm.

Yeah, I bet.

I have to assume that since they have it in Santa Fe...

That it's warm water?

Yeah. So, it's actually next door to the place that I'm staying at.

What does aqua yoga mean? I mean do they just do movements in water?

Yeah. It's better on the joints, because you have more buoyancy in the water. Also it makes people less self-conscious, because you're in the water, so nobody can probably see you.

Oooh.

Versus when you are on your mat...

Everyone sees you.

Yes.

I see. So, for the self-conscious it's a better form of movement.

Yes, and sometimes for the people with injuries and older people.

What do you consider to be an old person?

A person that's not doing a lot of movement.

Does age have anything to do with it?

No. Anybody can do it.

Now this is a pretty good little place to eat right here, Taco Foundation.

Wow! There's a place, I don't know if it's on this street, but...

What's the name of it?

I can't remember. I ate here...

Describe it to me.

They serve Spanish food and breakfast.

Spanish food and breakfast? Is it Tia Sofia's, downtown here, right down on this street?

No, it was kind of off.

Off the main track?

Yes. I think it was on the same street as Cat Meow...

Tortilla Flats? Next to Meow Wolf?

That sounds like it.

Were you doing yoga training last time you were here too?

Yes. I was doing pre-natal.

Oh, really?

For that one you do have to be pregnant.

I would imagine. I would imagine. For that one you got to be pregnant. That's funny!

And the last day it snowed but by the afternoon it was gone. It snowed overnight and then...

Santa Fe is a place where the weather changes frequently.

Well, sounds like Houston. One minute, on one side of town it's raining. In the middle of the day the sun is out, and at the end of the day there's sleet and ice. Where's the library?

The library, the downtown library is about four blocks over here, downtown.

Is this considered downtown?

Yeah. This is the Plaza over here. And the library is about a block off the plaza.

Okay. Did you have any snow all this past week?

Not this past week, we haven't.

This is still considered winter?

This is spring.

Oh my gosh, just like us.

They don't have this kind of weather down in Houston, do they?

We don't have snow, but we do have tornadoes and hurricanes.

Yes, I know, you got all the other kind of stuff.

Yeah, the other elements, sleet, ice.

Now how did you get into yoga?

I had an experience when I finished having my second child. I was a stay at home mom, and I needed some time to get away. I went into a yoga class. It felt great, and I've been hooked ever since then.

How old are your kids now?

I have an 18-year-old, 14-year-old, 9 and 4.

Oh, my Lord, you've been pumping them out. I have two granddaughters that are graduating from high school this year.

Are they twins?

No, they're from different mothers, but they both live in the same area.

Well, that should be fun. Do they go to the same school?

No, they go to different high schools, and they're going to different colleges.

Are they staying in state?

One of them is staying in state, Arizona, the University of Arizona. The other one is going to Brown, which is an Ivy League school in Providence, Rhode Island.

Yes, is she going to do literature or...?

I think they're both trying to figure out what they want to do. They're still so young.

Yeah.

She thought something in medicine, medical research, medical anthropology, doctor, being a doctor. I don't know what she's going to do. She's a bright kid though.

And the other one, Arizona?

The other one I have no idea what she's going to do. She's just going to go to school. She's a bright one too. Here is a picture of my lady's great granddaughter.

Wow, look at her. Does she like to dance?

Yeah, she's four in that shot. Now she's seven.

She looks like she's a lively one, all dressed up in that purple ballerina outfit.

Well, she's full of juice, let me tell you.

How many kids do you have?

I have three, and my lady had three. My daughters are in their fifties and my son is in his thirties. My lady's kids are in their mid-fifties; she had another son who died in his twenties. She has three grandkids. I have three grand-daughters, and then she has two great grandkids. Those ones right there. That's Aliyah. And the boy is Isaac. Yeah, kids are fun.

They are. They tell you a lot about yourself.

I guess you are right about that. Your little four-year old has got to be missing you.

Yeah, been my shadow for the longest. So, I'm sure he's going to be waking up asking, and then he'll start playing with his brother.

There you go.

Horse playing. They love to wrestle.

Do you have a girl too?

I have one daughter.

One girl. They are different than the boys aren't they?

They extremely are, and that's what I keep telling my husband. It's really pretty...

Yeah.

So, does this snow look fresh and new to you, or are you just like used to it?

We get five, six, seven good snows a year. This is nothing right now.

Oh, okay.

But from what I hear, we could, maybe, have some serious snow tonight, 6-12 inches. That's how much they are going to have out east. I don't know if we're going to get hit or not. Okay, are you sure this is the right address?

Yes. Okay, thank you.

Thank you.

∞

— HEC —

I never know what people are going to say. It's fascinating.

Yeah, you know, I mean, there are a lot of interesting folks out there. Sadly, I'm not adept at small talk.

You don't have to be. That's one of the more interesting things too. You're like a lot of people. I pick up people from A to Z.

I guess it's good to know that I'm not a rare beast in that aspect.

I have had many people get in my car and say absolutely nothing.

I can imagine that pretty easily. I try to at least say something.

Because you know with this app, I mean, it tells you where you're going, and so they don't really have to.

I try to keep some conversation if it's wanted, but I could only talk about the weather so often, and it's like, well, we've talked about the weather...

I've had that too.

I'm better at facts, would you like to know a random fact?

Well, let me ask you, how many ways does a banana split?

How many ways does a banana split? I guess it depends on what you define as splitting of a banana. You can turn it about sideways and all the different angles that you can split it that way, or you talk about the peel itself, or...

I'm talking about the fruit.

Okay, how many?

Three.

Three.

Banana is a three-ribbed fruit, and if you stick your finger up in the middle of a banana, it opens into three sections.

Interesting. I did not know that.

Try it with your next banana.

So right up, like directly in the middle.

Either end. But you will find that, one of the ends has a little deeper indent, that's the best one to go into at the very tip of the banana.

And then you just push it, right?

Just push and it will open up. It's a three-ribbed fruit. It opens in three sections.

I did not know that.

I've probably asked a thousand people that, and maybe 10 have known. I asked the president of Chiquita Bananas if he knew how many ways a banana splits. He said, "Three." He knew.

Well, it's good that he knows, at least.

That's right. I've thought about presenting the idea to Baskin Robbins or Dairy Queen for them to use in an ad for their banana split.

That's a good sign that a guy knows his bananas because I didn't know that. I'm much more into biology than plants, although that said, my papa is a... Oh, my god what's it called... I don't remember the English word, but I guess it will be something like a floral biologist. What's that called. The...

A botanist?

Yeah, a botanist. There we go. What little I know I got from him. But I got to admit it, it's very, very limited. He's much more educated on that end. Did you know that your eyes cannot see the color blue?

Really?

Yeah, because of the wavelengths. Blue wavelengths distort images, so the bluer there is on something, the harder it is normally for your eyes to be able to pick it up. From what I understand it kind of makes the other wavelengths less clear. So, what happens is that your eyes filter it out. So, every time you see blue, the wavelength that is there is being actively filtered out by the eye, and all other colors are being allowed in, which means that... I'm assuming you've heard the conundrum before of, 'is your red my red?' or 'was your red really my green?' or 'is your green really my blue?' in terms of what we actually see. And it's hard to know if that's true or not, but for the color blue, I would imagine that everybody sees blue differently, because it's an imagined color.

Do you know the one part of the body that never changes size?

You got me thinking. What's that?

The iris of the eye.

You know what? I could have guessed that. Well, at least I could have guessed the eye specifically, but, yeah, that makes sense. Do you know that the changing of eye color can actually happen, and do you know what causes it?

I'm not sure.

Unstable DNA. The color pigments in your eyes, some individuals have DNA that is very unstable and doesn't... to put it simply it really doesn't know what color it's supposed to be, so it constantly changes. So, for folks who say that their eyes change color a lot, it does happen. There's still a lot of people that don't think that's true, but it does actually happen. For some individuals it will change faster, because of unstable DNA, and the factors that can cause it are a bit varied. The common thing to go to is stress, but at the end of the day there are just too many factors that it could be. It's too hard to properly track down, at least so far, or at least I should say nobody's taken the immense amount of effort that it will take to successfully figure it out. But so far the biggest ones are either stress, or diet or...

As far as changing of the eye color?

Yes. Eye color changing

Stress or diet?

Stress, diet, or light sensitivity, or not sensitivity, but light stimuli. So essentially, being in the sun for a really long time versus being in the dark for a little long time. All those things can change the stability of the DNA, or, I guess, for the instability in the DNA that can change colors. And there might actually be a really easy fix for Alzheimer's and possibly dementia as well.

And what do you think that is?

I would like to take credit for it, but sadly I'm not even anywhere close to having found it out, but it made a lot of sense. There was a scientist in 1989 or 1990... something in that area, I've forgotten the exact time that he discovered it, and he had said that it has to do with something called a tau protein. Essentially tau proteins, or T proteins, create these little microtubes...

Tau proteins?

Yeah. And essentially what this protein does is that it creates tubes, microtubes they are officially called, and they're literally feeding tubes. And what they do is that they go to your neurons or your brain cells, and they feed them. These cells are called astrocytes and oligodendrocytes, and they are responsible for cleaning and feeding things like that in your neuron cells. What they found is a very strong link that these tau proteins will eventually sometimes corrupt, and then they get frayed, and essentially with these frayed tubes it can't feed the cell properly anymore. But the problem is that these tubes will then replicate perfectly, which means that you suddenly have a whole bunch of cells that go to your brain, pretend like they're feeding it, and then release a signal that says, "This has been fed now." So, when you look at people with Alzheimer's and what not, you realize that their neurons have starved to death.

Ok, here we are. Good luck to you.

You as well. Thanks.

I LATER TOOK A TRIP TO TENERIFE IN THE CANARY ISLANDS. THE HOUSE AT WHICH WE STAYED WAS LOCATED AT A BANANA PLANTATION. WHEN WE ARRIVED AT THE HOUSE THERE WAS A STOCK OF ABOUT ONE HUNDRED OR SO BANANAS HANGING FROM ONE STOCK. I LEARNED THAT A BANANA TREE ONLY GROWS ONE STOCK AND THEN DIES AND BEFORE IT DIES, IT SHOOTS UP NEW ROOTS AND TAKES NINE MONTHS FOR THOSE NEW ROOTS TO BECOME A BANANA TREE THAT PRODUCES ONE STOCK OF BANANAS, AND THEN DIES.

∞

— SYDNEY —

What inspired you to write a book?

The people who are my riders, for the most part they're all fascinating. Everyone's got a story.

Good idea.

Yeah, it's a great idea.

Where are you all from?

We're from Sydney, Australia.

Sydney. What did you think of Meow Wolf?

It was kind of cool. We learned to pay attention to details, like colors and stuff.

It's sort of got a story, but it could be more intriguing. If you really follow the stories through, I think it's quite amazing.

It's a pretty involved story.

Absolutely.

I was only there for two hours, but right at the beginning I read all about this character named Lex.

We were probably there about two hours as well. There was a big line, and they were very busy.

This is an off day compared to... You should see the weekends.

Really?

Oh my lord, they have lines around the block. I don't know if you're vegetarian or not, but they have good vegetarian and gluten free stuff at The Teahouse.

Really? I just heard it was a nice place, and we thought we'd go in there, and walk around and look at the galleries along Canyon Road.

Yeah, just walk down.

Yeah, that's what we'll do.

You just come on vacation to travel the states or...?

Yeah, I'm living in Colorado at the moment.

She's living there for a year. We like Georgia O'Keefe and those kind of museums and galleries.

My friend had a women's clothing store here on the plaza for many years. Georgia would come into his store.

Oh, really?

For 40 or 50 years something like this, and whenever she came in he locked the door. She didn't want anyone...

How interesting, and she always wore the same set of clothes.

He sold her everything, all of her undergarments, everything.

She always wore these long outfits and sort of the same look.

Right.

She'd come out of there looking differently.

He had more Georgia O'Keefe stories. What do you all do in Australia?

I'm a guide at the Museum of Contemporary Art, and I have four children, two in America, one in England, and one in Australia. That's why I come to stay there.

And you, what do you do?

I just finished university, so I'm kind of just hanging. Yeah, and then I've moved to Colorado for the skiing.

For your skiing?

Yeah. And then I'm staying for the summer though, because it's quite beautiful in the summer, lots of hikes and things like that.

She's got a job.

So, yeah, and I work in a restaurant. How is it all made, this adobe, how is it all made? Is it...?

Many different ways. The original adobes are just mud bricks. Sometimes they fire in the sun till they dry. I had a double adobe, so it had an air space in between. But a lot of them are frame houses that are plastered on with adobe stucco.

For the same look. And is that part of the building regulations now?

Yeah.

Our plane from Phoenix wasn't allowed to land at Santa Fe airport, so we had to land in Albuquerque. It took all day to get from L.A. Anyway, just got sunny every day. It's beautiful.

Does it get very, very hot here in the summer?

No.

Because of the elevation?

Ninety or so. But there's no humidity. Sometimes a little higher. You ever heard of Ray Martin?

Yeah, as an Australian journalist.

My lady used to be on his show.

Oh, really. What did she do?

She had an ordeal with her son down there in Sydney. She had to get all these volunteers and she wrote a book about it called <u>Hold My Hand: A Mother's Journey.</u> He used to interview her.

Is she Australian or American?

She's Welsh?

Oh, she's Welsh? And you met her here?

Yes.

Really. Nice chatting with you.

Yeah. Thanks.

∞

— HERTZ —

Good, I'll get it.

Thank you. Oh, perfect.

Morning.

Hey, good morning. We're just headed to the airport.

So, you're going to Hertz?

Yeah, at the airport.

We booked it, and then didn't realize there were actually some rental locations downtown.

How do you like that place where you were staying?

It was really nice. They do really good breakfast and...

What's the name of it?

Inn of the Turquoise Bear.

It's kind of a mouthful.

Yeah, right.

But very nice.

Where you all from?

We're from Salt Lake. Just thought we'd take a little trip.

Just to experience Santa Fe?

Yeah. I've been down here before. It's my husband's first time. We're expecting our first baby in July

You are? Congratulations.

So, it's a little bit of a babymoon. Yeah. When we first started planning this trip the weather was supposed to be in the mid-70's and 80's, and we got here in a snow storm. So, it was a little chilly our first night.

How about you? Are you from Santa Fe?

31 years

Oh, wow!

My boy was born here 30 some odd years ago. You know, we did a birthing class with eight other couples. Those kids have known each other since before they were born. We have videos of all their early birthdays. My son grew up here in Santa Fe with a very close group of friends, and to this day they are all very close.

Wow! That must be nice. Does it seem like it's changed a lot since...?

Not really. Parts of it. The county has. Downtown really hasn't. They have a historic district here. It manages the way that the downtown historic district looks.

We were wondering about that. Are there a lot of rules on development down there?

Yeah.

What brought you out 30 years ago?

A woman.

Yeah, they'll do that.

After we got married, she moved to L.A. with me for a year, got pregnant, and just said, "You know, we're not having the baby in L.A." She was from Santa Fe.

Oooh.

Where are you going to drive to?

We're headed to... We're going to head over to Taos, and then I have some family. My mom's side of the family is from the Mora area.

Where?

Mora. And there's some... There's a couple that bought the land that my grandmother owned, that her family owned forever, and they've, they've been very welcoming to our family. They have a cabin on the property that we're going to stay at for a night.

Have you been there?

I have, when I was younger.

Have you been to Mora?

Oh, yeah. Several times.

So, did your son stay in Santa Fe or did he...

He just moved to Sonoma County to be with his girlfriend.

That's nice.

What do you guys do in Salt Lake?

Oh, we're professional nerds. We're attorneys.

Attorneys? What kind of attorneys?

I do gas related work in the environmental field for the federal government.

Yeah. Represent the Feds.

So, we're enjoying playing hooky from work today.

Ah ha. You guys might want to check out Bandelier.

Yeah! We, we're... I would like to try and work that out tomorrow on our way back. I don't know

You should also take the back road, you know, go see the Earthships.

Yeah...

Okay, and take that road all the way, go over the bridge, and then down and go to Ojo Caliente.

Oh, I've read about that! Yeah.

It's fantastic.

And what's in Ojo Caliente?

It's a hot spring with all these natural mineral waters.

Oh, wow!

They've really developed it to where you can spend the

night there, and, or you can just use the facilities. They have a sister location down here called Sunrise Springs, south of Santa Fe, but it's not the natural hot springs.

Oh.

See that mountain up there?

Yeess.

That's where Los Alamos is.

Okay

And that mountain was like double its size or something like that and it exploded and created one of the country's largest calderas.

Oh, really?

And when you go up there now, you drive down to Jemez where there's a lot of hot springs, but on the way, you see all this hot water bubbling up and steaming. There's still magma underneath there that, you know, fuels the Ojo Caliente waters, and all those waters that are under northern New Mexico. Are you like a federal prosecutor?

No, I'm a... I represent the Department of the Interior, so...

Oh.

BLM and the National Park Service primarily.

Oh. My ex-father in law was director of the National Park Service.

Oh, really?

Wow!

Most recently?

No. He's like retired for 35 years.

Oh, really?

He's like in his mid-90's.

He must have some good stories from that time

He started as a horse concessioner at Mesa Verde. And then worked up the ranks and was superintendent of many different parks.

Oh, wow.

Then was Southwest Regional Director here in Santa Fe.

How long have you been driving Uber?

My daughter put the Uber app on my phone about a year ago, when I did a trade show conference up in San Francisco. I tried it in San Francisco just as a rider, and I was so impressed with the technology. I said, "You know, I'm going to drive in Santa Fe."

Yeah!

It works really well. Beats the cab company.

The cab company here went out of business a while ago.

Oh, did it? That doesn't surprise me. So, is Santa Fe growing a lot?

In the past 30 years it's gone from 60-80,000, so...

What's the mountain on our left?

Sandia Mountains. That's above Albuquerque

Okay. Does the train go this way?

Yes. People take the train to Albuquerque all the time, back and forth.

Yeah, we took it up from Albuquerque on Saturday during the snow storm. Is St. John's College part of the Santa Fe community, or does it sort of operate unto itself?

Oh, no, they're part of the Santa Fe community. People from all over the world go to St. John's.

I had an Uber driver once in San Francisco, and he was one of the first 10 Uber drivers.

Oh, boy.

He responded, uh, to a Craigslist Ad years ago, and, yeah, they actually gave him stock options for sticking with them. Yeah.

Oh, boy. Well, it's been a pleasure.

Oh, wow. Thank you.

Hey, thank you.

∞

— WRITING WORKSHOP —

Fascinating people visit Santa Fe and live here.

Do you get mostly visitors, or do you get mostly locals?

About 50/50.

Okay.

Where are you from?
I'm coming from San Francisco, and I'm here for a science writing workshop they have at the Inn.

What kind of science writing?

It's a mix. I think the instructors are mostly journalists from newspapers and magazines. But the students are... Some of them work for universities, others for researchers and, like, I work for a university. But they have it every May at this Inn.

Like, how many people attend?

About 40. I think we have 47 this year.

Is it to write white papers, or to write...

It's to write, like, magazine stories.

Magazine stories?

Yes, but it's a variety, you know. Some are probably more technical, and some are just for newspapers. I see you have a pair of binoculars.

Oh, yeah, I do. I look at birds.

Me, too. That's why I'm going to the Audubon. I'm actually skipping out of the workshop, because I feel it would be a shame to come out here and not see any birds.

I have a fascination with birds.

Yeah. What are some of your favorite bird spots around here?

Well, my porch!

Oh, okay!

We have all kinds of bird feeders.

Oh.

We are up against a meadow, a fairly large meadow, and a lot of wildlife come there and birds. A while ago we had a twelve-point deer come down in our property, and we are pretty close to downtown. We also get raccoons, skunks and a few other things. But it's the birds in the morning that are just fantastic.

I hope to see some things I don't get to see in San Francisco, like is there a canyon wren here? Have you seen them? Any canyon towhees?

Well, we certainly have towhees.

In your backyard?

Yeah. They're beautiful. And sometimes we have these gigantic woodpeckers.

Do you know what kind?

I think they're called pileated woodpeckers. Then we have smaller woodpeckers, too. What university are you associated with?

UC San Francisco.

Two of my granddaughters are just graduating from high school, and are college bound as far as interviewing for colleges.

Yeah, well, UC San Francisco is a little bit odd in that they don't have any undergraduate programs.

Oh, they don't?

No. It's all medical school and professional schools and graduate schools. And they are very good at that, but they don't have undergrads.

I see.

Are they looking at California schools?

One has chosen University of Arizona. The other, she looked at Claremont McKenna and USC, but she decided on Brown.

Oh, wow! Okay. Well, that's a good school. So, she's sort of excited that she's going to go?

Oh, yeah, both girls are excited.

I grew up on the East Coast, so I think Brown is a great school. Growing up, I wasn't even familiar with the West Coast schools. I kind of wish I'd applied to California schools.

Where did you go to school?

I went to Yale, so actually not far from Brown. I think she will enjoy it.

She texted me last night and said, "Well, I'm off into the great big world. What do you think I should major in?"

Oh.

She has no idea, really.

Well, I think most people don't really know, and, you know, college is a good place to figure that out.

Yeah.

And I don't think... I didn't figure it out until after college, really, so...

She's thinking some kind of medical research or something in anthropology.

So, more science?

Yeah.

Science-oriented?

Definitely. They have a lot of weddings up here at the Audubon Center.

Oh, really?

Yeah. Right up there on the grass by the visitor center.

This red building?

Yeah. In there someplace. Enjoy.

All right. Thank you so much.

— LITIGATION LAWYER —

I'm doing a book on my Uber riders and I'd like to record the conversation, are you okay with that?

Yes, are you serious? That's awesome.

Hi, I'm the older sister. What's your most interesting pick up so far?

I've had a lot of them.

Especially late at night.

I only work during the day. I had one guy though who was a Silicon Valley start-up guy. He started six Silicon Valley companies, and sold them all. He says his latest investments are in flying cars.

Flying cars?

Cars are going to be flying pretty soon.

Wow!

I've heard of that.

I've been seeing it all over the internet.

I've heard of that. I think I've heard him speaking.

Sir, are you from here?

31 years.

What did you do before this?

I still do. I have a company near Portland, Oregon. I make little parts for the semiconductor industry.

Okay.

But with Uber driving, I created a little project around this book.

How long have you been working on that?

A while.

Okay.

How much amount of raw material do you think you need?

I've got enough.

Okay.

I'm sort of editing it now. I've been working on the book project for about six months.

Okay.

It came to me, so I started doing it.

That's cool.

I had this one lady who was a sock designer; she's designed socks for 40 years.

Wow!

And she knew so much about socks it was unbelievable, as far as the medical and therapeutic side of socks, the way they gripped your leg on down to your toes, your heel. Where are you all from?

I'm from Miami.

Atlanta, Georgia.

What brings you all here?

Confidence.

Illegal confidence.

Are you all lawyers?

I am.

All of our husbands are too.

I see.

They are stuck inside all day, while we're entertaining ourselves. It's everyone's first time here. We love it. It's beautiful.

What kind of legal conference is it?

It's litigation. All the lawyers come from like all across the country right here to La Fonda.

We have a lot of interesting conventions here.

Yes, you have to go somewhere nice a little more in order to get people to drive. What's your favorite restaurant recommendation for a nice dinner?

Sazon. It's right downtown.

Okay.

Its two and a half blocks or something from La Fonda.

Okay.

S-A-Z-O-N.

All right, I'll have the reservation Sunday night to see if it's really as good as people are saying.

Geronimo's?

That's it, we are supposed to eat there Friday night.

Geronimo's is, you know, one of the spots around town that people go to, particularly if people are coming here. It's a very good restaurant.

How is it different that Sazon?

It's completely different.

Okay, tell us about Sazon.

The owner and chef is from Mexico City. It's a taste sensation from the minute you walk in. He provides these four or five moles with silver dollar size tortillas. You dip them in and get your taste buds going. Very, very unique menu. The way he does food is just different from anybody else in town.

Wow, is there a place called The Compound?

Yes.

Somebody told me about that.

The Compound is excellent. It's been up there for years. The Compound, Geronimo's and Coyote Café all serve similar kinds of food. They all do it very well, and a little different, but you can't go wrong with any of those three. Another great restaurant is Santacafe with their stuffed poblano pepper. Sazon is just in a class by itself. The place with the best view of the sunset though is Coyote Cantina. They also make a killer margarita.

Okay.

In my opinion.

Is The Compound the one that's like really romantic?

Yes, I think I heard that. He said that was like a really romantic spot.

Can be.

Yes.

I'm so proud. I've already had two liters of water today.

Good.

I've been trying to drink three liters of water a day. My doctor has recommended that to me. I guess there was, like my, what are the numbers that come out in your blood work and stuff, most people if they do the numbers they see that we need to drink more water?

Doctors say that if you are dehydrated your heart has to work overtime and your pulse rate goes way up.

What's the population of Santa Fe?

80,000.

The hotel concierge has recommended that we try this 10,000 Waves spa.

It's fantastic.

Ok. Thank you.

Thank you.

∞

— TWINS —

Good morning.

Hi. Hertz at airport please.

And how old are you girls?

Ten.

Both of you?

Yes, twins.

My lord, you're twins? That must be fun.

At times.

They always fight.

What grade are you in?

Fourth.

Fifth next year.

What happened to your car?

It's like five years old. It's an Altima, and we were just driving, and all the stuff started flashing, and then it died. It would stay on in neutral, but when you put it into drive, it wouldn't go. So I said, "Oh, my gosh, I'm going to blow the transmission." That's what I thought it would be, or a sensor is out.

That's right.

But it's not gaining any power, so when the tow truck called me they were like it might be the alternator, that happens in these cars. So, I said I hope it is, but at least I won't blow a tranny, so it won't be that much more than a new one. It's okay, now that they have Uber, its fine. I'll get a car rental now, go call Uber, and then call the insurance.

What school do you kids go to?

Turquoise Trail.

You go to Turquoise Trail? How do you usually get out there?

We drive.

Or by bus.

Is there a bus?

At my work, but usually we just drive, because it's so close. We have three generations. I have two other kids who went there too. They're 25 and 19. I have a famous international kid who's an artist.

As we speak, he's probably getting on a plane.

To where?

To Florence. Oh my god, it makes me cry, because that was my dream for him. His first international show was in Mexico, because he's famous all over the U.S. The art collectors, they would know who he is, but he flew to Mexico. He did his show there, and it sold out. He was supposed to take a cruise, and do an actual line show, and go into Barcelona, and then to the Greek island of Mykonos. But just like a week ago or so, it changed, and they said, "No you're going to go directly to Florence, and you're going to have a show there." I said," Oh, my god, Michael, that was my dream for you." I took him to see Michelangelo's paintings when he was four and ever since it has been my dream for him to be an international artist.

My lady and I are in the great grand baby business.

How many do you have?

Two great grand babies, six grandchildren between us.

Okay.

Three and three.

My mum has ten grandchildren, no nine grandchildren, and one great grand baby. That's from my 25-year-old. He has red, red hair and blue, blue eyes.

Oh, boy.

Yes, little ginger running around.

I wonder if that's where ginger comes from, when they call kids that. I was just thinking about that. Just think, with a twin you've got a friend for life.

You do, to share the company.

Two thirds of twins are fraternal, but of the other ones that are identical, 10% of them are mirror twins.

Yes.

And what that means is that their body organs are on the other side of the body. Like there heart can be on the right side of their body.

I did not know that part.

Google that, mirror twins, it's pretty fascinating.

When you're pregnant with twins, you have to go like every month to an OBGYN class where they send you to like a twin school.

Oh, they do?

Yes, and how things happen, and the possibility of having the fraternal, and blah, blah, blah. They say that sometimes you can have an x chromosome, which is interesting,

Thank you so much.

Thank you. You have a great day! Thank you for getting us here.

Bye-bye kids. I like to give my kid riders $2.00 bills, so here is one for each of you.

Thank you. Thank you. Bye.

Thank you so much.

You have a great day.

∞

— IOWA —

Good afternoon. Going to St. John's?

Yeah.

Where are you from?

Cedar Rapids, Iowa.

Really? That's where my parents grew up. I still have my parents Washington High School annuals. You know, year-books?

Oh, yeah.

Yeah, from I think it was, must have been 1932, 33, 34, somewhere around there.

Wow, that's really exciting. That's where I went to high school, except seventy some odd years later.

Amazing. When I was a little boy back in the early fifties, we'd go to Cedar Rapids every year for the summer for several weeks. I stayed with my grandparents. I'd go fishing for catfish off one of the bridges over the Cedar River with my

Grandpa. He had a pool table downstairs in the basement. His pride were the big red tomatoes he grew in his garden.

Yeah. Where did they live in Cedar Rapids?

On Ridgeway Drive. Not too far from Washington High.

Yeah, I used to live right over in that area too.

My mother used to tell me how the iceman used to come up and down the street selling ice for the iceboxes. You know, instead of a refrigerator, they had these iceboxes.

That's funny. Yeah, there's a pretty cool area of houses right around Washington High School.

My grandparents had a really nice house. I remember grandpa would sit on the front steps every evening during the summer with his hat on smoking a big cigar.

But then we all moved away.

My family has reunions every three years or so, where we all meet in Ottumwa. Even family members from Sweden come.

Oh, yeah.

Ottumwa, Iowa is where they all immigrated from Sweden, you know, back in the late 1800s to work in the meat packing facility. I remember going down there in the early 1950's and attending a fiftieth wedding anniversary with all my relatives. Afterward I went with my grandma to the cemetery where she laid a wreath on her baby Rachel's grave, who she had lost 40 plus years earlier. I don't think you ever get over losing a child.

I have a bunch of family there also. Yes, several aunts and uncles.

In Ottumwa?

Mm-hmm. Small world.

Really? You know Tom Arnold is from Ottumwa. Roseanne Barr and Tom planned to build a big mansion there. But then they got divorced. One of the oddest things is that my ex-wife, Sherry, her aunts and uncles on her mother's side also lived in Ottumwa.

Yeah.

And then we have a whole bunch of different relatives that live over in Fairfield.

Yeah, I know Fairfield.

It's where the Maharishi University is. But my relatives are either grain elevator operators, pig farmers or race car drivers. They build their own cars, you know, and do stock car racing. I've been to their pig farm. My uncle said, "Smell that. That's the smell of money."

That's funny.

Really. My parents both went to the University of Iowa. My mother was a Pi Beta Phi.

I went to Iowa State in Ames.

All right.

Thanks for the ride.

Thank you.

∞

— LIGHT LANGUAGE —

What kind of conference were you here for?

I think this is something you're actually really going to like. We went to what is called a Stardreamer workshop forty minutes away from here where there are different intergalactic portals. We had a meeting with people speaking light language and ...

A meeting with people that speak what?

Speak light language.

Speak light language?

Yeah, this is Aucturian. "May the peace be with you," they were saying. We had two different ceremonies. One was in the temple of the 13 grandmothers, where we brought the energies of the grandmothers for the blessings and joy for the rainbow race, and yesterday we opened up a Stargate in a very specific light language ceremony with all these Aucturian starships. It was really profound. We had 44 people. It was amazing.

Was it in Dolce?

No. Stardreaming, that's the space. His name is James, and for over 20 years he's been creating these spirals and temples. It's like a very magical place, and people go there for ceremonies, and, I mean, it's like high vibrational. The place that he has created, he chipped every stone by himself - it's mind blowing, temple of magic, the temple of the sun, the temple of the moon. He's also an artist, and he's using Fibonacci sequencing in his paintings. We are just regular people, but then we get the call. Then you start having the connection, and start speaking light language, and start following what spirit wants you to do. It's very interesting. It's coming up right now – it's like it's just coming through... They're saying "We all speak light language. It's something that's very normal for us, because we're all from a very specific star system. It's just about vibration. When we enter this vibration, we can communicate with everyone. It's also happening on a telepathic way, and people are waking up to this higher vibration." So even you, just sit down, make a tape, start speaking. And if you go to this place, it's called Stardreaming. It's on Southern Exposure Road about forty minutes away from Santa Fe. It just kind of opens a lot of things for you. "It's already there. They are watching us all right now, because we are the only species who has spirit and body in one. And the way we are evolving – evolving is in fact now very profound. We can see the magic besides the fear and the terror. If we could see the light coming into this planet right now, what a privilege it is to be on this planet right now, if we are awake. If you're not awake, you got to be stuck down and thrown at the deep end with the fear. But if you start waking up to your divine essence, that is mainly what you're here to do, to give service, to bring this higher vibration into being. We're all one. All right." So, 40 minutes away from here - Stardreaming. This man, he might be your age. It's amazing what he's created. He's also going to create a temple in Hawaii. I think it's what they're calling him out to do. They asked him to make 20 paintings. So, he finished, I think, almost all of them. Must be fun for you driving Uber.

Yeah, I love it. I've had over 3000 rides in the past year. Met all kinds of people. Even doing a book about it.

Wow, that's wonderful. Actually, I wrote a book too. I just published last December.

What's the name of it?

It's called <u>Inside World,</u> and it's by me, Saharra White-Wolf.

Can you get it on Amazon?
Yeah.

Great.

If you want it, you can have it. I'll give it to you. It's based on my own experience. I do some light work, and it's based on my own experience with how I got the connection to spirit, and it's in three colors. Black is the 3D world; blue is the spirit world; and purple represents the inside, where our spirit goes out and connects with the inside world. It's about the chosen boy, who was chosen by spirit to bring the vibration of love on the planet. Their spirit started connecting all the way with him. That was actually what I experienced in my life, and he had to face self-doubt. Of course, the negative spirit wants to prevent this from happening, and at the end he overcame self-doubt and found compassion for himself. So, this is the first one. They were telling me it's a trilogy. It's called the Inner Knowing Trilogy. The first one is about finding out who you are and overcoming self-doubt, like being aware that you are a divine powerful being in the co-creation process, and that love can shift everything. The second one is about really reconnecting to spirit, and the third one is about the revolution, of changing like the essential process. Changing and awakening people to higher vibrations on the earth. So, I just thought if you're writing already ...

Yeah.

So, you're almost done?

Well, I've got all these different recordings, and I'm just transcribing them. Then I'm going to edit them. I was going to change everyone's names. Just sort of like edit some of the stuff like that, but you know with someone like you, maybe I should do it with your real name and your book name.

Whatever you want to do is fine. You are a channel.

You know I like to manifest stuff that comes through me. I've got to be careful what comes through, because I like to manifest so much, and it all takes time.

I think it's all about discernment and timing.

I work with great people all over the planet in different fields.

That's wonderful. You have a very calm presence. Do you meditate?

I try to make life a meditation. I don't formally meditate anymore. I used to live in an ashram with a guru named Muktananda. He died in 1986, I think, but you know we'd meditate and get up at four, meditate, chant the Guru Gita. He sort of taught me, plus some shamanistic type experiences, just to be in that meditative space as much as you can be. Be of service to others. Be a guide to the Light for others. We invite people to be guides to the Light. Some people, when they know, they know that's their highest path.

I learned through my shamanic experiences with ayahuasca about being baptized by Light. It's an experience you will never forget, and from my eye is true baptism. I have learned from the shaman about Jesus and the Christ Energy. I have been blessed with personal visitations with Jesus. Muktananda used to tell me to read the Bible. Finally, a couple of years ago I read the Bible from cover to cover. I know Jesus in a different way than most people.

My mother always told me not to read the Old Testament, only pay attention to the New Testament. I couldn't believe how gruesome the Old Testament is. Millions of people have lost their lives over whether or not they were circumcised. And then King David, who I had always idolized, sent Uriah into battle knowing he would be killed, so that David could marry Uriah's wife, Bathsheba. King Solomon was born from that marriage. But then Jesus came along and told another story.

Wow, I think our meeting was planned. I feel like it was profound what this weekend was for me. I could sleep for five days, two to three hours a day, and like my cells were completely aligned. Everything was so moving! We were saying that we are actually changing with the weekend, and I really feel like it's really happening. It's my diet. I'm already now vegetarian. I don't want meat anymore. It's like very interesting how I speak differently. It's just very interesting. And supposedly a lot of gifts came in for us, but it's going to take several months until they come out and reveal themselves. It's such an exciting time to be alive! And when you are in this meeting with all these people who are like you, being of service for others and on the healing path, it's great. They feel they can really be of service. It's beautiful. And we had so many different light languages being spoken. Twenty people came from the church in Pennsylvania. They followed this woman here; she was one of the organizers. So, you are very fortunate to live here.

Yeah. Where do you live?

New Jersey, but I'm from Austria. I live one block away from the Delaware River. It's beautiful. Yeah, but I feel like I got to move. We are going to be uprooted. I got a sense that I got to move. Let's see.

My lady has a non-profit here in town that provides free home care for people who fall through the gaps and cracks of our medical system.

How beautiful.

Particularly towards the end of life, long term care and stuff like that. She's trained over 500 people to be her volunteers.

No way.

Yeah. They are providing a real service.

Where does she get the money from? Through donations?

Through donations, foundations, grants, she's never done any invoicing, any billing whatsoever. People who have money, they contract directly with her nurses. But the same nurses are her volunteers. They care for people with no money. Now she is opening a social model hospice house

here in Santa Fe called Scott's House, named after her son. She provides the residence for free.

Wow, I work in hospice. I'm a hospice nurse. And I had a psychic reading like a year ago, and she said you have two options. You can go this way, or you can start being an entrepreneur in hospice and create something that doesn't exist.

You should be working with Glenys. Her name is Glenys. I'll hook you guys up. She has a book called <u>Hold My Hand: A Mother's Journey</u> published by Macmillan. I'll get you a copy. One of the reviews on Amazon said it was the most spiritual, non-spiritual books, she had ever read.

Wow! This seems like we were really supposed to connect. Alleluia.

Thank you so much. Nice chatting with you. Have a good flight.

∞

— HATS —

You're okay?

Yeah, they put me in a wheelchair because I went to sleep.

You went to sleep?

Yeah, and I really was so deep in sleep I didn't want to wake up. And so, they said we don't want you going home if you're asleep. Yeah, so, I couldn't go home sleepy.

You're on San Mateo there?

Yeah.

Are you feeling okay now?

Yeah, well, they gave me something. Well, they gave me...

You want me to help you? I will get it for you, okay?

394 · EVERYONE'S GOT A STORY

Yeah, they gave me something to eat.

Oh...that's good.

They actually, you know, if you are there for several hours they will give you half a ham and cheese sandwich on white bread.

Oh, boy.

And a drink of Kool-Aid.

Are you doing okay?

Yeah, I'm doing okay. I just don't want to go there anymore.

I know.

Because really it's difficult to...

Well, that's good.

Well, it's only temporary. So, I guess I just have to accept the temporariness of it. So, how are you?

Good.

Good.

Do you use the GoGo Grandparent thing?

Yeah.

There you go. Are you going to be able to walk okay to your door?

Oh, yeah.

Okay.

So, hats. I'm ordering lots of hats.

Lots of hats?

Yeah.

What kind of hats?

Hats to wear to cover my head, because they told me I'm going to lose my hair.

Oh, with the chemo?

Yeah.

You can really get creative with hats.

Oh, I have. Right now, I have five hats on order.

Oh, cool.

From two different places, and then they told me this thing I don't think I'm interested in. They said if you need a wig, we will give you a free wig.

Oh, boy.

I didn't really say just what I wanted.

But, you'd rather go the hat route.

Yeah.

∞

— MALAYSIA —

You found me!

I found you, yeah.

Okay. It's raining - that's why I bring my umbrella.

I'm doing a book on my Uber riders. Are you okay if I record the conversation, our trip down?

That's fine.

Do you work at the massage place?

Yes, you can come to try it before I am leaving. But I'm leaving

next month, by the middle of the month, or maybe the last of
the month, like that.

Where are you from?

I am from Malaysia. But now I'm going to London.

London?

Yes.

How do you like Santa Fe?

Yeah, it's good, but it's not for me, you know. Yeah, because...
Maybe when I get a bit older, maybe I can stay here. I'm still
young, so I still want to have fun. Because here, they don't
have nothing to do, you know? I get bored.

When did you leave Malaysia?

11/11.

11/11? Last year 2015, 2016?

2016.

What's Malaysia like these days? Is it strict?

It is too much about, you know, religion thing. It is like a little
bit close-minded. For me, it is a bit hard to live there, because
I am open-minded, you know? I don't care about any religion.
It is a bit too closed for me.

Is it a Buddhist religion?

No, it is Muslim. But I don't believe about religion, you know,
so... I want to be free. There, it is more about religion things,
so it is not the place I want to be forever. Yeah, maybe I stay
for 30 years, but now, no more. It's kind of dead, you know?
You have to find the place that fits. So, I choose to go to London - there I want to be free forever now.

You want to be free forever in London?

Yes.

Because you can be free where ever you are.

Yeah. I can be free and be odd, because I am a specialty, you know, so I just want to be who I am, what I born to be, you know? It is not like someone asks me to be what they want me to be. Yeah, that is kind of my country. Yeah. So, it's hard. So, it's good I go to find my way, you know? Some people, they live in the suffer because they have to be what others ask them to be, you know? But I don't want to be like that forever. I just live once. I want to live my life. To be happy, to be love. That is my life purpose. It is said "expect nothing and you will never be disappointed."

Did you have any problems in traveling to the United States? Visa problems or...

No, no. I have the good blessing with my traveling all the time. I mean, I've been to a lot of countries, but I don't have any problems in my life. You know, like, maybe God blessed me with that, to go to see the other cultures, you know? Because maybe this I have to learn to born to be with, be what I have to. See the truth, you know. I recently read this book called The Four Agreements by Don Miguel Ruiz. Let's see, the Four Agreements are: Be impeccable with your word, don't take anything personally, don't make assumptions, and, always do your best. It's a very good book. I am learning to let go of things that do not serve me.

Yeah, right. I've read it. There is another book called The Journey of Souls by Dr. Michael Newton you might be interested in.

Yeah, the hypnotist guy. I read that too. It's amazing how he gets similar responses from everyone under hypnosis. For me, I get down and I find the truth, but I have to fight with the truth now and then, especially when it's about me giving things up that do not serve me. That is a bit harder, but I'm not giving up. Right now I am learning how to master intuition. And my family is going to come to me in London, because I told them that. They are going to come to meet me in London, because I told them that maybe I'm a long time I'm not going back, so you all have to come to meet me. I'll buy the ticket, anything for them to come, when I get there in London. Because I have my cousin in London, so I stay with her for a while. My mother, she taught me everything.

My mother taught me a lot too. She was extremely bright. But when she didn't know the answer to something, she always told me, just sit down and be quiet, or sleep on it, and the answer just comes to you. So, you have your cousin in London?

Yes, she met up with an English guy.

She met a guy from England?

Yeah. And I will stay with her for a while until I find my own place, and I find my own job then, and I start my life. Step by step, you know?

How did you happen to arrive in Santa Fe?

Actually, I arrived in New York. After that...

Oh, you were in New York?

Yes. And I worked there for a month. And my boss had a friend here that needed a girl to work, so I came here. It's fine. I enjoy the U.S. I mean, I go to most of the places in U.S. I've been in New York, in Philadelphia, L.A. A lot of places. It's the first time. Yes, right. But it's good. I mean, I enjoy it here. But it's not the place that I want to settle down, and so for now I am off to London. Yeah. Thank you so much.

You're welcome.

∞

Epilogue

Most of us go about our day interfacing with all sorts of people, but not really knowing a lot about them. This book is an intimate glimpse into the unique world of everyday people, including me, who are either residents or visitors of Santa Fe, New Mexico. I have purposely left out any reference to dates of the interviews as I feel the stories are timeless.

I came to realize while interviewing the riders that approximately 50% was about them and the other 50% about me. It became a stream of consciousness about my life, in no particular order, just depending on which rider I picked up next. That's why I call it An Anthropologic Memoir – you've really got to dig to discover the memoir.

When I told my Uber/Lyft riders that I was doing a book and wanted to record them and keep notes, everyone, for the most part, was very curious. During this particular six weeks there was a huge anthropologic convention in town, a DNA biology convention and several other conventions. All of the anthropology people, they loved to be interviewed. That's what most of them do for a living, so they were more than happy to reciprocate.

I became fascinated with the intimate details that all my riders were willing to share. It became a slice of humanity that most of us rarely, if ever, see. Santa Fe, the City Different does have its share of unique individuals who both live here and visit, and they all have a story. It was my honor to interview them.

For me, life is a spiritual journey and one of continually learning more of who you are. This book brings up all those feelings of growing up, the discovering of the world and then becoming the person I've eventually become.

Blessings and love to You on your journey.

John Bishop

Index of Interviews